OFFICIAL
BOOK CLUB
SELECTION

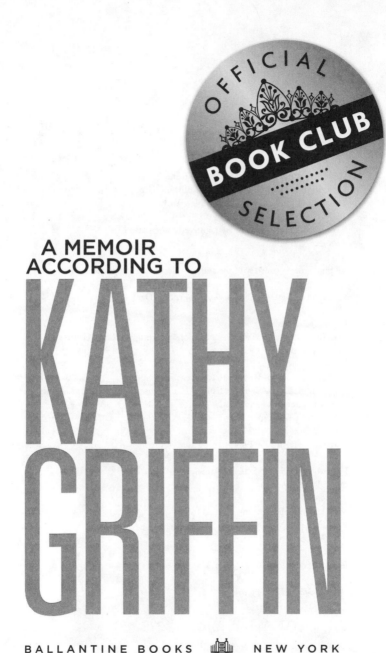

OFFICIAL BOOK CLUB SELECTION

A MEMOIR
ACCORDING TO

KATHY GRIFFIN

BALLANTINE BOOKS   NEW YORK

Published in the United States by Ballantine Books,
an imprint of The Random House Publishing Group,
a division of Random House, Inc., New York.

BALLANTINE and colophon are registered trademarks of
Random House, Inc.

All photographs courtesy of the author unless otherwise noted.

Library of Congress Cataloging-in-Publication Data

Griffin, Kathy.
   Official book club selection : a memoir according to Kathy Griffin.
       p.   cm.
   Includes index.
   ISBN 978-0-345-51851-4 (hardcover : alk. paper)
   1. Griffin, Kathy. 2. Comedians—United States—Biography. 3. Actors—
United States—Biography.   I. Title.
   PN2287.G6955A3   2009
   792.7'6028092—dc22
   [B]   2009029845

Printed in the United States of America
on acid-free paper

www.ballantinebooks.com

9 8 7 6 5 4 3 2 1

First Edition

Book design by Liz Cosgrove

*"Kathy, don't take any crap from those people.
I don't care if you never work again."*

John Patrick Griffin

1916–2007

CONTENTS

FOREWORD: DEAR OPRAH   ix

1   THE LITTLEST GOSSIP GIRL   3

2   GROWING UP GRIFFIN   7

3   THEY BARKED, THEY LAUGHED   25

4   KENNY   39

5   LA IS MY LADY   53

6   TO LIVE AND BOMB IN LA   75

7   HOT CUP O' TALK   91

8   I'M A STAR! (OKAY, A GUEST STAR)   105

9   BROOKE SHIELDS, DON'T READ THIS   121

10   TALK SHOWS: LET THE BANNING BEGIN   139

11   FROM WORCESTER, MA, TO DICK: STORIES FROM THE ROAD   155

12   NIP/FUCKED   171

13 REINVENTING MYSELF:
     I'M JUST LIKE MADONNA!   187

14 REALITY CHECK   203

15 MY MARRIAGE BEGINS   217

16 MY MARRIAGE ENDS   237

17 A WIN, A LOSS   253

18 FANNING FLAMES IN HOLLYWOOD,
     AND YES I MEAN DAKOTA   269

19 THE WIZARD OF WOZ   285

20 HOW PARIS HILTON CHANGED
     MY LIFE   319

     EPILOGUE   329

     ACKNOWLEDGMENTS   333

     READING GROUP GUIDE   335

     INDEX   349

FOREWORD

Dear Oprah,

Hi, how are you? How's Gayle doing today?

Nice to hear.

Get ready, cause after you read this barn burner, you're gonna want me on for sweeps week. You're gonna want to open a school in *my* name, and have a special edition white ladies' legends ball, just for me. Barbara Walters can cater. Maybe.

I know you have questions about what's wrong with me. Call Dr. Oz, he can be on with me during my hour, too. You don't have to call Nate. He's already on my team. But don't act like you don't want to see my post-op plastic surgery photos, if you haven't already flipped to that chapter. You probably don't remember that I was actually a guest on your show. Once. I'm on a lot of shows once, for some reason. But just know that if my house ever catches fire, I'm grabbing my two dogs, my picture with you, and running for my life. My mom is on her own. By the way, don't even think about Skype-ing my mom for this episode. She'll throw me under the bus in a heartbeat. She's got a thing for Gayle. Ring a bell?

Let's establish some ground rules for my much-anticipated appearance on your show. First of all, I'd like to sit on your lap, at a moment of your choosing. Please wear peach. I love you in summer colors.

We're going to cold-call Steadman, because I'm no longer convinced he even exists. And you will have to introduce me using your signature vowel-elongating bellow. Repeat after me: "KAAAA-THAY GRA-A-A-A-FF-A-A-A-A-A-N!" I already have chills.

Here's my promise to you. This will be the most talked-about episode of your career. Well, after the one where Dr. Oz showed pictures of your poo. And maybe the one where the Olsen twins shocked the world with their tales of the difficulties of living in the public spotlight while trying to sell their sassy-themed tween fashion clothing line.

I know that you like to do episodes that help women put themselves "first on their list," that inspire "lightbulb" moments, and that lead to revelations that are big. "BIG, PE-E-E-PUHL!" Our hour together on camera, in front of your global audience, will surely motivate, challenge, and most important, help the children. After all, it is about the children. They are our future.

Here is what you will admire about me. I'm living the life you secretly wish you could. I've got the dysfunctional family story just like a lot of people. I've bitten, scratched, and clawed to get where I am, just like you. But I don't have to be nice about it. I'm naming names and telling tales out of school. I will be your guilty pleasure. I will be your new showbiz confidante. I will be your new Julia Rob-iston-altrow-avolta-angelou.

So strap yourself in, O. You may be the only person who will still be talking to me by the end of this journey. Keep a bunk open at that school in South Africa. I may need to lay low for a while.

Come to think of it, I'm not sure you can handle this book. I'm going to Tyra.

XXOO
Kathy Griffin

OFFICIAL
BOOK CLUB
SELECTION

1

THE
LITTLEST
GOSSIP
GIRL

Have you ever looked at the online photos of Britney's peesh?

I probably shouldn't start my book with that question, but I just can't get enough of those photos. I find it nearly impossible to turn away from an online snapshot of any celebrity's peesh. All right, Kath. Focus. This is the story of your life.

Wait! Have you seen that TV commercial with Wynonna Judd where she hawks diet pills? Look, I don't mean to be rude, but maybe a gal with a big voice and a bigger . . . um . . . talent shouldn't be hawking diet pills. Come on, you *know* those pills are just tiny donuts. Teeny, tiny powdered donuts.

All right, that wasn't very nice. In fact, it was inappropriate, and nothing short of cheap gossip. But let's face it, that's why you bought this book. That's right, I'm bringing it: gays, women, and the occasional DL (down-low) husband. The pages you are about to read have a lot of gossip, but guess what? Most of it's about me. I'm going to try to make this book a recipe (shout-out to Paula Deen!) of equal parts shit-talking about myself and others. Yeah, I go down pretty hard on myself in this book. Not as hard as Steve Martin does, or my drunken Irish Catholic relatives do, perhaps. But I've had some heartaches and bumpy passages on this road to notoriety. Basically, I take great pride

Left: "Go fuck yourself."

in the fact that I'm a professional. You're in good hands. This is a job I've been training for my entire life.

How did I get here, then?

I'll start with a statement so shocking you might have to burn this book immediately:

I was a kid who needed to talk. All the time.

I mean, what's a beleaguered Mary Margaret Griffin to do when her mouthy little daughter won't shut the fuck up? Breathe a sigh of relief, for one thing, whenever I would bolt out the front door of our house on Home Avenue in suburban Oak Park, Illinois.

But Mom was really of two minds about my exit. While part of her was thinking, *Thank God, get her out of my earshot,* the other part surely thought, *Uh-oh.* That's because I'd just go next door to the Bowens' house, where I first learned the power of juicy material.

The Bowens were an older couple, and they lived with Mrs. Bowen's mother, Mrs. Tyres. The Bowens, Mrs. Tyres, and I had a mutual understanding. They would bribe me with Pepperidge Farm Milano cookies, and I'd freely spill our family secrets, all to my mom's horror, of course. She knew exactly what was going on because she could see it all through our kitchen window, which had a perfect view into the Bowens' formal dining room. Mom would be doing dishes, occasionally nursing a nice highball—boxed wine innovations hadn't arrived yet—then look up, see my mouth moving, and then see the Bowens shaking their heads.

It was good stuff I was slinging, too. I'd reveal how one of my older siblings would have had a kegger the night before, and I'd run right over with the latest. "Yeah, Joyce had a party and one guy just fell asleep right on the lawn!" I'd excitedly report. "He was real drunk and everything! There was puke everywhere! My mom made me promise not to tell anybody! I don't think she meant you, Mrs. Tyres! Boy, these cookies sure are good!"

From my perch at the Bowens' table, I could see my poor mom waving me over, mouthing, "Get back here! Get back here!" If either Mrs. Bowen or Mrs. Tyres looked over, too, my mom could turn on her party face instantaneously and be all smiles: "Oh hell-o-o-o-o-o-o, Mrs. Bowen!"

Everything was so prim and proper at the Bowens', with doilies on the table, and cookies neatly laid out on a plate. It was like high tea. At our packed house, it was a bag of cookies thrown out and all of us diving for them like animals, with no Kate Gosselin there to spank some sense into us. So naturally I thought it was my job to go next door to these fancy people and try to tell the most graphic, shocking, and horrible stories I could. I mean, haven't you sold your soul for a good slice of cake? (More on that later.)

Mr. Bowen, of course, wanted nothing to do with me. Typical straight-guy audience. He would come home in his suit, grab the newspaper, and sit in his Barcalounger, tolerating the freckly, redheaded, seven-year-old spinning top who came over and just talked *constantly*. Poor Mr. Bowen. The ladies, however, knew what was important, egging me on with widened eyes and a gently prodding "What?"

"My dad swore FOUR TIMES last night!"

"Joyce got kicked out of school again!"

"Keith Norman let me watch him pee in his yard today!"

"My brother had a party where everybody was drunk and my dad had this antique sword and it was stolen and my mom is FURIOUS!" (By the way, my family is *still* talking about that damn sword.)

This arrangement with the Bowens went on for years. It started when we moved into that Home Avenue house and continued till I was in high school. If the Bowens had had Flip cam technology, they could probably sell it on eBay for tens of dollars. Today, the story of my trips next door is one of my mother's favorites, but I guarantee you it caused her no end of grief back then.

"What are you airin' our GAHDDAMN dirty laundry for?" she'd always unload on me, her Chicago accent in full flight. "Mrs. Bowen and Mrs. Tyres, they don't want to hear your GAHDDAMN mouth, for CHR-EYE-SSAKE. JEEZ-us CHR-EYE-ST."

Sorry, Mom. You and everyone else in the family might call it tattling. But to me, they were my first live shows. From the Bowens to Madison Square Garden, it's been quite a ride.

2
GROWING UP
GRIFFIN

With all the craziness this past year surrounding the Octomom and her fourteen kids—I'm on suicide watch for her, by the way—it's worth noting that my mother was herself the youngest of sixteen. Suck it, Octomom. Before fertility drugs let Nadya Suleman set some kind of land-speed record in childbirth, there was good old-fashioned Irish Catholicism.

Of course, I've told Jesus to suck it, too, which earned me a certain measure of notoriety, because you have to make fun of any religion that would let you have sixteen kids and say it's God's will. I mean, bless my grandparents. They seem like they were wonderful people. I didn't know them, really, because most of them had passed away before I was born. But that amount of children is clearly insane. They were big believers in the rhythm method, and you can see how well that worked out for them. I don't even know my grandmother's first name, because my mother only refers to her as "The Saint." For instance, I would say, "Mom, don't you think it might not have been the best choice to keep on having children, one a year, like she was punching a clock?"

She'd reply, "NO, don't say that! The woman's a SAINT!"

My mother's father was just called "The Governor," or "Himself." Which, if you have sixteen kids, probably isn't as crazy as it sounds.

Left: Who knew the one in the overalls would cause all the trouble?

"Himself is comin' home!" Grandma would supposedly announce in her Old Country brogue. I had to clarify with my mom who exactly she was talking about when she'd use this term. I would say, "Mom, do you mean your dad?" And she'd say "Of course. Himself."

Apparently, "Himself" liked to get into fistfights with his sons, *well into their twenties.* That's right. My mother would talk about this as if it were cute and adorable. Um, no. There isn't supposed to be any fisticuffs as a matter of everyday parenting.

I know I'm making fun of my family—mostly because I love teasing my mom—but there was also real tragedy in that situation. For one thing, you can't keep track of that many kids, and the likelihood of something horrible happening because of that just increases. This is a true Irish Catholic story: One young child in my mom's family died when he pulled a pot of boiling water off the stove and was scalded to death. Her sister Angeline died of tuberculosis when she was twenty-one. This was a time when scurvy and polio were real dangers, when a family member would go into a veterans' hospital and never come back.

My mother's family came over on a ship in steerage class from Ireland, but she and her four siblings nearest in age were born in America, so I'm second generation. They settled in the west side of Chicago, and life became all about the parish, or church community. Presentation was the name of the Catholic church they attended, and this is what I love about the Irish: My mother became known as the *second* prettiest girl at Presentation parish.

"Why was that okay?" I once asked her.

"Oh, because everybody knew Mary Griffin was the most beautiful girl at Presentation," she replied.

My mom was happy to be on the D-list! Just like I'm not trying to be Brooke Shields, she wasn't trying to be Mary Griffin. Now, she did go and marry the prettiest girl's brother, my father, John Patrick Griffin. That probably helps you accept the mantle of second prettiest girl at Presentation.

My dad's family, on the other hand, was something of an embarrassment at Presentation, because—get ready—my dad was the youngest of *only five* kids. You can imagine trying to be happy with only five children in the family. I'm sure you're dampening this page already with tears of pity.

We don't know if Mr. Griffin the elder was shooting blanks, or somebody was partially barren, which is apparently the worst thing you could call a woman in those days, but it gets crazier. After my grandmother had five children—six, really, since one baby sadly died after a week—she said, "I don't want any more kids." To which Grandpa said, "Well, the only way to not have kids is to not have sex, because we're not going to use condoms or anything."

"Yeah, that's the deal," my grandma agreed. "No more sex."

"No sex? I'm out of here."

I love that this was apparently a very religious man, too. What, a "bad" Catholic uses birth control, but a "good" Catholic leaves his wife over it? So-o-o-o religious. Anyway, Mr. Griffin moved out and relocated one parish over, where he checked tickets on streetcars for a living. But here's the kicker: Because it was such a shame to have a man leave you or get divorced, for years my dad had to tell the whole parish that his father had *died*. Mrs. Griffin would say, "Yeah, my husband passed away."

I just want to reiterate: He was *one parish away*. We're talking two miles. It was such a small-town culture that no one knew. How could they not just run into him?

It gets better. As my grandpa on my dad's side got older, he took ill. So the woman he abandoned, my grandmother, actually took him back, and took care of him! Then they had to tell the town, "Oh, right, he's . . . actually . . . not dead." But the best part is, when my grandparents reunited, they vowed never to speak to each other until the day they died. She nursed him in silence all the way to his deathbed. How sweet a deal did he get?

When his dad returned, my father was still living at home, and he had begun dating my mom. According to my mom, their first date, which took place at the blindingly romantic setting of his family's home, went something like this:

"Tell your mother to pass the butter."

"Tell your father to get his OWN butter!"

"Tell your mother I want some more soda bread."

"Tell your father he can have the soda bread when I'm good and ready!"

Maggie just looked over at the son of these two, and ten minutes later realized, "So this is the gig." But when she tells the story now, Mom makes it sound as if it were par for the course. So freakin' Irish Catholic.

Before they started dating, my parents first met at the Formfit bra factory. Dad was a stock boy, and Mom was a secretary. Somebody introduced them, and as the story goes, that somebody said, "John, you know Maggie, the second prettiest girl at Presentation?" And he said, "No, I don't know her."

My mother was incensed. "What do you mean you don't know me? I'm the second prettiest girl at Presentation! And by the way, you're not that hot, anyway. How can you be related to a beautiful sister like Mary, the prettiest girl at Presentation?"

Well, the sparks flew. Mom was very intrigued that Dad wasn't just following her around drooling. But he really got her with his sense of humor. He did the smart thing in the beginning: He would go out on a "date" with her and a few of her girlfriends or sisters. It wasn't heavy dating. They didn't have any money, so a night out was a bottle of booze and a trip to the park with plastic cups in the middle of winter. Now, this is Chicago. That's a fucking cold night out. It was usually Dad, my mom, her friend Rae, and her sister Irene, and they'd all just get hammered. Then, it would be too cold to walk home so they'd go from building to building, and Dad would ring the doorbell of each one. Then they'd be let into the foyer, warm up some, and then he would ring the bell of every apartment as a joke, and the girls would be mad at Dad but they'd laugh anyway. "Johnny, stop it!" they'd say, and he'd promise not to do it, and then do it again. Just so you know the level of entertainment we're dealing with here. This was a hot Saturday night for them.

According to my mom, she and Dad dated almost two years before getting married. Dad was home on furlough from the war for just a few

Dad hams it up even on his wedding day.

days, right before Pearl Harbor, after which he had to get back to his base right away. Mom went to meet him in Denver, hoping they could get married on St. Patrick's Day, but due to some army regulations, they had to wait until March 20 (at that time, soldiers kinda had to get approval, or so Maggie says)—lucky for them the army approved! They had their first child, Kenny, nine months and four days after they got married. We kids like to tease Mom: Perhaps she was a naughty girl? But she's very proud that that four-day window proved Kenny wasn't an "accident baby." The rest of us came afterward in four- or five-year increments: Joyce, Gary, John, and then me, on November 4, 1960. Right next to Election Day! (I then went on to retroactively elect my mother the prettiest girl at Presentation.) I'm the baby, just like my mother and father were in their families, and I never heard the end of it. I got away with everything, according to my siblings. But Mom doesn't think I was spoiled. Precocious, okay. Annoying, yes. But not spoiled. She will also happily admit that I was an accident baby,

This is me after my second face-lift.

and that by the time I came along—eighteen years after their first child was born—Mom and Dad were too tired to worry about me.

But get this: When my mother was pregnant with me, it turns out she was on amphetamines. That's right, speed. This was a time when doctors thought a woman shouldn't gain more than fifteen pounds during a pregnancy—and when doctors spoke back then, mothers listened—so to keep her weight down they gave my mom amphetamines! She took them while she was pregnant, *and* after she had me to lose the few pounds she had gained. Plus—I love this—she's actually guilt-ridden about it. She thinks that's what made me crazy, or shall we say, the accomplished person I am today. Let's just take this in for a moment, shall we? In 1960 there were two doctors in Forest Park, Illinois, who were just doling out methamphetamines to pregnant Irish Catholic women with part-time jobs. Where's *my Dateline* episode? I like to picture my mom with a baby on the way, bouncing off the walls, scratching her neck, and fiddling with the rabbit ears on the TV set in a frenzied manner. This, by the way, is how I write my act: I get an idea in my head and I run with it. So granted, I was a fetus at the time, but I *was* there. You can't deny that. Also, the way I tell it is probably funnier than the way it actually happened. But in any case, she now believes I'm her crack baby.

I love holding it over her, too. It's really the only thing I have on her. "Well, maybe if you hadn't been taking DOLLS all day!" But in my mind, she's Judy Garland and I'm Liza.

Really, my mother wasn't alone about crazy '60s and '70s parenting. I remember the excitement about the DDT pesticide truck, how its arrival on our street was a big event. The parents on the block would alert us: "Hey, kids, the DDT truck is coming!" Then we'd all go knock on our friends' doors, because the truck would come and leave this giant haze that smelled awesome, like incense and Fourth of July. We'd run around in it and yell, "We're in clouds! We're dancing in clouds!" Later on I saw Meryl Streep on a commercial talking about the dangers of pesticides, scrubbing fruit vigorously with soap, and I thought, *Oh, you mean dancing in the clouds was bad? Meryl, pass me the scrub brush.*

In any case, we were a very typical middle-class household. When I was in kindergarten, we moved from a small house in Forest Park, Illinois, to a bigger house in Oak Park, and I remember my mother thinking our new place was very grand: four bedrooms, a sun room, wood floors, a galley kitchen with a breakfast area. There was a fireplace that may not have been operable but could be made to look like a working fireplace, and that was fine by us. I'm pretty sure my parents got the house for under $30,000, and Mom thought it was the Taj Mahal. They worked hard for it, too. Dad was managing a hi-fi stereo store six days a week, which meant all of us kids each had full-on stereo systems, with woofers, tweeters, receivers, and everything, and that

Easter Sunday! Candy! Do I have to go to church?

helped us seem cool to our friends. Mom, meanwhile, worked as a cashier at Oak Park Hospital. It was really the administrative office, but back then it was "cashier," because this was when people would actually pay for their hospital stay in cold, hard dollars and cents.

Obviously I wasn't around when my parents got married or were starting a family, but I can tell you they were a great couple. They have many stories about singing songs around a friend's piano, going to block parties, and attending the occasional pancake breakfast at church. I honestly never once heard them fight. They yelled at us kids all the time, but never at each other. My siblings and I joke to this day about how the reason we have trouble in relationships is because we never learned how to fight from our parents. However they worked out their problems, they kept it between themselves. My dad had such respect for my mom, even though she was only the second prettiest girl at Presentation. He definitely taught me the old cliché, that a sense of humor really is the most important quality in a man. That, and how to mix a nice Tom Collins.

Which brings us to the drinking portion of our show. My parents never thought they were alcoholics, but they sure got used to me calling them that in my act. Drinking was so prevalent in our home, it was a daily thing. Now my parents would argue that it was a different time back then, but as a kid, I definitely remember them having beer and "the hard stuff" on a regular basis. My mom still loves to say, "It's five o'clock somewhere!" Often at noon.

Did I ever see my parents wildly drunk? No. They never fell down. They never missed work. They never yelled at me or embarrassed me in front of friends, none of those classic stories. Did they drink every day? Absolutely. It was really my older siblings Gary and Joyce—who would, in typical teenage fashion, have beer bashes—who exposed me to what being visibly drunk looked like. Their keggers were legendary. Just ask the Bowens.

The funny thing was, we all only thought of my uncle Maurice as the "real alcoholic." I vividly remember my parents talking about how hard it was for Uncle Mo and his wife, because he couldn't get off "the drink." Dad would even take me to visit Uncle Mo in the "hospital." I didn't know at the time that that was code for rehab. I don't think they even called it rehab in those days. He was a Chicago cop—he once worked on the famous Leopold and Loeb case—and the legend in my family is that Uncle Mo is what we used to call a bagman for the Chicago police department. Allegedly. A bagman was a cop who went to the local merchants and collected payments from them to look the other way about certain legal issues. But in any case, for a cop to have to go to "the hospital," he must have been drinking a lot.

I saw all different kinds of drinking going on at our house, from my brother John's occasional beer to Uncle Mo teaching me how to make him a Manhattan when I was in grade school, something my parents never would have condoned. But when Uncle Maurice had me assemble a drink for him in the kitchen, it did make me feel like a grown-up.

I'm halfway to a bad sunburn, and Uncle Maurice is half in the bag.

I, on the other hand, have never had a drink in my life. Never. Voluntarily, that is. Once when I was about ten years old, I was choking on something at the dinner table, and my mom yelled, "Give her something to drink!" My dad grabbed the closest thing, which was his stein of beer. I took one big sip, and while it startled me out of choking, it also led me straight into thinking, *My throat is burning. This tastes disgusting! Why would anyone want to drink this stuff?* That really was my first and last taste of alcohol.

When my pals in high school were starting to drink, it always looked unappealing to me. I would be at a big party and see one of the popular girls or football players completely wasted and puking and acting a fool, and think to myself, *There's nothing cool about that.* I never wanted to be that out of control.

I had friends who would drink because they were nervous, or they were shy. I wasn't really nervous, and I certainly wasn't shy. It's weird the way many guys over the years have said to me, "I'm going to be the first to get you drunk!" I'd say, "Why? What are you possibly going to gain? I'm going to loosen up *more*?"

But I also remember thinking, with so much alcoholism and addiction around me, that I didn't need to be starting any vices. An inner voice was telling me, "How are you not going to become an alcoholic with all these drunken micks around you? Don't play with fire. If you have one drink, you'll be an alcoholic in a week." I still think that.

Because both of my parents worked, I was the classic latchkey kid. When you're in a family with a bunch of kids, you never get quiet time. So when it was just my older brother John and me still in the house—Kenny was married, Joyce was teaching, Gary was at college—I made the most out of this unsupervised time. I would get home from school at around 3 p.m. and have the house to myself for about two hours. I was in fourth grade then and that's when two things started: my eating disorder, and my love for all things Hollywood, a lethal combination that has skyrocketed many stars to fame, from Tracey Gold to—allegedly—Calista Flockhart.

We didn't really use the term "eating disorder" back then. It was just eating. We also didn't have the term "BFF." But I had one, and it wasn't Paris Hilton. My BFF was a lady named Food. I wasn't the kid who came home and made a sandwich or had a few cookies. Instead I had a routine that was, I have to admit, particularly sick. Binge eating is all about the rituals. It began after school. On my way home I would stop at Certified Groceries, the mom-and-pop grocery store on Madison, where they all knew me. It was kind of like my Cheers. I would get two staples: Pringles and a blue-and-white box of Jiffy cake mix, with a frosting mix kicker sold separately. Because, when binge eating, I felt very strongly that it was important to combine salty with sweet.

Food technology was moving at such a rapid pace in those days that potato chips had been remolded to conform to one shape, so they could be stacked vertically in a can. Their scientific name: Pringles. Pringles are not even potato chips. I believe they're actually called potato crisps. They are to potatoes what McNuggets are to chicken. I had a can-a-day habit.

Now, on to the sweet. Oh, Jiffy cakes. Jiffy used to have these cake mixes that came in little boxes. They weren't Duncan Hines big, but they were really for people who essentially want to eat their own cake, even if the package claimed to serve four.

On these specially designated days after school, I would run home with my stash, turn on an afternoon movie on the tube, and start with the Pringles. When I had finished off my last Pringle, the Jiffy box on the counter would catch my eye. My favorite flavor was white cake with chocolate frosting. Yellow cake was okay, but I thought the white cake was better. I put a lot of thought into it. I can tell you, there were tense times when Certified ran out of white cake, and I had to get the yellow with chocolate frosting. That made a great day into just an okay day. Keep in mind, a Jiffy cake was one layer. That's what made eating an entire one in a single sitting seem normal to me. Believe it or not, in my mind, it would have been really weird to bake myself a two-layer birthday-style cake five days a week. However, you'd have to be a pussy not to be able to comfortably slam a Jiffy cake a day. Right, fellas? Who's with me?

Even though I didn't have a name for this ritual, I knew it was wrong, because I would never throw away the garbage from my private feast in the kitchen wastebasket, or even our garbage can in the alley. I knew a savvy CIA operative like my mother would have nailed me. So I actually gathered the hollow Pringles can and the empty Jiffy boxes, put them in a bag, walked down the alley, lifted the metal lid of the Schumachers' garbage can, and placed it in there. I owe the Schumachers an apology. If Mrs. Schumacher was any bit as astute as my mom, one of those poor kids probably got grounded for nothing.

Looking back, I know I was "filling the void," as a psychologist might term it. Part of it was surely the feeling that in a house with five kids, I could have this thing that nobody could take from me. My own secret. When I'd go to somebody's house, and there'd be a cake made a day or so earlier with only two slices missing, I'd say, "How is that still standing?" At our house, we'd turn into a pack of dogs. We'd be lucky if the plate wasn't lying in shards on the floor after we were done with it. But I've always had a low tolerance for loneliness, too, and binge eating was maybe a result of that loneliness.

The photographer asked me to say "cheese," but my word was "cake!"

Thankfully, I was a skinny kid, so nobody really noticed these indulgences. I didn't barf it up, either. The binge eating was definitely symptomatic of my not knowing when to stop, though, an affliction I still suffer from today. Verbally, that is. I wish this was one of those stories that ended on a self-help note, kind of a he's-just-not-that-into-you tale about cakes. But it's not. I was and am into them. I've dealt with food issues my whole life, and eventually I acquired the tools to deal with them, as you'll find out later. But I'll admit it, last November 4—I reveal with no small amount of shame—I asked my friends for one thing for my birthday: my own cake, one that they were not allowed to touch, eat, or look at. That's right, last November 3, I could barely sleep because I knew the next day I was getting my own cake that said "Happy Birthday, Kathy," that I could eat with one fork while watching *Oprah*. I was even tempted to put the empty cake box down the street in Forest Whitaker's or Drew Carey's garbage can. By the way, did I mention they're my neighbors? Snap. I'm famous.

When it came to the dinner table of my childhood, though, or family parties, it was probably more important to be full of knowledge and snappy comebacks than food. The great thing about growing up Griffin was that you had to have all your ducks in a row to keep up with everybody's rapier wit. All of my family members were smart, and they all read the *Chicago Times,* the *Tribune,* and the *Daily News.* They watched all the television news programs. At dinnertime, they would wipe the floor with you if you didn't know which alderman was on the take, what was going on in the country, state, city, or neighborhood, or what the leading religious issues were. I don't recall a single relative from my immediate or extended family—and that's a lot of people—who wasn't up on everything. And that includes Hollywood stuff. I have an eighty-five-year-old aunt Florence who can name all the Jonas brothers, plus the release date of their next album. She just likes to keep up with it all. So I may have been into *The Brady Bunch* like every other kid, but I also wanted to watch John Lennon and Yoko Ono on *The Dick Cavett Show,* and every minute of the Watergate hearings. It was fear of the dinner table that got me hooked.

In addition to sweet-and-salty binge eating, television dominated my life. I was into total pop culture consumption, but I have to say, when it came to my passion for showbiz, Mom was not only a great enabler, but an eager and willing participant. Back then we weren't aware of any studies that said kids shouldn't watch eight hours of television a day. Mom openly talks about the advent of television and how wonderful it was to just stick the kids in front of it. And I was happy to oblige.

I lived and breathed movies and television. Rona Barrett was the big entertainment gossip columnist of the day and we always had her magazines around. Kitty Kelley's scandal-packed books, too. Mom was the ideal audience for Hollywood dish. To this day, her dream gift for Christmas is some kind of juicy, unauthorized biography, preferably about Princess Di or any of those damn Kennedys. Uncle Maurice had a joke that he hated the Kennedys so much, he wanted to go to Washington, DC, and pee on the Eternal Flame until it went out. Can you believe it? Irish on Irish crime. Oh, Uncle Mo, how you loved the drunk tank.

But I digress. I remember one night at home when Mom and I watched the movie *Suddenly Last Summer,* that outlandishly dramatic Tennessee Williams adaptation starring Montgomery Clift and Elizabeth Taylor. Mom kept a running commentary on the stars' lives.

"Did you know that Monty Clift had a gorgeous face? And then he was in a car crash, and poor Liz Taylor was in LOVE with him, and kept making sexual advances? But he was one of THOSE men!" My mom really felt like this had happened to one of her friends.

"Really?" I said.

She'd set the scene for you, clearly putting herself in Liz's shoes. "Can you imagine being as beautiful as Liz Taylor, with that tiny waist, and Monty Clift just turns you away in the bedroom? Can you IMAGINE?"

"Um . . . no?" (Gays weren't on my radar yet.)

We loved to watch medical shows together, too—*Medical Center* with Chad Everett, and *Marcus Welby, M.D.* with Robert Young—and again, what she'd read would dribble in as we were transfixed by all the on-screen illness and healing. "Did you know that poor Robert Young cannot sleep at night because as big a star as he is, he's afraid his show is gonna get canceled?"

Me, again, entranced: "Really?"

"That's right. So just think about that, when we're watching *Marcus Welby* next week, and Consuelo comes in with the appointment sheet, that Robert Young didn't even SLEEP last night." Then, because she knew where my career interests lay: "That's how cold show business is. Be careful, Kathleen. Be careful of the biz."

Mom's a hypochondriac, too, so the best part was that every week she would get the disease that the medical shows were dramatizing. I'll never forget, they did an episode on sickle cell anemia, which as far as I know, is almost exclusively an African-American affliction. But Mom was convinced she was the first white person to get it. It's not like we could just Google it in those days and clear her mind, either. She would just walk around until the next week's episode, thinking, *Aaugh! I got this sickle cell and it's really wearing me down. I gotta call Lena Horne about this.*

Mom thought she had debilitating diseases, but I wasn't immune to delusional thoughts, either. Yes, I had my television crushes, like every starry-eyed girl. But they weren't obvious ones. Dark, brooding, and handsome Rod Serling from *The Twilight Zone* and *Night Gallery,* anyone? Mom would make fun of me for that one. "Who the HELL wants to marry that crazy Rod Serling? He looks like a SERIAL KILLER!" But I thought Rod in his leisure suit was the sexiest, most badass thing I'd ever seen. Actually, I was torn between him and David Janssen as Dr. Richard Kimble, that poor, innocent victim of blind justice on the classic chase series *The Fugitive.* I didn't really get into trouble as a child, but when I did, it was usually for staying up late because *The Fugitive* reruns were on at 1 a.m. I would drag my sorry, tardy ass into school the next day because David Janssen had me up way past my bedtime.

Excuse me, but I had priorities. The three things I still live my life by: television, insomnia, and delusions of grandeur.

3

THEY
BARKED,
THEY
LAUGHED

Let's just get this stuff out in the open: As a kid, I was ugly, I was freckly, I had short, wiry orange hair, and when I walked down the street, boys in my class would bark. (To this day, when my dogs do it, I turn my head.) And the torture didn't end when the school year did. One summer, my parents treated my brother Johnny and me to a horseback-riding lesson. The instructor said to Johnny, "Let me get a smaller horse for your little brother." Ouch. It was a blur after that, because I literally became hysterical and cried at him, "I'm a girl! I'm a girl!" for about twenty minutes straight. That guy really earned his five bucks. It's why I wear lots of makeup and fake eyelashes today: I know that there's a horse instructor walking around somewhere who thinks I'm Andy Dick. I'm a girl! I'm a girl! I have my period and everything!

And it wasn't as if I was going to find comfort and solace at Catholic school for being different from all the other girls. At St. Bernardine's the nuns never liked me. Especially Sister Mary Bitch-and-a-Half. I think that was her biblical name. She really tortured me. I'm telling you, she was out to get me. It really gave me an education in how to deal with people in authority who have it in for you, something that would occur again years later when I started doing plays and

Left: Mom must have spent a fortune on these three carnations for my eighth-grade graduation.

had a director who really hated me. But I can thank those nuns, just like the lyrics of that Christina Aguilera song, for "making me a fighter," because they knew how to pick on someone. If it wasn't me, it was Brian Czech, the shy kid who'd spend his time drawing all day. This nun would gun for him just because he was vulnerable. It's one of the reasons I don't like organized religion of any kind. They have too much authority. There was no oversight committee. No Barney Frank.

Now, I never saw a kid get physically abused by the nuns and priests, which my siblings claimed to have witnessed, but I do remember something that happened to one boy that really chilled me. He was being rambunctious, and the nun said, "Go get your coat." He had a winter jacket with a thin fabric hook on the back, and she hung him by that hook in the cloakroom until lunch. And there he was, just hanging by his own jacket, and nobody questioned it. No parents ever came and said, "Did you really hang my kid in the cloakroom?" At that time, it was, "Whatever you say, Sister."

Never mind a nun coming to a kid's defense against other kids. It was a dog-eat-dog world at St. Bernardine's from the get-go. Starting in first grade I had to band with other outcasts to protect myself from the cute, straight-haired mean girls. I may have been a dork with Bozo hair, but those girls were vicious. I remember getting my ass kicked by them one time when I'd said the wrong thing to piss off a couple of the mean girls. I don't even remember what it was, but when they decided it was payback time, you were done for. This was on the school premises—on the *stairs*—that I was being roughed up, and I swear a nun nearby did fucking nothing but watch. I mean, they were kicking me in the *ribs*. I'm not saying I had to go to the hospital, but when I could see an adult—who could have stopped it in a second—wasn't going to do anything, I had what Oprah would call my "lightbulb" moment: "Oh, I see. Nobody saves you." Then immediately I started thinking, *I have to see them in homeroom tomorrow!* It was like learning a tribal mentality. How am I going to survive with Mary O'Hanrahan and those bitches?

I knew I wasn't physically strong enough to fight back. I couldn't kill them with kindness, because that doesn't come naturally to me. I couldn't kill them, either. Which *really* felt natural. But I did think I was smarter than them, and was pretty sure I was more clever. So I decided I was going to be openly sarcastic, and make a joke to their faces in class. I did my homework, too. I remembered that once in class, Mary had been chosen to answer what the capital of Romania was and had gotten it wrong.

So the next day when my ass kicking was being savored by Mary and her gang, I said loud enough for all to hear, "Well, Mary, I guess I'll have to move to a place you've never heard of . . . like Bucharest?"

It was my EF Hutton moment. Remember that old commercial? "When EF Hutton talks, people listen." There was a beat of silence, and then her friends laughed. The class laughed, too.

(Very important point, by the way. *Everyone* has to laugh. Otherwise you just get your ass kicked again.)

There was something like a tacit agreement after that. They never made me their friend, but they did something better. They left me alone. And in return, I would occasionally make them laugh, and not necessarily at their expense. But I just thought, *If I can keep them laughing, they'll get off my back.* And they did.

Brian Czech, the boy who sketched all the time, who I swear didn't talk for eight years, became one of my good friends in grade school, and he had his own way of protecting himself. He would draw guitars all day on thick pieces of cardboard, cut them out, and put them on his pens with tape or a rubber band, so they all looked like guitars. And he did it for all the kids in the class. Even the most popular kid would come up to him: "Hey, Brian, would you make me one?" He would just nod, and then produce this incredibly ornate cardboard guitar for the kid to put on his pen.

To this day, if I have a type, it's quiet guys. Guys like Brian. Turns out, I do enough talking for both of us. Of course, back then I was determined to get Brian Czech to talk to me. I just persisted until I found out our common ground was that we both *loved Night Gallery.* (Perhaps you remember my crush on Rod Serling?) Brian would come in on Monday and I'd say, "Did you see the new one? With the twins? The dead sister who had the tap-dancing school and you could hear

I can explain. I was in a play. Honest.

her tap dancing after she died?" (I never did see Brian after St. Bernardine's. Hey Brian, if you're reading this, you can find me on Twitter. Twat me!) I make fun of my mother for her sympathy illnesses from *Marcus Welby, M.D.*, but like I should be talking. After that disturbing *Night Gallery* with Laurence Harvey as the guy whose murder plot with a brain-penetrating caterpillar backfires on him, for ten years I thought I had an earwig. AND IT LAID EGGS!!!

Did I mention I watched a lot of television?

My dream to be in showbiz took all forms from a young age. If there was any reading aloud in class to be done, my hand shot up first. Even the corny Nativity pageant bullshit every year got me all psyched. Outside of school, I was always dragging kids from the block to do plays with me in the yard. Anything for attention.

For the Griffin household, I naturally had my own one-woman shows that I would perform each night during dinner. I'll be honest, I just stole my theme song from *The Tonight Show*. Then I'd move into a topical, cutting-edge monologue about what happened to me that day—lemonade stands, five cents a cup, you call this a living?—and then go into my tap number. I was a kid living with a lot of denial about my tap-dancing abilities, when all I was really doing was stomping my foot around the floor. Then there might be a reading from my favorite Judy Blume book, or a dramatic reenactment from *Love Story*. (I played all parts.)

The family, meanwhile, would just be anxiously eyeing their Hamburger Helper, wondering when the floor show was going to end.

It was *The Mary Tyler Moore Show*, though, that gave me the first inkling of what place I could have in the entertainment world. When that legendary sitcom first came on, I naturally had to check it out because I loved Mary from *The Dick Van Dyke Show*—that hilarious Dick Van Dyke was, like Rod Serling, another husband candidate in my mind—and I'll never forget that awesome apartment with the big M on the wall, and how beautiful Mary was. But when Rhoda burst through the door in her Gypsy headscarf, billowy caftan, and hilariously abrasive delivery, I was like, "Who is *that*? Oh my God!" That's when I fell in love with wanting to be the sidekick. Everything out of her mouth was hysterical, yet she was vulnerable and human. I remember my family fell in love with her, too.

That's who I wanted to be. She had all the jokes.

I knew I could never be Mary—just like when I watched *The Brady Bunch* I knew I could never be Marcia. Let's face it, I was Alice even when I was ten years old. (It doesn't help when your mother has this horrible expression she unleashes every once in a while: "You'll always be cute, but you'll never be pretty." The Irish think it's just like saying, "Hi.") But in any case, I knew I could totally be Rhoda. She battled with her weight and had funny comebacks, and things didn't go her way, but she always got the laugh. I loved her.

Before I had gays to do my hair.

After eighth-grade graduation, my parents were hell-bent on sending me to the local all-girls parochial high school, but I wanted to go to public school. It was a lot bigger, and there was a huge drama department. And it had boys. Hmmm, how was I going to win this argument? I tried crying. That didn't work. I told them about all the plays I would try out for. That didn't work. Then it came to me: "Public school is free!" That got 'em.

When I entered Oak Park High School, my mind was blown because I was going from a graduating grade school class of thirty-four to a freshman class of over a thousand. The school had three theater programs, and I signed up for all of them. The auditorium held 1,700 seats, and I remember seeing Mary Elizabeth Mastrantonio—remember *Scarface* and *The Color of Money?*—and Dan Castellanata—the voice of Homer on *The Simpsons*—in *Camelot* there when they were seniors and I was a freshman. They were the queen and king of the drama department. When Mastrantonio went on to Broadway from Oak Park, I told myself, "Don't fuck around. There's good people here."

The numbers game is intense at a school that big, so when there was only one picture of me in the freshman yearbook, I was determined to get my picture in the sophomore yearbook so many times they would have to add another line for me in the index. Pathetic, I know. It's really no different than how I am with *US Weekly* today. I guarantee you I went to maybe one meeting of student council, but I was there on picture day! I was a cheerleader, too. Don't get excited. I was a *soccer* cheerleader. It doesn't get nerdier than that. I was fired from the soccer cheerleading squad after one year, which I believe to this day is unprecedented. You have to understand, no one went to the soccer games. In fact, I believe part of my duties as a cheerleader was to bake brownies for the team. Then I became the only person who couldn't read music to get into City Chorus. I joined everything I could. I also told myself that when I graduated, I was going to speak at the commencement service, no matter what. And sure enough, I'd bullshitted my way into reading some ridiculous poem. That was my big thing, getting my name out there, a credo I still live by today. You may not like me or embrace me, but I'll bet you've heard of me. The best thing about the *D-List* show is that people who didn't like me so much, or simply found me annoying, watched the show and came around to my side. But step one has always been, "They're all going to know my name!" Looking back, it sounds like I was going to go postal on my school, but I wasn't. I was just focused!

I make jokes now about Hollywood being like high school, because it is. It's the same hierarchy. You had to know your place, but you could easily be fooled into thinking somebody was your friend when they clearly weren't. If I were alone with any of the jocks or popular girls, sure, they'd talk to me. I could even have a conversation with someone like homecoming queen Christie Grisaffi. But every time I'd walk through the hall and be like, "Hi, Christie!" she'd act like I hadn't said anything. Or I'd be in science lab next to a football guy, and think, *He seems cool in class! Maybe I shouldn't judge people!* The next day, he would act like he didn't know me. I know, John Hughes nailed it, right?

This is how I discovered what I now lovingly refer to as "my gays."

I'm lower right, and my boyfriend Tom is in the blue-and-white-check shirt. Why doesn't he want to go all the way with me?

I sought refuge in musical theater. The safe haven! I truly loved the drama clique, where I felt welcomed. I tried to be involved on any level, from watching rehearsals to printing programs. And the cliché is true, once you're in and you look around, it's a bunch of straight girls and gay guys. (You'd think one of those football players would have half a brain and sign up for the play and get laid constantly.) Tom Murphy was my high school boyfriend. When I look at his yearbook picture now, he does remind me a little of Zac Efron or Chace Crawford. Mom would say to his face, "Tom, you're so damn pretty, it's a shame you're a boy!" Good old Maggie. Always direct. He was sort of flamboyant, and my friends and I would tease him about being gay, but he did make out with all of us girls in the drama department. We just . . you know . . . never went all the way. For some reason. I'm pretty sure people didn't start being gay until I was in high school. I'll have to check with GLAAD about that.

Today it's different, of course. If I meet a guy and I think he's gay,

I'd probably just come out and ask him. So my girlfriends and I may have good-naturedly ribbed guys like Tom about boys he had crushes on, but we didn't pursue it, and we certainly weren't mean-spirited about it. It was all pretty innocent. (Although I do think the guys were all fucking each other.) My idea of a date, meanwhile, was Tom picking me up from my job at Farrell's Ice Cream Parlor and walking home in my gay-nineties' outfit and Styrofoam hat through the cemetery, talking about theater, dance, the Bee Gees, the Donna Summer concert we were going to stand in line for, how we both wanted to be Karen Lynn Gorney in *Saturday Night Fever*. Other times we would hang out in the Griffin family den singing songs from *Gypsy, Guys and Dolls*, or the ultimate, *Funny Girl*. Yes, the gay boys and I could lip-sync the sound track to *Funny Girl* in its entirety. Sometimes we would try to copy a dance routine that we saw on a variety show: the Osmonds or Jackson Five. We did plenty of gay stuff; we just didn't know how gay we were at the time.

I was so used to hanging out with gay guys that when I had a real high school boyfriend, I couldn't believe that he wanted to actually fool around and have sex. His name was Nick. He was shy and cute and third string on the basketball team. And I couldn't believe he liked me. One time we had a date and he tried to feel me up over my paisley button-down shirt and olive green elephant bells, and I was appalled. Tom Murphy never tried to go that far with me. To this day, the behavior of straight men is something I've never been able to wrap my head around. Have you ever met one? They're really weird. Sometimes they want to have sex without *A Chorus Line* playing in the background. Yuck. How is that even possible?

So while straight guys may have mystified me, I was a girl who knew what she wanted in terms of fame and recognition: a lead in the school play. I scratched and clawed my way to starring in the big shows my senior year. I was Rosemary in *How to Succeed in Business Without Really Trying*, the part that Michele Lee played in the film. (Now, of course, I'd never take that role, because it's not the funny sidekick.) I was also Hodel, one of the daughters in *Fiddler on the Roof*, a production in which I believe there was only one Jewish girl. Very multi-culti.

Even then, I wanted my school to think outside the box. Why weren't we doing *For Colored Girls Who Have Considered Suicide When the Rainbow Is Enuf*?

My senior year I started having vicious, tearful fights with my parents about why I didn't want to go to college. They couldn't figure it out. They'd saved for it. Joyce, John, and Gary had all gone.

But I knew that I had to try to be a real actress, and start as soon as possible. I certainly wasn't going to follow the paths imagined by my parents, who never took my show business yearnings seriously. They kept trying to talk me into being a dental hygienist, so I could meet a nice dentist, who would then take care of me. That was after I got braces, which means it probably occurred to Mom after she bitched and moaned about the price. The second option to consider was being a "stew." In other words, stewardess. They said if I became a "stew," I could fly for free. You can see where this is going.

"That sounds like *you* just want to get free plane tickets," I said.

"No, no, you'd be great!" They beamed.

In any case, I'd already had a taste of "the biz" when I got to appear in a commercial while I was still in high school. My parents had a friend who did local voice-overs, and that friend's son announced one day that he was going to be an extra in a commercial for the Chicago White Sox, and did I want to do it, too? "You come, you sit in the seats, they film it, and you get twenty-five dollars."

I'd be rich! Sign me up!

The shoot was held at the old Comiskey Park, where the White Sox played. I was outfitted in braids, a red-and-white-check gingham shirt, and a Sox cap. I got to sit in the crowd and sing the team's anthem, which was the oldie "Na Na Hey Hey Kiss Him Good-bye" but with a chorus that ended in "good times." That day I had the time of my life, and then, sure enough, they decided to put me in a small group shot. So out of the whole crowd, they zoomed in on me, my parents' friend's son, and two other people. I didn't even know I was recognizable until the commercial started airing. "Hey, you were in the Sox commercial!" I'd suddenly hear when I was at school or walking

My first award, for second best singer in a talent competition. Yeah, I rocked Genoa City, Wisconsin. Next stop, Hollywood!

down the street, which thrilled me to no end. I had become a famous face!

My parents may have pooh-poohed my career aspirations, but they were cool enough to foot the bill for my first headshots. I needed them, too, because after that commercial I went and signed with every talent agency in Chicago. (No one cared about exclusivity there.) They were corny shots—me with a handbag in a Sears catalog pose, as a counter girl in a generic fast-food restaurant, and as a tomboy in OshKosh B'Gosh overalls—but the idea was to show a range of what I could do.

Despite my efforts, I didn't get booked for anything else.

I knew I had to move to Los Angeles. That was where it was going to happen for me. I had talked my parents out of college, and now other factors made the notion of relocating also attractive to Mom and Dad. Kenny was already out in California touting the place, Joyce was looking for a change of scenery, my parents were now old enough to retire, and the winters in Chicago were really starting to kick my mother's ass. So after living six decades in one city, my parents up and moved to a place where they didn't know a soul. Joyce and I headed out a month later, driving across the country together. I was eighteen.

LA may have been the home of movie-star mansions, big studio lots, and the expanse of the Pacific, but the Griffins found a way to live there like Depression-era Irish. We were all enmeshed in a run-down apartment building at Pico and Lincoln, to this day a hinky area of Santa Monica. I was living with my parents in a two-bedroom apartment, Joyce was in the unit closest to the street, and in between us lived a guy named John who worked for the General Accounting Office and who I ended up dating for five years. Yes, men, you could have had me as your girlfriend if you'd lived close enough.

It really was some fucked-up white version of *Good Times*. I had just come from such a typical suburban environment that our street in Oak Park, Illinois, was called, if you'll remember, Home Avenue. Medium-sized middle-class houses, children, dogs, block parties, relatively quiet. Now, we lived across the street from Santa Monica High, so urban teenage rowdiness was a daily fact of life. Occasionally we'd go downstairs to the communal washer-and-dryer room and find some Malibu trust fund ne'er-do-well or poor Mexican teen smoking pot. Then there was the homeless contingent in Santa Monica. Being a beach town, my mother's theory was that we shouldn't spend money on air-conditioning. She would prop open the front door to our apartment and plug in the Builders Emporium box fan to cool the place down. One time a big, scary-looking, stanky-smelling vagrant just walked into our apartment and started yelling at my dad, caught unawares in his boxers and Sears T-shirt.

"I wanna take a SHAWAH! I wanna take a SHAWAH!"

He did actually need one, by the way. He was filthy. But that doesn't mean you do what my dad—who wasn't having any of it—did next. My five-foot, six-inch, roughly sixty-year-old father, without batting an eyelash, took this guy on. He repeatedly poked an angry finger in the homeless guy's chest. "You're not takin' a shower HERE, pal!" The guy backed up and Dad slammed the door in his face.

I'm not saying it was the hood, but it definitely wasn't the safe suburban enclave to which we'd become accustomed.

No matter, though. I was in California. I was excited. And I had a plan. I was going to work as an extra, take acting classes, then become a professional actress! I was going to get in the door! I was going to pound the pavement! I was going to go from agency to agency! I was going to be a star!

I ended up living with my parents till I was twenty-eight. (Sigh.)

4
KENNY

Moving out to LA meant that my family and I were going to be in close proximity to my oldest brother Kenny. My memories of Kenny are perhaps the most difficult part of writing this book. My recollection of him just doesn't line up with those of family. What follows is my version of my relationship with him, and I've decided to get it out in the open for the first time. He was really the dominant male figure of my formative years, for reasons that started out good and eventually turned very bad.

Early on, Kenny was living the life I hoped to one day lead, and as an impressionable young girl with a dream to be in show business, I looked up to him for that. It was clear as I was growing up that Kenny was the star of the family. He was very bright and very charming, and he became something of a minor celebrity as an actor and musician. He was in a band—okay, a cover band, which back then seemed glamorous—but when I was a kid what was more important to me was that he had the lead in a celebrated production of *Hair* at the famed Shubert Theatre in Chicago. That was a big deal. At the end of the musical, when the song "The Age of Aquarius" segues into that chorus of "Let the sun shine in," they would have the audience come up on stage. I remember I was too young to see the play, but one night Kenny brought me up anyway and I got to dance in the finale with everyone, and that's one of those bitten-by-the-bug moments I'll never forget.

I would hear about Kenny getting to meet local celebrities, actors at the Playboy mansion (which was then a Chicago hotspot), and he was getting offers to sing commercial jingles. It all seemed so fantastic. Part of me really did have a bit of idol worship with him. And when I was a snotty little kid who annoyed the family by singing and dancing around in the house every night, he was the encouraging one. He'd say, "You know, you could do this if you want to." A comment like that, as simple as it sounds, can really fuel the optimism of a starstruck kid.

Kenny's behavior at other times, though, offered up contradictions. He had a terrible work ethic, for instance, which really burned itself into my brain as something very negative. He was an "artist," he'd claim, so he always felt he was above a regular job, and because he was a charmer, he could always find a hot chick or girlfriend to support him. His attitude, though, would shock me. I remember one time when Kenny was between road gigs and staying at the house, I was in my room and someone called the upstairs phone. It was an offer for Kenny to do a voice-over. The job was short notice, though, as in, happening in a few hours.

"What? I'm not going to do some stupid voice-over! I'm in a band!" he yelled into the phone.

I overheard that the pay was $300, which seemed like an instant windfall to me. I gasped and thought, *Get out of bed and go do that voice-over for three hundred dollars! What are you thinking?*

But he hung up. Then he got into a big fight in the hall with Mom, who also couldn't believe he was turning down that kind of cash. Then of course two months later he'd be asking her for money.

As talented as Kenny was, he was a troublemaker from as early as I can remember, always causing Mom and Dad a lot of heartache. He was getting arrested for one thing or another, and because our family knew the local cops, he'd be let off easy, after which Mom would go off and cry somewhere. He was always asking for money from Mom—never Dad, who would just explode on him if he tried—but instead of just borrowing it like a normal person, he'd turn it into a confrontation that would end with him in her face screaming, "I don't want your goddamn money!" and then throwing it on the floor. He could be physically frightening in every way, and easily spin out of control.

But sure enough, he found a beautiful, sweet girl to marry him. Her name was Kathy, a red-haired knockout who wore fashionable clothes and was really cool, and I thought she was a superfox. But shortly after they got married, she would take me aside and tell me that Kenny beat her. I know: There's a boundary issue here, and you can debate the appropriateness of telling an eleven-year-old these things. She would tell me about the time Kenny threw her out of their apartment naked in the middle of winter to humiliate her. But Mom and Dad would say, "Oh, she's being dramatic." I'd look at the tightly wound Kenny and easily believe it happened.

Then it happened in front of me. We were hanging out in Joyce's room upstairs, and Kenny and Kathy got into an altercation. They started yelling, and in an instant, it seemed, Kenny threw his wife across the room. She hit the wall and slid down to the floor. It knocked the wind out of her. I was horrified. Joyce tried to stop it, and I ran into my room, terrorized. I couldn't stop shaking. My brother Johnny came in, asked me what was wrong. I was trembling, too scared even to talk at all, fearful of escalating the situation. After a few minutes, I stammered out the words, "Kenny beat up Kathy."

As a result of all the shouting, Mom and Dad ran up the stairs and Kenny was already in the hallway. But what surprised me was that the commotion afterward focused on me, the crying little girl, and not the woman who'd just been abused. I was overcome with guilt, and I remember thinking, *No, look after her! I saw her get thrown across the room!* But Kathy didn't have a mark on her, and she was quickly tamping out the fire with "I'm fine! I'm fine!" Kenny, meanwhile, wasn't saying anything, just tapping his thumbnail repeatedly against his teeth. My father went off on him, of course. "How do you hit a woman?! What the hell are you thinking?" But they kept making a fuss about me. "Is she okay? Is she going to be okay?" Even Kenny's wife, the victim here, was taking it upon herself to comfort me by saying, "I'm so sorry you had to see this." By the end of that night, everybody in the family was acting like Kenny had shoved his wife a little, there was some hysteria, and it would never happen again.

But Kathy continued to tell me about beatings. And when they got divorced, and Kenny got another girlfriend, she told me privately about his being violent with her, too.

Then there was the extremely inappropriate sexual energy that came from Kenny. This older brother I worshipped would crawl into my bed and softly say to me over and over things like "You're so pretty" and "You're the prettiest girl I've ever seen." If you saw this, if you'd been in the room, you'd stop it from happening. He never molested me, but a twenty-eight-year-old guy whispering sweet nothings into his ten-year-old sister's ear like a lover is out of line in any sane person's book.

Another incident occurred with a creepy friend of Kenny's when I was around thirteen. Our house was always pretty welcoming, and friends staying over was never an issue. So Kenny brought home a guy he knew. When he and Kenny were in my brothers' back bedroom, I was singing and dancing in front of them and being a general show-off. My brother left the room, and in two seconds this grown man pulled me onto his knee, and before my preteen brain could even process what this was, he jammed his tongue down my throat. Our teeth tapped. It's odd, the details you remember. It was over in a minute maybe, and my thoughts ran to *Bleeccch! What was THAT?* I stood up, and then he casually went downstairs like nothing had happened.

This guy ended up cooking dinner for my family that night. Tacos, I recall, which we all thought were pretty exotic. This guy had it down. The whole family liked him, which is what pedophiles know how to do: charm everyone. Meanwhile, as the evening wore on, I started getting angrier and angrier, reliving in my mind what had happened upstairs. I wanted revenge. After dinner, when it was family talk time in the living room, he was sitting on a chair, and I deliberately chose to sit on the arm of his chair. I didn't know what I was going to do, but I could at least start to make him uncomfortable. At one point he was holding court, telling a story, when out of the blue I made a fist and punched him in the stomach as hard as I could.

"What are you doing, Kathy?" everyone yelled.

I'm sure this asshole knew what was up, because he tried to laugh it off, to make sure I didn't talk about what he did. "Oh, don't mind her!" he joked. "Look out for little Attila the Hun here!"

Later that night, I was too scared to be in my bed alone, so I told Mom what he did, and insisted on sleeping in her and Dad's room. Mom, to her credit, kept saying, "Oh my God," and told me that this guy would never be allowed in the house again. But she couldn't bring herself to say anything directly to him, so he spent the night. This upset me for so many years that in my twenties I confronted Mom about it, and yelled, "How could you have let him spend the night in our house after what he did?" My mom burst into tears and said, "I'm sorry, I didn't know what to do. We didn't really know what that was!" She was trying to explain to me that that kind of behavior was something you saw on the news, or happened to other families. She obviously didn't know how to process it.

I do remember that she had the wherewithal to protect me that night, to the extent that I got to sleep in my parents' bedroom, and I specifically remember her locking the door. But she wasn't able to confront this guy. She later told me that she wanted to tell Dad, but she knew a chain reaction would start, and this is where Kenny comes in, as an unstable force that nobody wanted to unleash. It was the fear of the wrath of Kenny that prevented her from doing more. If Kenny were to be upset—God forbid—Mom knew this would lead to one of his inevitable rages. The cops would come. Somebody would end up in jail or the hospital. With Kenny you never knew. It was a call she made. Maybe not the best call.

Plus, how do you prove what had happened to me? That was when I began thinking, if Kenny's friend is doing this, then Kenny might be doing it as well. When Kenny's wife told me later that during the production of *Hair* she came home to their apartment to find Kenny hanging out with two thirteen-year-old girls, I started to put things together.

Later, after I'd moved to LA and was performing regularly at the Groundlings theater, I had a conversation with my brother John and mentioned the incident with Kenny's friend. John said he didn't know about it. "Really?" I said, surprised.

He said, "Kathy, I would remember if you'd told me that."

So I filled him in on what had happened. Then John did something I'll never stop loving him for. From Chicago, where John lived, and totally unsolicited, he tracked the guy down in another city and confronted him by phone. The guy's response was that the call caught him off guard and he'd have to get back to him. Which is a sure sign of guilt, don't you think? If someone asked you if you'd molested a child, you wouldn't reply, "Um, I need a minute," if you were innocent. Anyway, John called me back and said, "That fucker, he did it." But he also told me that the guy wanted to take me and my mother out to lunch to explain. This threw me into a tailspin. I didn't want to see the guy. I thought the request was categorically weird.

Well, that Friday I performed at the Groundlings, and afterward I got flowers backstage with a note from the guy saying, "I'm here, and I want to take you out for a drink after the show." This seriously creeped me out. Naturally, I was dating some loser at the time who wouldn't go outside for me and find him and ask him to leave. So I had to walk out in front of the theater and confront the guy. I was shaking from head to toe.

"You want to talk this out?" he said.

"No," I nervously replied. "Please don't ever contact me again, and certainly don't contact my mom." And that was it. I never heard from him after that. John and I may have fought a lot as kids, but I love that he felt protective enough of me to stop everything in the middle of his workday and freakin' cold-call this guy from years ago.

Hearing that Kenny was a pedophile, though, was what set me on the path to cutting him out of my life. Again, his alleged pedophilia is something that there is no record of, as is sadly the case with many passed-on stories like this. No child has come up to me, either, and said, "Your brother molested me." But here's what I know: independently of each other, women deeply involved with Kenny—his wife Kathy, and then later a longtime girlfriend—told me about his being caught with minors, then his admitting it to them and crying.

Kathy once told me about a phone call she got from a guy who wanted to kill Kenny because he'd caught Kenny with his underage daughter, and by underage I mean a child. These women I knew had graphic stories that, coupled with how I knew he'd been with me in bed when I was very young, were convincing enough for me. Kenny would eventually get locked up for drug charges and theft, but I wanted him to go away for being a pedophile. For ruining lives.

"How can you be so hard on him?" I'd hear from members of my family, who just didn't believe me.

I couldn't get these kids out of my mind. You think fucking a kid doesn't ruin their life forever?

Those were the crying, screaming arguments I'd have with my family. Unfortunately, the cheese stood alone.

It was so difficult for me to understand why the rest of my family wouldn't consider the possibility that Kenny was a pedophile. My mom and dad would constantly say, "Kathleen, that's a horrible accusation to make." And I think it's a worse crime to commit than an accusation to make. This caused a great divide between me and the rest of my family, resulting in everything from separate holiday gatherings in one day—one where Kenny saw the family, and a later one that I attended—to the mere mention of his name by anyone else in my family, setting me off.

The final straw for me came a couple of years after my parents and I had moved to Los Angeles, when I was in my midtwenties. Kenny, as you know, had been in LA already. I gave Kenny the benefit of the doubt for a couple of years. Then, I heard another story from his longtime girlfriend involving my brother confessing to sexual relations with kids. On separate occasions, he had molested one boy and one girl in the apartment building he managed. His explanation, according to the person who told me, was that *they* were coming on to *him*. Typical pedophile logic. In any case, I had the apartment numbers of the victims, and this may sound odd, but I actually tried to get my own brother arrested. I never told my family this. Blood is not thicker than water, not when it involves the abuse of kids. I was dating an attorney at the time, and he checked LA county arrest records for me. Kenny had never been arrested for molestation. There was no record of anything. I called the LAPD, and I told them that my brother was molesting kids—and then I provided the addresses. To my surprise, they told me that unless the children or the parents themselves contacted them, they could not investigate it.

It was frustrating to me that there was no recourse for these accusations that I believed to be true. Though this led me to cut off all contact with Kenny, I stepped up my crusade with the rest of my immediate family. You have to understand that they simply didn't want to believe that he was a pedophile. They still don't. They would say things like, "You're exaggerating," or "You're being overly dramatic," and about my break with Kenny, "He's the only oldest brother you'll ever have." But I took a hard line. My crusade continued in the form of years of arguments with my parents.

Cutting off contact with Kenny wasn't the answer, though. It didn't get him out of my life, as I hoped it would. It may have been easy for me not to have contact with him, but because he was my brother, I was still hearing about what he was up to from the other family members, whether intentionally or not. When you're dealing with someone as dangerous, damaged, and volatile as Kenny, it shouldn't have surprised me that his life spiraled even further downward, very quickly. He was living with a woman who was a registered nurse—of course, he'd found a woman who could take care of him—and he started using drugs while he was with her.

And then, in what seemed like an instant—either she kicked him out or he left—he was homeless and hooked on crack. It was devastating to watch the effect this had on my parents. They tried to use logic with an out-of-control addict—getting him on food stamps, for instance—but he wasn't willing to work. "I'm too good for food stamps," he told my mom once.

It had been some years, but I did see Kenny again, in the weirdest of circumstances. I was driving to an audition at the CBS Radford lot in Studio City, and as I was getting off at the Laurel Canyon exit from the freeway, there he was. My brother was holding a sign: HOMELESS, NEED FOOD, NEED MONEY.

Maybe you're hoping this story ends with a tearful reunion. Well, it doesn't. I'll never forget that the sign *didn't* say, WILL WORK FOR FOOD. I remember thinking, *that fucker would rather be homeless than work!* The sight admittedly shook me. I knew I had just witnessed something nobody should ever have to see.

Yes, I went to the audition. No, I didn't get the job.

Then, things got even worse. I remember the day Mom and Dad returned to their apartment only to find Kenny had used his key to let himself in and burglarized them. And the panhandling that I had seen was, it turned out, to support his habit. Apparently in those days you could buy some rock cocaine for $5. He told my mom he would panhandle till he got enough for a rock, as he called it, then go back and beg strangers until he could get another $5 for another rock, and on and on. He would also go missing for days at a time, and my mom and dad would then drive around the streets of LA trying to find him.

It killed me to see my parents go through all this with Kenny. One time when I was at their apartment, the phone rang, and I picked it up. It was him. Keep in mind, I hadn't talked to Kenny in many years at this point. But I just started screaming into the phone: "Stay away from Mom and Dad, you fucking child molester! I'm on to you! I know who you are! I know what you did! Stay away from them!" I remember saying to my mom after the phone call, "This isn't a poor troubled drug addict to me. This guy is a child molester. That's a whole different animal."

Eventually he was arrested, I believe, for drug-related charges: burglary, etc. Then I had to watch my parents go through the excruciating process of going to court with Kenny, vouching for this middle-aged man like he was a child, and later making the sad trips to visit him at the state penitentiary.

My not shutting up about Kenny was always a sore spot with the family, but I held firm about what I knew, and the subject of Kenny never ceased to potentially turn any gathering with my parents into a volatile argument. But then my dad did something surprising. He was talking to Kenny on the phone, and Kenny—ever the victim—asked him, "Why does Kathy have such a problem with me?" And Dad told me he said to Kenny, "You know, she thinks you're a child molester. Is that true?"

I couldn't believe it. Dad had actually, finally, asked him flat out.

According to my dad, Kenny replied, "Well, I do what I do."

After Dad told me this, he said to me, "So you can take that whichever way."

Huh? *"I do what I do?"*

"DAD!" I responded, my jaw on the floor. "If someone accused you of having sex with children, your answer would not be, 'I do what I do'! Your answer would be, 'That's outrageous!' ANYTHING but 'I do what I do.' "

And that's where my family and I reached our separate peace, because that was the moment they stopped dogging me for separating from Kenny. Something might have finally clicked for my family. Not enough to admit it to themselves, but enough not to fight me about it.

I eventually learned that John had been suspicious about Kenny for a while, as well. When John's daughter, Claire, was born, he and his wife were terrified that if they brought Claire out to Los Angeles for a visit, that there might be an instance when Kenny would be alone with the baby. John had held out hope that I was exaggerating, but when it came right down to it, he had to tell Mom, "Tell Kenny that he can't ever come over when our kids are there." When Kenny died, Claire was around twelve, and she never knew she had another uncle. Like me, John had come to realize that it was necessary to cut Kenny off.

Mind you, it was never like I insisted Kenny be cut off. I only wanted everyone to cut the bullshit and admit what my brother really was. How could anybody have begun to help Kenny if they wouldn't face up to it? As it turned out, later in life Kenny admitted to my parents that he'd been molested by someone associated with his junior-league baseball team. We all now think a cousin of ours who used to babysit Kenny might have molested him, too. This cousin went on to become a priest who got moved from parish to parish each time he was caught with a kid. He eventually died of AIDS.

When I put myself in my mom's shoes, I can see why being the parent of someone like Kenny leads you to think of his transgressions as symptoms of an illness, rather than criminal wrongdoing. I know the only time I've ever seen my dad sob was with guilt over Kenny. "What did we do? What did we do?" he cried, putting his fists to his forehead. They'd question everything about their parenting, and how could you not? I was hard on my parents about their denial, but they get a free pass from me now, and here's why. After Kenny got out of prison, word was he tried to right himself. He even got a job as a deliveryman for a restaurant. My mom's version of this story is that at the end, he had finally cleaned his life up. I don't know about that, but here's what I do know: He literally died in my mom's arms. After years of living on and off the streets, he contracted pneumonia, and while on a visit with my parents at their condo, he took seriously ill. But before the paramedics could arrive, he collapsed in my mom's arms.

When he was in Cedars Sinai hospital, he was declared brain-dead, and my parents had one last request for me: They wanted me to go to the hospital and say good-bye. I had not laid eyes on Kenny in several years, but of course I couldn't deny them this request.

There he was, thin, frail, and finally harmless. It was easy to say good-bye, and even to forgive him, but only for the effect he had on me. I could never forgive him for what he did to those kids, and it wasn't up to me, anyway. That's an important delineation. Also, there's something about seeing the lifeless state of someone who really did terrify you that finally allows you to stop feeling afraid. It was perhaps an illogical feeling at that point in my life—because for years I'd had no reason to be scared of him—but at that moment I was able to put the fear and angst that I had suffered for so long to bed as well.

I'd be lying if I said Kenny wasn't a big influence on me. I don't do drugs. I'm not homeless. I'm not an addict. I know what serious fucking up looks like. Kenny turned down the voice-over. I'd do the voice-over. Kenny called in sick to *Hair* all the time. I think, *Don't ever miss a performance.* That's a form of influence, for sure. Negative, perhaps, but an important one, nonetheless.

My parents probably wouldn't have even considered retiring in California if Kenny hadn't convinced them it was a beautiful place to live. So say what you want, but Kenny tangentially set the stage for my parents and me to come to Hollywood. I'm looking for positives here, people. Hopefully you'll cut me some slack.

5
LA IS
MY LADY

I wasn't always a whore. There was a time when I was actually naive about things—like when I first moved to LA—and just barreled through life like it was mine for the taking, without thinking about the consequences.

Most people new to a city on the ocean would probably go to the beach during the day when there are people around. I, on the other hand, decided to try a midnight swim at the somewhat gamy Santa Monica pier, by myself. That is, until a nearby guard kicked me off the beach for my own safety.

Most people unfamiliar with the men in a new town might search for love until they find it. I picked out some guy on my second day in LA, who worked at the local bicycle shop, and handed my virginity to him. "You can fill a tire? Sounds good to me. Let's call it a date." Needless to say he wasn't Mr. Right.

Then there are the ballsy moves that pay off. In that first week as a Los Angeleno, I read in the alternative newspaper the *LA Weekly*—which quickly became my bible about goings-on in town—a review of the latest show at what had become a comedy hotspot, the Groundlings. This was a place I'd heard about, something in the vein of the famed Chicago troupe Second City. So I went to the Friday late show, and thought it

Left: My typical '80s dance club outfit . . . What's the problem?

was fantastic. The group did improvisational songs, sketches that involved the actors in costumes and wigs, and most important, included the crowd in a lot of the skits.

I was sitting by myself in the front row, and got picked for a bit involving audience interaction. I was so excited. *I have to get in this group,* I thought. *This is where I want to be. This is the greatest thing in the world.*

So at the tender age of nineteen I marched backstage by myself, past everyone's lockers, through the girls' dressing room—I can't believe it now, it was so rude—all the while telling myself, "I'm going to just go up to the performer I think is the funniest and ask advice." He was taking off his makeup, and I must have had a deranged determination on my face because he turned to me and said politely, but with that "uh-oh" sound in his voice, "Can I help you?"

"Sorry to bother you, but you're so fantastic. Please, how do I get to do this?" I said.

He was so patient with me. "Well, there's a school here, and first you have to go through all the levels of the school. . . ." He continued talking as he got up and led me to the director of that night's show, a guy named Tom Maxwell. "Here's a girl who's interested in classes," he said, introducing me. I'm telling you, he could not have been sweeter. This guy was the star of the show, and he calmly spent a good ten minutes explaining how the Groundlings worked to this brassy, boundary-crashing audience member who he could have easily dismissed.

That man's name was Phil Hartman.

Years later—I mean it took me *years* to get into the goddamn Groundlings—I would do shows alongside the great Phil Hartman. But until then, apparently I had to pay something called "dues." More about this later.

When it came to pestering show folk for career tips, I wasn't the only Griffin looking out for me. I had eager lieutenants in my parents.

Mom and Dad were always starstruck. In the early years of living in Los Angeles, they were unable to stop themselves from pulling the car over whenever they saw television shows or movies being filmed.

This is a Groundlings photo showing the cast for a particular skit. That's Lisa Kudrow upper left. I'm the tough guy in the center. (Photo: David Siegle/Courtesy of the Groundlings Theater and School)

The line of trailers was always the tip-off: hair and makeup trailers, wardrobe trailers, and moveable dressing rooms.

They would come back home, my mom saying, "We saw the trailers! We saw the trailers!"

One day my parents returned with complete delight in their voices, because they had happened upon (or stalked) a location for the then smash hit show *Hart to Hart,* starring Stefanie Powers and Robert Wagner. My mother told me the story of going up to Stefanie Powers on location in a way that if someone did that to me today, I'd punch them in the face. But mom showed no visible signs of bruising. Apparently Stefanie Powers, the victim in this scenario, was sitting on her director's chair with her name on the back, and my parents saw this action as an invitation to lunch.

My mother went up to gorgeous and talented Stefanie Powers, fawned over her beauty, and told her how much *she* loved Bill Holden, too. But most important, Mom asked Stefanie Powers if she had any advice for me, her fledgling starlet daughter.

> Mom: Oh, Stef, you have such beautiful features, and such a DA-A-A-ARLING figure. Do you have any tips for my daughter Kathleen? She's got this crazy notion of becoming an actress in Hollyweird.
> Stefanie Powers [under her breath]: Security.
> Mom: I mean, you've just done so great. With all your TV shows and your movies, and all that and everything else. What advice can I give Kathleen that she can follow forever?
> Stefanie Powers: Tell her to take *everything*. Never turn down work.

I listened without irony as my mother relayed this encounter, because Stefanie Powers was doing something I wanted to do. She was starring in a TV show. Not only did I not blow this advice off, but I clearly take it to heart to this day. In fact, I take it to heart to heart.

Unfortunately, Stefanie Powers, I didn't have any work to turn down at that point, but I knew I could sign up with a talent agency and work as an extra. It was a crappy job, but I had to start somewhere. This is where the dues-paying comes in, with an assortment of acclaimed roles as an extra in some of the finest motion pictures of our time. I was a concert audience member in the Diane Lane musical *Streets of Fire*. Don't know that one? Here's one reason. D-list fun fact: That was the film that named itself for a Bruce Springsteen song, and then when Springsteen didn't want to give them the rights to it, they still kept the title. Ouch.

I also stood outside of Grauman's Chinese Theater for a crowd scene in the horror film *Fade to Black*, which obviously faded to black upon release. It chaps my ass to this day that no camera got an acci-

dental close-up of the top of my head so some agent could see an aer-
ial shot of my bangs and go, "She's got the stuff! That's our new It girl!"

And when I think about the now-famous-in-my-head shot of me
as an alien extra reacting to a spaceship landing in that sci-fi gem *Battle Beyond the Stars,* starring Richard Thomas, it's pretty amazing I
wasn't singled out for stardom. Movies with aliens became huge after
that. You'd think I would have been in a few *Star Trek* movies by now,
or at least on the spin-off series *Star Trek: Now Voyager.* I could have
that title wrong. But again, where was the agent saying, "She's got the
stuff! That's our new alien It girl!"?

The reality was, as an extra I wanted to absorb anything I could
about the television and movie world. I'm surprised I never got fired,
because I was always really obnoxious and always bothering the
celebrities (sound familiar?), peppering them with questions:

"How did you get started?"

"How do you stay thin?"

"Do you know Stefanie Powers?"

It didn't help that being an extra is humiliating work at times. You're
treated like cattle, and the second assistant director really keeps you in
line. If you take one step out of the holding area you're put in, you get
screamed at in front of everybody, and because they don't know your
name, they'll just pick on what's least flattering about you.

"You with the ugly yellow dress!"

"You with the big nose!"

"You with that stupid retarded look on your face!"

It was like high school that way, just brutal. Plus, everyone around
you is in the same boat you are, wondering how to get into SAG
(Screen Actors Guild). The long-standing catch-22 you always hear is
that to get into SAG, you need to be working, but to get work, you
need to be in SAG. One day I heard somebody mention something
about being "Taft-Hartleyed" into SAG, and I remembered signing
something about that when I did that Chicago White Sox commercial.
Well, this person explained that Taft-Hartley was an exemption law
that means that if you're an extra in something, but your face is distin-

guishable, you're considered a principal, which is one of the requirements for SAG eligibility. Bingo! That Sox commercial—where, if you recall, I dazzled the city's television viewers with my quasi close-up—was my ticket all this time and I didn't even know it!

Getting the money to join SAG, though, was another story. At the time it was $1,750, and it wasn't like we were rolling in it. In order to support myself (while still living at home), I temped (badly), and bused tables at a diner (because I wasn't even good enough to waitress). I didn't have any extra money lying around. And it wasn't like I had an allowance from my parents. But after I convinced them I needed to do this, they paid the whole thing. That's because my mother the master negotiator—able to scream any utility employee into being reasonable about a bill—worked out a payment plan with SAG. It's all about the payment plan with her.

In addition to helping me gain access to SAG, my parents were smart enough about fiscal responsibility that they figured out a way for me to go to the prestigious Lee Strasberg Theatre and Film Institute on a bullshit scholarship by way of a loophole in a company that my dad hadn't worked for in thirty years. Genius, huh? So for two years I went full-time to Lee Strasberg, which was founded by and named after the acting school giant who helped make the Method—a kind of memory-based acting that drew on what was unique about you to bring life to a role—into one of the leading acting disciplines in America. This guy taught Marlon Brando, James Dean, Marilyn Monroe, Al Pacino—all my favorite stars—and now his techniques were going to turn me into a serious fucking actress. It was dancing, singing, Method classes, elocution to get rid of my Chicago accent, the whole nine yards.

When I was there, Rebecca DeMornay had just been in the school, and suddenly she was in movie theaters everywhere getting raves for the movie *Risky Business.* That was mind-blowing to me. I remember I was in a tai chi class at Strasberg with Maria Conchita Alonso. She was serious about the movement exercises. I thought they were dumb. Two seconds later, she's starring opposite Robin Williams in *Moscow on the Hudson,* and I'm in a movie theater watching her going, *There's the girl*

I made fun of for being dedicated while I was ditching class to eat Cheetos across the street at 7–Eleven with my girlfriends.

We were always naked in class, too. We did these exercises where you'd have to enact your most private moment onstage. You might get somebody popping their zits, but mostly every guy pretended to jerk off, and for girls, it was stripping down and taking a fake shower.

One of my teachers was Sally Kirkland, who had been in *The Sting*, and would later get an Oscar nomination for a movie called *Anna*. She was awesome, because not only was she a very good acting teacher, but she would casually tell us about every famous guy she slept with. She talked all the time in class how she had met, you know what I mean by "met," De Niro, Pacino, all the hot Method guys. But the amazing thing is, she'd get them to come speak at the school! Pacino came in right after he'd made *Cruising*. Perhaps to apologize to the gay community. Strasberg would come to the Institute, too. We called him Yoda (his looks had a little something to do with it.)

The Institute was located in Hollywood, and because I didn't have a car, I had to take the bus from our place in Santa Monica, which took forever, and categorically sucked. I would jump on the number four bus bright and early in the morning in my unflattering Danskin spandex outfit, and then stay at Strasberg all day till the last class ended at 11 p.m., then catch the number four at 11:22 p.m. to Santa Monica and 4th, and walk eight blocks home. That bus was a funky cross-section of LA personalities, too. Everybody from trannies to drooling kids to surfer dudes to weird guys hitting on you to the occasional nice person. You got a little bit of everything on the number four. As Denise Richards would say, it's complicated.

Between dedication to acting classes and the transient nature of Los Angeles, it was hard for me to make and keep friends during this period. I'd be really close to somebody for a year, and then they'd move away. One girl I was friends with got married, became addicted to cocaine, and just seemed to vanish. Another girl in acting classes with me also got married, but she became born again, decided she didn't like show business, and moved. I was used to a close neighborhood, like

Me in my first crib. Where was MTV?

back in Oak Park, and the spread-out quality of Los Angeles was a hard lesson in acclimation those first years.

I was also pretty lost during that period when it came to guys. I had sex for the first time at nineteen. Okay, I know I waited a good long while, but I've been making up for lost time ever since. I became pretty promiscuous, and not with a whole lot of winners, because as I've always said, my vices are junk food and bad men. I screwed a million really gross, sleazy guys. Is a million a lot? I'm surprised I was never killed. I remember being at Carl's Jr. at La Brea and Santa Monica in Hollywood late one night, meeting some motorcycle gang member, and just climbing on his bike and leaving with him. I never drank, but I'd go to nightclubs and bars all the time to go dancing, then just go home with a guy and think nothing of it.

One time, a girlfriend and I were in a club—I was probably sporting my mind-blowingly sexy Madonna-inspired crinoline-over-tights look—and she pointed to a pair of guys in the corner. "See those two over there?" she said. "They have matching 280-Zs!" I was like, "No fucking way!"

They were busboys. And we fucked them. That's how low the bar was. But remember, I never wanted to get married or anything. It's not like I put a lot of thought into where these magical interludes might go. I wasn't exactly looking for love.

Here was my problem: My type was pretty much any guy who said "hi" to me. That was my type. It's important to have a type. "Creepy" was another one of my types. This one guy Roland was so weird that during sex his voice altered—as if he were a fucking alien—and he started talking like a baby in a bizarre high-pitched voice. He'd start screaming shit like, *"I just want to fuck my baby! I'm your baby! Will you be my baby? Baby? Baby?"* For one thing, he couldn't decide whether he was the baby or the daddy. Make up your mind, freak. I had to force myself out from under him and flee the apartment undressed, clutching my clothes.

Point of interest: Mr. Baby, or Mr. Daddy, whatever he considered himself, was a donut fryer. I'll be honest, I've probably fucked five donut fryers overall. I love donuts. It's my happy place. So this was clearly the action-packed sequel to my after-school eating disorder— *The Perfect Storm* if you will—when having no boundaries about food meets Roland the donut-shop fryer giving you free bear claws at three in the morning. I didn't wait to get to his apartment, either. I banged him in the back of the donut shop. He waited till he had me in his apartment, though, to unleash his disturbing goo-goo-gah-gah blathering. Not great.

I once told a therapist the following story from my childhood. My older brothers Kenny, who you now know went on to be quite deranged, and Gary thought it would be fun to take turns holding each other outside the upstairs bedroom window upside down by their ankles. It became a tradition, and it happened with my brother John, too. I'm not kidding. We called it being "dangled." I was always whining, "When am I gonna get *dangled*? This is *ridiculous*! Just cause I'm a GIRL I can't get *dangled*?"

So one day my brother John says, "I'll dangle ya." Yes!

We opened the window, I climbed out, and my brother got me by the ankles. I'll never forget the feeling of being upside down, bouncing against the stucco wall, and giggling. I was having the best time. He'd say, "I'm gonna drop ya!" and I'd yell, "Don't!" Over and over, that was how it would go.

Now imagine that you're walking down a back alley, looking up, and you see a kid holding another kid upside down by the ankles, outside a second-story window. If YouTube had existed back then, my parents probably would have lost custody of us. Well, a neighbor finally caught us. He ran to tell our mother, who then bolted upstairs in her muumuu and screamed, "What the CHRIST are you GAH-DAMN kids doing?" John freaked out enough that he let go of one ankle, and I'm just like, "Johnny, cut it out!" But he pulled me up instantly and everything was fine, except for our being punished, of course. Actually, I think John got punished, not me, which is a shame because he was a pretty darned good dangler. I think he had to spend an hour in the garage. Or, as my mom calls it when I asked her about it recently, "Oh, we got after him. We gave him heck." I feel kinda bad that he got "heck" and all. John, I love you and I forgive you. You're not a damned good dangler. You're the best dangler I've ever had.

So when I told that little nugget of childhood roughhousing to this therapist, she said, "Well, don't you think that's kind of what you do with the men in your life? You let them dangle you out a window and you don't really know it's dangerous?"

I'd never made the connection. "So dangling was a bad idea, huh?" I said.

I always thought of it as the equivalent of parents throwing their kids up really high and catching them in their arms. But there was a big difference. It's not like I was running to Mom and saying, "Will you get John or Gary to dangle me?" So I knew it probably wasn't right. But that was the problem. I liked being dangled.

Immaturity and low self-esteem also played a part in my less than stellar relationships with men back then. But I wonder if my attitude toward sex and men also had something to do with how career-driven I was. Was I unconsciously choosing guys who I knew would end up being only interested in silly affairs that would never lead to anything permanent because I didn't want anything to get in the way of my career track? Like my calculated decision never to touch a drop of drink or get mixed up in drugs, I might have intuited that marriage was another impediment, and that a crappy one-nighter wouldn't deter me from my true love: performing. And since a guy was going to come second, anyway, maybe that led me to men who were clearly never going to be number ones in anybody's book.

It would take me a while, however, to realize that nice guys were better than bad boys. There I was in a crazy situation with a baby-talking donut fryer, and not ever saying to myself, "Um, maybe things aren't working out so well for me. Maybe I could find someone better."

Instead it was, "Okay, back to acting class tomorrow!"

So on the one hand, while I wasn't too concerned about who I slept with back then, I was pretty consumed with my weight and my continued binge eating. Since childhood, I had developed a rigorous cycle of bingeing and starving, with an erratic schedule of compulsive over-exercising on top of that to *really* fuck me up. After a bender of a toxic combination of junk foods, I'd feel so shitty the next day that I could barely function: nauseated, unable to fit in pants I'd just worn yesterday, consumed with self-loathing, and unwilling even to look at food until evening. That would then put me on a cycle of having my first meal of the day at 6 p.m., and my last meal at probably 3 a.m. Really healthy, Kath, when you have to get up for your temp job in El Segundo at 7:30 a.m.

I could never barf, by the way, although God knows I desperately wanted to be bulimic. One time I ate a whole pie—not too much pie, cause "too much" implies there's some left, it was an entire fucking pie—and I went to the bathroom I shared with my parents in our little Santa Monica apartment and tried sticking my finger down my throat like I'd seen drunk girls do after a crazy night at the bar. I had no girlfriends with me to hold my hair back, though. Well, it was just too disgusting. I couldn't do it. I can honestly say, with complete disappointment, that I have never purged in my life, because I have what I call a barfing disorder. Every time I puke, even when I'm sick with

"Do you have a to-go box?"

the flu or from food poisoning, I think I'm going to die. Weird, I know. No disrespect to you, Mary Kate. Rock on.

But it's certainly not as if starving was a sane alternative. After a bad binge, I might do crazy things I'd read about in so-called women's magazines, like spend all day drinking only water with five lemons squeezed into it. *Everything's going to be okay now!* I'd think, and then of course I'd be starving the next day. The problem is, when all you've allowed yourself are clear soups or elixirs as a corrective, it's not like the craving for pie goes away. My eating habits were so shitty that even when I could suspend the cycle and eat okay for a week, I'd never develop a craving for healthy food. I remember once when I realized the healthiest thing I'd had all week was a pint of Häagen-Dazs, because in my mind, it was part of the dairy food group.

Diet pills never worked, either. They made me lose my appetite for maybe two hours. But I did try speed for three weeks! (I blame Mom, from her wild-eyed amphetamine freak days whilst I was in utero.)

And may I say, you don't know how proud I am to have this revelation in a genuine celebrity tell-all memoir. Let the bidding war begin between Tyra, Oprah, and Maury (just to get the price up) for the Kathy Griffin exclusive. I promise to sob on air. I'm crying right now.

A-a-a-nyway, what happened was, a guy I was dating named Phil—okay, I just banged him twice—got a bag of "black beauties" and "speckled eggs" for $40. I don't even know if anybody makes those anymore. I'm pretty sure people jump straight to crystal meth now. Anyway, my trial period with speed didn't work, either. They were basically jacked-up diet pills, and all they did was make me jumpy and irritable for a day, followed by me being three times as hungry afterward. I ended up going to a doctor, who gave it to me straight, albeit in the context of me asking, "Um, I have a . . . friend . . . who's, um, having trouble with her weight, and might take 'black beauties' and 'speckled eggs.' What would the health implications be?"

She calmly replied, "Tell your . . . *friend* . . . the reason diet pills and amphetamines don't work is because all they do is put off your hunger. Your body just stores your fat for a day, and then you wake up the next day twice as hungry. You'll never be able to keep up with the speed."

All right, all right, so much for speed. It was back to plan B. As I couldn't afford Bally's Total Fitness and I had a desperate need to over-exercise, I realized I was in luck because the YWCA was much cheaper. Do you remember a little phenom called step aerobics? If you do, then you know how crazy it was to take two ninety-minute classes in a row. It's incredible that I didn't die from a blunt injury to the back of my head from slipping on my own pool of sweat.

I was much clearer-headed when it came to what *was* working for me in my life, and that was my career. After two years of plugging away at acting classes, it was pretty obvious that I was never going to be a serious thespian. I knew that the Groundlings were my calling, so I started taking classes there as I was finishing up at Strasberg.

I could immediately tell that what I was learning at the Groundlings would undo everything I learned at Strasberg. For one thing, at the Groundlings I was never naked. Bra, maybe. But not naked. The big difference, though, was that at Strasberg it was about reaching deep down, and at the Groundlings, it was about whatever got a laugh, and if that meant superficial characters, so be it. Fine by me.

I started in the basic class, which is just improvisational training. But I was going to the main company's shows all the time to soak it all in, and because the instructors were also cast members, I could see what they were teaching in action. These people were stars in my eyes. The hot names in the group back then were Laraine Newman, from the original cast of *Saturday Night Live;* Paul Reubens, who had just left, but who'd become the biggest star in LA since taking his incredible Pee Wee Herman show to the Roxy on Sunset; Cassandra Peterson, who was Elvira, Mistress of the Dark; and Edie McClurg, who had gone on to do a lot of John Hughes movies. But once I was familiar with all the members, I'd go to something like a Cheech and Chong movie and recognize Groundlings people in small roles, and get excited about what lay in store, possibly for myself. So being at the Groundlings, I just wanted to hang out as often as I could and get backstage to mingle with the actual troupe members.

When you reach the intermediate class, you start to develop characters. Some people would do composites of types, maybe by imagining, "What if Abraham Lincoln was a punk rocker who worked at the Mall of America?" Or "What if the Heisman Trophy winner was ten years old and had a facial tic?" Or today, it might be, "What if one of those *Twilight* freaks could actually form a sentence at an awards show and didn't have gray skin?" I was better at playing characters that were simply based on people I knew. So my first characters were Mom and Dad. I worked as a bank teller at the time, so when the exercise was, "Play someone you know, but as a different gender," I'd think of all the characteristics unique to my dad—sarcastic wit, eye-rolling, and strategic swearing—make him a woman, and put her in a bank. My sister Joyce was another character, a negative preacher of doom and gloom who also loves the Ronettes.

Moving up at the Groundlings was about getting through the lev-

This is from the Groundlings days. That's Mindy Sterling of *Austin Powers* fame on the right. And apparently I'm fighting the power. (Photo: David Siegle/Courtesy of the Groundlings Theater and School)

cls of classes, and then hopefully making it into the performing groups. There's the Friday and Saturday group featuring the main players, and the Sunday show they'd call the B company, or farm team. Getting into the Sunday group is one thing, but you needed to get voted into the Friday-Saturday gang. It's a really touchy line they walk with that policy, because it allows for criteria other than pure talent (i.e., jealousy) to determine who gets in. If you were a main company player, maybe you'd think a really funny farm-team guy or gal would steal your spot. The trick, therefore, was trying to dazzle the Friday-Saturday people, but not threaten them. Sometimes you'd tell them, "If you vote for me, I'll write scenes for you." You'd try anything you could. But ultimately if you were the one getting the most applause, the biggest laughs, they couldn't deny you. That quality trumped everything.

Well, once I got into the Sunday group, I was parked there a long time, as in two years. The normal run in the Sunday B company is six months to a year before moving on to the Friday-Saturday group. But my problem at the Groundlings was I wasn't a chameleon. I was always a variation of myself. The people from my peer group who had a kind of unstoppable popularity and moved quickly to the next company were Jon Lovitz and Mindy Sterling, actors who were great at coming up with a million different faces and voices. Jon originated the liar guy and his Master Thespian bit—characters he made nationally famous on *Saturday Night Live*—back at the Groundlings. Mindy, meanwhile, who went on to play Dr. Evil's fraulein in the Austin Powers movies, had this great rubbery face and pliable voice that she could adapt to any wacky part. Me, I was stuck with this face—okay, former face— and one inescapable voice.

My two strongest characters at the Groundlings then were what I do now in my stand-up act: some version of myself, or my mom. You did well at the Groundlings if you were the biggest and the broadest. But I would make the stupid mistake of writing a skit for three char- acters, and I kept casting myself as myself—because usually it was about something that had happened to me—and then I'd ask Julia Sweeney or Jon Lovitz to play the other larger-than-life, crazy charac- ters I couldn't do. I gave myself the straight person in my own skits. That wasn't the way to get noticed. I didn't know it then, of course, but that whole time what I was doing, being myself, was more appropriate for stand-up.

So while I didn't exactly help myself gain access to the Friday- Saturday company, it also didn't help that I had a series of B-company directors who just didn't think I was funny. And if a director doesn't think you're funny, you're not in the show as much, and then how are you going to prove to the main company that you're worthy of admis- sion? If you've watched *Saturday Night Live* over the years, it's the same thing with that show's reigning monarch, Lorne Michaels. If he doesn't like someone, they're just not in the show, or they're only doing small parts.

In my case, it really felt like I was part of a blackballed clique. I was friends with a guy named George McGrath, who could be a diva, but I thought he was really funny. Well, this one director *hated* him. And because I was always trying to do sketches with George, you could say I backed the wrong horse. (George would go on to win an Emmy co-writing *Pee Wee's Playhouse,* incidentally, so if anyone deserved to say "Suck it" before me on an Emmy telecast, it was George.)

But what that experience really taught me was that I was just going to have to work harder. *I have to be so good,* I thought, *that this director* has *to put my pieces in.* But because no one wanted to work with me, I had to learn to write monologues. After writing and writing and writing—bad pieces, then mediocre ones, then good but not good enough stuff—I finally hit upon my first successful character.

Once when I was back in Chicago, I went to a midnight screening of one of the Rambo movies, those Sylvester Stallone shoot-'em-ups about the crazy Vietnam vet. I was sitting in front of an African-American woman, and she talked to the screen the *whole* time. And it was hysterical, certainly more entertaining than the film. So remembering that moment later at the Groundlings, I started trying to think like that woman. She took that movie so personally, it was funny. "Ooooooh, Rambo!" she'd yell out. "Looka Rambo *cl-i-i-i-mb*-in' up dat tree like he an *animal*! Looka Rambo! RAMBO, WHERE YO KNIFE?" Thankfully, we live in a world where one person's intimate exchange with a ludicrous movie character can be another person's ticket to comic notoriety, and when I presented this monologue to the director of the show, he put it in, and it absolutely killed. I even got written up in the *LA Weekly,* whose reviews could make or break a Groundlings show.

It was also the only sketch I did for six months, and suddenly I got a taste of pigeonholing. That's right. I had pigeonholed myself as a thirty-year-old African-American woman from Chicago who goes to Rambo movies at midnight. My spirits would soar because this bit started to get me auditions with casting directors, sometimes for a big network show, but then I'd go in and they'd say "Do that Rambo sketch!" I'd do it, and they'd say "Bye-bye, thanks! Isn't she great?" I was now performing for free in offices around town, for people who had nothing to give me in return.

It taught me a lesson about going in to read for roles. Are television and film executives and casting heads calling you in for their own amusement? Or are you really appropriate for the part? That's when I started trying to find out as much information as I could before I went in for auditions or meetings. It's something I think all actors should do, so you're not wasting your time. If I'm sitting there at an audition all dolled up in high heels and a cute outfit but I'm surrounded by tall, gorgeous blondes, I'm thinking they're calling me in because I'm the performing monkey. At the Groundlings I was surrounded by girls who looked like me, yet they would waste all this time and energy being upset that they weren't up for the role of the ingénue in whatever it was they auditioned for. This line of thinking inhibited a lot of careers, in my opinion, because instead of being happy about being up for the best-friend role, they'd be crying, "How come I'm not the girl who gets the guy?" Let me tell you something; I knew I was never going to be an ingénue. At eighteen, I wasn't that girl. My thinking was, don't ever try to be anything but the homely, wisecracking girl. Be Rhoda, and go balls out for it. Find the meeting or audition where they're looking for someone who's able to be funny on their own, quick on their feet, rather than think I'm going to be able to compete with the tall, stupid, gorgeous girls. Hooker with the heart of gold, quippy secretary, nosy neighbor, that's what I wanted to do—and knew I could do it better than anybody else—and so I'd go into casting offices and say, "I want to be second banana."

Even with this more realistic goal, it took years for me to get an agent. I tried answering ads in every industry publication that existed: *Hollywood Reporter, Variety, Back Stage West,* you name it. I went to public casting calls that I would hear about on local television commercials or read about in the *Los Angeles Times.* I had my ear open at all times, and in all situations, in hopes that I could at least overhear a conversation between a couple of people in acting class or audience members when I attended a play, or at dinner parties, hoping to get some kind of a tip on where auditions might be held at any time.

I went to several talent agencies, and the drill was always the same. I would paper Hollywood with invites to the Groundlings, or any underground play I happened to be doing on the side, and about once a year, some little down-and-out, *Broadway Danny Rose*–style agency— usually one that sat above a resale jewelry shop, the kind that boasted client pictures of Linda Blair fifteen years after *The Exorcist,* or Erin Moran long after *Happy Days*—would "sign me." I would go in for the meeting, filled with hope that this would be the agent who would believe in me and send me out on real live television auditions. But invariably, I would have a less than promising meeting, keep working away in the Groundlings, and never hear from that agency again.

I soon learned that the agency business is simply a numbers game. In my opinion, 98 percent of all agents sign up unknown actors hoping the actor will have a gig that just falls into their lap, so they can then collect their commission. And guess what? In my case that's eventually what happened. In defense of agents, I will admit that it is difficult for an agent to promote an actor if that actor really doesn't have anything going on. So it is kind of a chicken-and-egg situation. That's why I don't count on agents for very much these days, except to negotiate contracts. I learned early on that a very important thing to let go of was the notion that anyone was going to get me work except me. I wasted a lot of time waiting for the phone to ring, when the most important thing is to generate your own shows, your own performances, get out there and do it, anyhow, anywhere, until they can't help but notice you if you're good. And even then, you better not have a big nose.

Of course, the term "work" in show business is a loose one. In those days, I had bizarre notions of what a real acting job was. One time I was sitting around the Groundlings with a bunch of girls, and someone came in and said, "Hey, there's a dentist in Marina Del Rey, his office is calling, and they need an actress to come over and pretend they're coming on to him for his birthday. They'll pay thirty dollars." The idea was, a bunch of his friends would be in a nearby room and then they'd yell "Surprise!"

Dentist humor. "I'll take it!" I shrieked.

I dolled myself up Robert Palmer-video-style in a totally cheesy $19 powder-blue minidress, fuck-me pumps, and a hot-pink sock in my hair, and drove down to Marina Del Rey in my beat-up Toyota Corolla with 100,000 miles on it. I walked into that office thinking, *I am a professional actress.*

Really, to me, it was another improv. This was a cake walk, I thought. And it was. I strolled in, sat in the dentist's chair, and when the guy came in, I crossed and uncrossed my legs about fifty times à la Sharon Stone in *Basic Instinct,* and just started making the most horrible double entendres. "Can you fill my cavity?" "Are you gonna root around in my canal?" "I don't spit. I swallow."

I'm pretty sure I took my top off, too, when I said, "Can you do a breast exam?" That's when everybody barged in with the "Surprise" and cake and I said, "Thanks, everybody," and took my $30 in cash in an envelope—*like a whore*—and left.

I was still thinking, *I am a professional actress.*

Let's hash this out for a second. Why didn't I bring a friend? I was so stupid I didn't even have the wherewithal to grab a gay and say "Drive with me." If you were a predator, how easy would it be to call up a theater company and get some dopey girl to come down to Marina Del Rey for cash so you could get her alone in an office?

And there's no telling how far I might have gotten lost in my craft if that little party had donuts. . . .

Let me tell you one more thing about dues, and I'm talking to you, LC, or any of you bitches from *The Hills.* Like taxes, sooner or later, we all have to pay them.

6

TO LIVE
AND BOMB
IN LA

Why do I make fun of Hilary Swank?

After I couldn't seem to cut a break after working my butt off for nearly a decade, hearing Ms. *Boys Don't Cry*'s "I moved here and slept in my car for four days with my mom" sob story all those years later just chafed my ass. I wanted to reach into the screen when she unloaded that poor-me crap on Oprah and slap her in the face. Cry me a fucking river, Hilary. You star in a Karate Kid movie at nineteen, and win two Oscars by thirty. Go fuck yourself. I was banging guys in donut shops. Try being an extra, going to Santa Monica City College acting classes with bored housewives, working as a Kelly girl temp, and doing endless Method exercises where you're pretending to hold a cup of coffee until you sweat because you really believe it. Then talk to me. If somebody had said, "Okay, you can either do it the way you did it, or you can live with your mom in a Toyota for a year, and it's filled with your own feces," I'd take the poop car. Not an issue.

And don't even get me started on "I yodeled in a van." Boohoo, Jewel. How horrible. I'll bet you liked winning that Grammy by twenty-five.

Sometimes you'll read about stars who can look back and realize how shocking it was that it happened so quickly for them. John Corbett is like that. He started off as a hairdresser, and when I was at the Groundlings he used to be our lighting guy, running the follow spot (the light that stays on a performer when they're onstage) for ten dollars a show, while I sat on his lap. He was supernice, thought all of us in the Groundlings were really talented, and because he was hot, all the girls wanted him. I remember him saying once, "Oh, hey, the other night I went to a play and some agent came up to me and asked me for my picture."

The whole time I'd been in LA, I'd prayed for that agent-approaches-you moment, and never gotten it.

"You're kidding," I said, barely disguising my despair.

John said, "I didn't know what to do, so I gave her my phone number."

He sent in one picture responding to a casting ad in the trade paper *Dramalogue—one* picture—and got a giant Mitsubishi commercial. Suddenly the follow-spot worker was the cute guy in car ads, the face of Levi's, and then he was on *Northern Exposure*. I love John, but boy, do I hate those stories. "I was here a week, and Robert De Niro came up to me in a restaurant and said something about a movie!" Ugh. I consoled myself with the fact that at least John could act. Don't get me started on the fucking Heidi Montags (oh, I mean Pratts, since when you have three weddings, I guess you might as well take the guy's last name) of the world, who are just handed a show like it's a flyer for a goddamn nightclub. Where's the talent? Where's the hard work? Unless you count getting blowouts hard work.

I'll admit it, it was hard watching everyone else at the Groundlings make it into the Friday-Saturday group ahead of me, people like Jon Lovitz, Mindy Sterling, and my good friend Judy Toll. It felt like being held back at school. I'm pretty sure I was in the B company at the Groundlings for longer than anyone I know of in the history of the place. I would just always hear that I wasn't there yet. So I hunkered down and worked even harder: writing more, going back to classes, trying to be funnier.

When I finally made it into the main company in the mid-1980s, though, I did have the great fortune to perform with the man whom I had hopelessly pestered as a total nobody all those years ago: the awesome Phil Hartman. Phil had left the Groundlings, but came back after years of doing television pilots that never got picked up to be series. Everyone was mystified that he hadn't broken out. Of course, *Saturday Night Live* was looming for him, but until then I had the distinct pleasure of being in the same show with him in that ninety-nine-seat theater on Melrose Avenue. I remember that the *LA Weekly* came out and they said the highlights of the show were him and me. Phil came in and set the paper down and said in that distinctively mock-serious tone of his: "Well, well, well, look who thinks we're the standouts." I tried to be cool—"Oh, hey, congratulations!"—but inside I was like, "Wow, I'm mentioned in an article with Phil Hartman!"

Phil was so obviously brilliant and hilarious, but he was also an incredibly good guy. When I just wasn't getting any traction with auditions in LA, I went to Chicago for a month. John Hughes was making all his hit films there, and I had this idea that maybe I could make something happen. Well, one time I came home at the end of the day to my brother's apartment and my mom called.

"Ooooh CHRIST, I've been trying to get you since yesterday," she said breathlessly. "Phil Hartman called us with a little part for you, but it was something you had to run over and get that day."

"You're kidding!" I moaned into the phone.

My mom said, "You know, he was so sweet. We had this nice conversation, and he said, 'I think Kathy is really talented. She's really standing out, and when this part came up, she was the first person I thought about.' "

I was so touched. For him to think of me like that—when I just assumed I wasn't even on his radar—meant the world to me. But missing that opportunity just wrecked me. It made me realize I couldn't leave LA. If you wanted to work in television, you couldn't live in Chicago. I'm not Tommy Lee Jones or Sandra Bullock, who can live on a ranch and expect people to track them down. Even if nothing's happening, it didn't pay to be somewhere else.

I went on to watch Phil become a huge hit, with immense pride and joy. I would later run into him at NBC events when I was on *Sud-*

denly Susan and he was on *Newsradio.* I remember my last conversation with him like it was yesterday. I had gotten a chuckle out of him, and felt honored to make the great Phil Hartman laugh.

Sometimes I got to know famous people before they were famous from my stint teaching classes for the Groundlings. It became my day job toward the end of the '80s, and I did that for about five years. I led five improv classes a week, and it was really fun except I lost my voice frequently during that period because you're doing a lot of yelling over your students for four hours at a time. I consider myself to be single-handedly responsible for the success of any and all of my famous students: Will Ferrell, Cheri Oteri, Chris Parnell, Mike McDonald, and Kenny G's wife (don't ask).

I have deep shame, though, about one of my charges, a young Mariska Hargitay. This was before the beautiful Mariska would go on to achieve Emmy fame on *Law & Order: Special Victims Unit.* I was getting ready to start a new class in a hot, sweaty, rented storefront in Hollywood—because the Groundlings had so many classes that not all of them could be at the theater itself—and before the first day I remember my mom recognized her name from my list of students, because of course she knew everything about every celebrity.

"Hargitay!" she crowed. "Mickey Hargitay's DAUGHTER? Holy Mary Mother of God, JAYNE MANSFIELD'S KID?"

Naturally I was excited now. Anyway, this tall, gorgeous girl comes into my class, and she's in no way acting like the child of a celebrity. She was just very sweet and normal. We started class, and in the Groundlings curriculum, one of the first exercises you do is the clichéd "trust" game. I made everyone stand in a circle, with me in the center, and I said, "Being onstage, you have to trust your fellow actors, especially when you're an improviser. You're going to be there for each other, and they're going to be there for you. For example, I'm going to fall back, knowing that you'll catch me."

Then I let myself fall backward, and sure enough, I was caught. Everyone gets out some nervous laughter, and then they all took turns doing it. By the time it got around to Mariska Hargitay, we'd already done it with ten or eleven students, and they clearly had gotten the point. Then it was Mariska's turn. "Okay, Mariska, cross your arms in front of you and gently fall back," I said.

She fell back and nobody caught her. She fell flat on her ass.

I was horrified. This had never happened in one of my classes before. I don't know if there was a fly buzzing in front of our faces, or being typical actors, we were just distracted. People must have turned their heads at the wrong time, but as the teacher, I took full and complete responsibility. And this was a 5'10" girl, too. It's true, the bigger they are, the harder they fall, and BOOM, she went right down on her coccyx. Like a ton of bricks. No, not a ton of bricks. A few very beautiful bricks. She giggled and got right back up like a pro, but it looked like it just fucking killed her. I mean, everybody else got caught except Mariska Hargitay. Nobody else wanted to do the trust exercise after her. Nobody trusted anybody. It was a terrible way to start that class.

To this day, whenever I see Mariska, and it's probably been ten times, I apologize. I let her down that day. Let her fall down, if we're being specific. If she has any lingering trust issues since becoming a big star, I blame myself. Whatever medical problems I read about her having, I point the finger at me. I mean, come on, she joined a show called *Law & Order: Special Victims Unit*. Was this not a call for help? Was she not my very special victim?

When I told Mom later, she didn't help any with my towering guilt.

"As if she hasn't been through enough," she said.

Gee, thanks, Maggie.

Things started to pick up for me career-wise when I finally began getting commercials. I had a commercial agent long before I got an acting agent, but I probably auditioned for about seventy national and regional commercials before I actually booked one.

The breakthrough in that area came in the early '90s when I nabbed a TV spot for Kenwood, the stereo brand. As explained to me

I Cher-ed this Bob Mackie outfit for the Kenwood commercial.

at the audition, the setup was a futuristic world, and I was supposed to perform the '70s funk hit "Play That Funky Music, White Boy" as if music had never existed. They said I could do whatever I wanted, and since I heard all these people before me singing crazy versions of it, like they were amateurs at a talent show, I just looked at the camera completely deadpan and spoke the words in a halting monotone, totally rhythmless, like a zombie. If you've heard Paris Hilton's album, you know what I'm talking about.

Anyway, I got the gig! I showed up on set, my first really big professional set, and it was huge, meant to look like the '70s. (Really, it just looked like my high school.) The guys were all in bell bottoms, and they put me in this wild orange jumpsuit that the wardrobe guy told me was a Bob Mackie that Cher actually wore on *The Sonny and Cher Show*. I was like, "Holy shit!" Chastity was probably conceived five minutes after this outfit fell to the floor.

The director was a guy named Joe Pytka, and he was the king of big-time national commercials. Chances are everyone in America has done three things: breathed, taken a shit, and watched an ad Joe Pytka directed. His reputation, though, was not so good. I kept hearing, "Look out for this guy. He's a monster. He fires people all the time. Don't take it personally." But I knew if I played my cards right, he could do a lot for me.

So we start shooting, with the client and my commercial agent there. They cue me, I do what I did in the audition and—whew!—the director's nice to me. But he was vicious to everybody else. He starts firing people, screaming at them. Then, without notice, he'd leave to go play basketball for an hour, leaving everyone standing there, and come back all sweaty and pick up where he left off. After he launched into another of his tirades, I started talking to somebody about how mortified I was by him, and then a crew member ran up to me and said, "You're on mike! You're on mike! Everyone with headphones can hear you!"

I said, "I don't care."

I then went up to Joe Pytka and said, "Just so you know, you're a freak, and if you keep screaming and having these fits around me, all that's going to happen is I'm just going to cry and leave. So really, take it down a few notches."

There was this hush. And then Joe said, "I like her!"

And that was it. I was golden. He was the first powerful person whom I took a risk with by calling him out, and he didn't penalize me for it. He got my sense of humor, and it made me realize that if I could make that happen with the people in charge in this business, I was home free. He single-handedly gave me a commercials career, and helped me get out of the yearly pittance I was making as a temp, and into a real living. To have Joe Pytka in your corner was fantastic, and he championed me in a way for which I'll always be grateful. Over the years I've done at least seven major commercials with Joe, including some Super Bowl ads.

But I have to admit, it also gave me a false sense of security about who I could tease. On subsequent shoots with Joe, it was common for me to talk back to him during his fits—which the crew loved—and he'd jokingly say, "Ah, fuck you," back to me. Or I'd go yell at him during one of his basketball breaks, and he'd laugh. But much later, when I did an elaborate commercial with Joe that starred Shaquille O'Neal, I learned the real pecking order of power. Shaq had to pick me up at one point, and while I was in his arms in between takes I made some inappropriate joke at his expense, and Shaq gave me this death stare, like, "Did you just fuckin' talk to me?"

And just like that crew member running up to me years ago when I spoke out of turn about Joe, now it was the seemingly all-powerful Joe Pytka in the damage control position, covering for my big mouth. He had to touch Shaq gently and keep saying, "She's a comedian! She doesn't mean it! She's a comedian!" People really do lose their shit around athletes. So thank you, Joe, for the commercials career, and for preventing me from being tossed like a free throw.

Shaq's not going to read this book, is he?

Shaq! I'm a comedian!

I was in the Groundlings, I was doing commercials here and there, but it still wasn't happening for me. What else could I try?

Commercials are great, but when you're in the Groundlings, it's *Saturday Night Live* you want most. Especially when your classmate Jon Lovitz gets plucked from the main company so fast he leaves a little puff of smoke like in cartoons. The problem was I could never get Lorne Michaels to laugh. I had two private meetings with him that I'm sure he doesn't remember, but it was the opposite of my success with Joe Pytka: Being myself and trying to shock him into laughter wasn't working.

It was always best, though, if Lorne could come see you perform, and thankfully he decided he was going to see me, Lisa Kudrow, and Julia Sweeney. In my case, I was one of the three because somebody at Brillstein/Grey, a very powerful management company, thought I was worth seeing. I wasn't represented by them, but I sure wanted to be. My impression is that if I got the job on *Saturday Night Live,* I would have been represented by them very quickly. So the Groundlings essentially

Lisa Kudrow and me with our old noses.

geared the late show so that the three of us rotated scenes: It was all about Julia, Lisa, and me. I remember there was one Groundling girl backstage who wasn't chosen to audition, and she was throwing costumes into a bag saying, "This is ridiculous! As if you're any more talented than I am!"

I thought, *What an awful thing to say to someone before the biggest tryout of their career.* But her reaction certainly hit home how important it felt, because that's what it was: the biggest audition of our lives. I had heard Lorne had a no-Groundlings policy for many years, so we considered this a make-or-break moment.

Well, sure enough, I had a bad night. My sketches were bombing. I was dead in the water. Especially when the audience—all too aware of the TV starmaker in their midst—held their laughter to see how Lorne reacted, as if they were scared of enjoying the wrong thing. It just stressed the fact that this was a performance for one, not a typical show. Ultimately I failed to do my characters as well as I had hoped that night. Nerves got the better of me. Even Lisa, who before the world knew her from *Friends* was great with role playing and a true standout at the Groundlings—always doing something off the beaten track, always a little better than everyone else—couldn't get it together the way she usually did. My dear friend Julia, though, rocked it. She knocked it out of the park with all her characters, including Pat—her soon-to-be-famous gender-nonspecific nerd who she'd developed at the Groundlings—plus her improvisations were amazing. That performance secured her *Saturday Night Live* gig.

Meanwhile, I was crushed that I couldn't make it work. After all I'd done to get some recognition there, it was easy to feel that I'd blown a golden opportunity, that I'd hit a ceiling. But Lisa and Judy Toll felt differently about my abilities, and each one independently told me the things that would help change my life and career for good.

The late Judy Toll was one of my best friends, and was the only friend of mine who was an actress and a comic, living in those dual worlds. She was always one clique ahead of me, which was kind of good, because while we were pals—getting into misadventures, going to Carl's Jr. at three in the morning to eat four orders of fries and then compare stomachs: "I'm fatter!" "Shut up! I'm fatter!"—there was always a little part of her that was mentoring me. I used to follow her around to her stand-up gigs, where I got to meet the top comedians of the day, like Richard Lewis and Andrew Dice Clay. She'd finish up at the Groundlings on a weekend night, then say, "I have a fifteen-minute set at 1:40 a.m.," and run to the Melrose Improv. I'd go and meet the most interesting people at the Improv bar. I even got into a conversation once with playwright Sam Shepard.

One day Judy said to me, "You know, you should try stand-up. I think you can do it."

My first reaction was "No way. I do characters. I can't tell a joke to save my life. I can't do what you do. I'd get heckled. At the Groundlings nobody gets up to leave. There's no dinner served. I could never per-

My good friend Judy Toll and me all dolled up.

form for people who are given drinks. That's my alcoholic family, bored and wishing they could just eat their food instead."

She was persistent. "No, this is your thing."

Here I was, saying that doing characters was my thing. But Lisa Kudrow gave it to me straight. "You're *okay* with characters," she said. "But you're really funny as yourself. When you talk to me as you, you're funnier than anybody I know."

Whoa. Okay. I always enjoyed making my friends laugh by just talking about my day, my parents, some stupid TV show I was watching, something crazy that happened at an audition, or my less than stellar love life. But that certainly wasn't the stand-up I saw being done on local stages. It was one-liners and screeds about men versus women, or observations about pets and airplanes. But with Judy and Lisa's encouragement, I convinced the show director at the Groundlings to let me open the late show each week with a monologue, a five-minute story. Which invariably became a twenty-minute story. (The one downside was that everyone in the Groundlings company backstage began to hate me for making the show start so late.) It put me out front in a way that I was comfortable with—in other words, outside of the sketch format where I could start to develop my own persona with my own point of view—and I started to get good feedback.

As for what I would talk about in those openers, believe it or not, I did no celebrity material back then. My act has pretty much always been retelling whatever happened to me that week in a funny way. I didn't begin ragging on celebrities until years later when I would actually be in the presence of them, experiencing them firsthand. So I started out mostly talking about my crappy day jobs, some new guy who'd just dumped me, or my family, but celebrity referencing didn't kick into high gear until I started getting parts on television.

Meanwhile, Judy was trying like hell to get me sets at the Melrose Improv or the Comedy Store on Sunset Boulevard. She got me an audition with Mitzi Shore, who ran the Comedy Store (and who birthed Pauly), and the cool thing was I got my first crack on a regular stand-up night with the other name-brand comics instead of on the night usually reserved for beginners: open mike night. Picture gang members, bigwigs, and banjos.

My first night at a real comedy club, though, I left out personal stories and the retelling of my week and basically just did my Groundlings act. I went onstage at the Comedy Store and said, "Hi, my name is Kathy Griffin and I'm from the Groundlings!" Then I would turn around, put a wig on, turn back to face the crowd, and then talk as my mom for a minute. Then I'd put on my cat's-eye glasses and do my old Jewish lady at the Farmer's Market. Nobody did characters at the Comedy Store. It was completely inappropriate. But I got laughs. Maybe there was something to this!

Then I bombed for two years.

Open mike nights categorically sucked, at least for me. The problem was I was doing my act like I was still trying to get on *Saturday Night Live*. (I've still never been asked to host that show, although one of my recurring D-list moments is when people stop me in the airport

Andy Dick, Janeane, and me at a coffeehouse where we often performed.

and tell me they loved me on *SNL*. I never know if they think I'm Molly Shannon, Cheri Oteri, or Chris Kattan. I just say "Thank you. I'm glad you enjoyed me as Mango.") But Lisa and Judy continued to encourage me with their support, saying, "Just be yourself. Try to do the stand-up that comes naturally to you, which is more like story-telling."

Okay, then. No more doing wacky characters. I'm never going to be on *Saturday Night Live*. I was going to go up onstage and just talk about the shit that happened to me that day.

In the early '90s, stand-up comedy was in a boom time. Stand-up shows were on several cable networks, from MTV to Lifetime to, of course, Comedy Central, and people around the country were getting to know the names Kevin Meaney, Judy Tenuta, Julie Brown, Emo Philips, Bobcat Goldthwait, Richard Jeni, Richard Lewis, Brian Regan, Ray Romano, and Rita Rudner, among many others. When it came to seeing these comics live, all anybody knew were the big-name clubs, and if you wanted to break in as a comedian, those were the places to be. The Improv chain was popular then, and there were so many of them. Open mike night at the Santa Monica Improv was so humiliating, though. You had to go and stand in line in the afternoon and get a number like in a lottery, and then you just went on. I knew I'd hit the stage between the prop comic and the comic who talks about how he wants to kill his wife. Plus, you had maybe five minutes tops, or sometimes only three. Brutal. Really, really short sets. Afterward, you'd get notes from the co-owner of the Improv, Mark Lonow.

I would go there, talk about whatever happened to me that day, whatever I thought was funny, and of course I'd tank. One time, Mark said to me afterward, "You just talked about what happened to you today. You have to talk about things people can relate to."

I remembered that the comic before me had started his act saying, "So, I got a ticket on the way over here!" I was pretty sure that hadn't happened. So I brought that up. I said to Mark, "When that comedian said that, I as an audience member know he didn't get a ticket on the way over here."

"Well, yeah," he said, "but you've got to make up stuff, make it relatable to people. Tell people you got a ticket on the way here."

I said, "But I *didn't get a ticket* on the way here. This other funny thing happened, though."

"People can't relate to that. Everybody's gotten a ticket."

"But I fucked a guy in a donut shop. No one's with me on that?"

That was a weird conversation, like we were speaking different languages. But it lets you know the problem I have to this day. I'll sit there and say, "As if I'm the *only person* who's fucked five guys from donut shops." I always think what I'm saying is funny and relatable, but really it's just funny and not necessarily relatable. And this wasn't passing muster with two-drink-minimum crowds who want routine jokes from a woman that start with "Men, can't live with 'em, can't shoot 'em!"

It was during this time that I was struggling with the club scene when Judy said, "I have this girlfriend who does exactly what you do. Her name is Janeane Garofalo, and I want you to meet her."

Judy was set to perform a set at a bookstore on Beverly called

Big & Tall Books, and she asked me to do a set as well. This was the furthest thing from a comedy club. There were maybe seven people in the audience, and two of those were comics: Colin Quinn and Janeane. The latte machine kept drowning us out, and there was a guy with a bunch of books and papers splayed out in front of him because he was studying for the bar exam, and he would keep looking up at us like, "Ugh, why are you bothering me?"

But it felt right. It was a casual setting where we each took turns doing about fifteen minutes of new material, sometimes looking down at our notes, simply trying to tell a story and make it as funny as possible. Janeane came up to me afterward. Five foot two, jet black hair, Doc Martens, tattoos, and thick black eyeliner. She kind of looked like a gothic gang member. She was so cute! "Don't change one thing about what you do," she said. "Don't try to be a joke teller. *Stop* going to the Improv. You're not going to do well at the Improv. You need to perform at alternative spaces."

That's when I said, "If I can get theater space, would you do shows with me and Judy?"

She said yes.

And by the way, I still don't think that comedian got a ticket on his way to the Improv. He was just making that shit up.

7

HOT CUP
O' TALK

When I got into stand-up in the early '90s, it was a time when the brick wall era of comedy—named after the backdrop always used for comedy clubs—was so prevalent that for certain audiences, that style of rigidly formatted joke telling had become dull. People were beginning to feel they'd heard all the differences between New Yorkers and LA people, between men and women, between cats and dogs, and all the setup/punchline combos as well. Plus, the scene was a breeding ground for hackery. I knew people who would scrape together ten, fifteen minutes of material, do it over and over from club to club, and get a million-dollar television development deal.

I didn't know how to write a one-liner to save my life. I still don't.

The scene Judy, Janeane, and I were a part of, though, felt like something special. I wanted to take advantage of this emerging buzz for what was being called alternative comedy that was happening at bookstores and coffeehouses and showcases like Un-Cabaret, which comedian Beth Lapides would set up from week to week in a different place. It was a niche market waiting to be tapped. Taking a cue from my mother's scholarship-hunting abilities, I found a loophole in the Groundlings membership book that said a member in current good

---

Left: My good friend Margaret Cho, who was a big supporter of my efforts at stand-up.

standing could have the theater for free on Mondays—when there were no classes or show—"if no one else has used it for any other reason."

I booked the theater for every Monday in July. Judy and I made flyers, copied them at Kinko's, and called our night Hot Cup O' Talk.

The setup was four comics: me, Judy, Janeane, and one other person. We tried to make it all girls—Margaret Cho, Laura Kightlinger, if they could—but occasionally it'd be guys like Dana Gould or Taylor Negron, who were always welcome. We charged a dollar at the door, because we were convinced nobody would come if we asked for two. We also hoped that being scheduled on a weeknight might make it easier for industry people to show up.

The concept I came up with for the show was that I would go on stage first with an egg timer and set it for fifteen minutes. I'd tell the crowd, "When the bell goes off, I'm bringing out the next comic." Then it was a baton pass, with the next comic doing fifteen minutes and bringing out the one after her or him. This way, people knew that it would literally take only an hour of their time. (Industry people loved that. And it only made them one hour late for their lap dances.)

The rules for performing at Hot Cup O' Talk were that if you had a forty-five-minute set that killed at the comedy club, you were not allowed to perform anything from it. People like Janeane were stoked: "Awesome," she said. "I don't have a comedy club set." But even comedians from the conventional circuit said, "Great." Guys like Dana and Andy Kindler enjoyed it because they had other material bubbling up inside them that just didn't work at the Improv or the Comedy Store or the Laugh Factory. They wanted a safe place to try something new. Another rule we had was, you could never repeat material. Ever! You had to have a new fifteen-minute set every time. I would usually tell one long story, but someone else might do a bunch of little bits, or a character. Sometimes somebody would have a guitar.

I realized that I bombed at clubs because I disrupted the standard listening rhythm of setup/punchline, setup/punchline, and the crowd just couldn't or wouldn't switch gears. What was great about Un-Cab and Hot Cup O' Talk was the audience walked in with the understanding that they didn't know what to expect. They might get seven minutes that slay, then eight minutes that ramble. At the clubs, there's a feeling of "We've paid this much, we're forced to buy two drinks, they're crappy drinks, the comedians don't know each other, it's not a community, and you'd better fucking deliver those laughs per minute." I remember once I was talking to a comic I met at an open mike night—okay, okay, I banged him, too—and he told me, "I have to get a laugh every twenty seconds, and when I'm doing my act, I count the seconds in my head." He said when he got to twenty, if he hadn't gotten a laugh, he knew by twenty-one or twenty-two he had to start a whole new topic.

Holy fuck, who has the time or concentration for that bullshit? I could never *count* while I was telling a story. That doesn't mean I didn't sweat if I wasn't getting a laugh. But to be so precise seemed robotic. I mean, I know there are technically proficient comedians who are great. But we were the anti-technicians. Janeane's big line to me was, "Kathleen, you can't possibly care what the audience thinks." It's so liberating to think that. It doesn't mean you don't want the audience to laugh. It means you're driven by what *you* think is funny.

Besides, when you see a regular stand-up, they probably aren't as revealing as we were being. I was going up onstage and innocently talking about how I'd taken seven laxatives because I felt bloated and thought it'd be great to just go to the bathroom for an entire day. Or my fear of camping: I'm convinced bugs will crawl up my vagina and lay eggs. Isn't everyone? We all had audition horror stories, although mine were mostly about auditioning and not getting jobs.

The reason my stories about auditioning were, if I might say, hilarious, is because I *suck* at auditioning. And I don't mean I blow the casting director. I wish it were that easy. I mean I am a terrible auditioner. What I'm good at is the kibitzing, so when I go into an audition, I'm so concerned with making the room laugh—which I invariably do—that I forget the pesky details, like preparing for the role, or memorizing the lines. Every so often, I would even have an audition for a real live movie that would come out. Once, years later, I auditioned for a big-budget movie called *The Whole Nine Yards,* starring Matthew Perry and Bruce Willis. I guess I should have prepared for my audition like a normal actress, but all I could think was, *What if Bruce Willis is in the room and makes one of his dumb jokes that leading men always make when they think they're funny? What will I do? Will I have to pretend to laugh? Yes, Kathy.* Was I serious about my craft? No. *But,* get this! Guess who was sitting next to me on the folding chair at that audition? Soon-to-be Oscar nominee *Laura Linney!* I was so excited to talk to her that I just folded my script and put it in my purse. I tried to act very casual, not starstruck in any way, as if I auditioned for several major feature films a week. But really I just wanted to tell my mom and dad that I met her. She was so nice, too, I couldn't get over it. And the best part is . . . right before it was my turn to audition, she said, "I just have to tell you, I think you are so funny." The rest was a blur. I think some really fat, unattractive girl named Amanda Peet got the role. I don't think she ever worked after that. It's really kind of sad when you think about it. Have I mentioned that I *totally know* Laura Linney?

Anyway, audition stories were a big part of those stand-up nights. As for the others, if Janeane had had a tough day on the set of *Reality Bites* with Winona Ryder and Ben Stiller, it would come out onstage that night. Then you had Andy Dick talking about bingeing on drugs, or getting into a fistfight with Wesley Snipes because he used the "n" word, Wesley overheard it, and punched Andy in the face outside the bathroom of a nightclub. How does "I got a fake fucking ticket on the way over here" top that shit?

Hot Cup O' Talk and the Un-Cab started to attract people who were into doing things differently. Word got out that there was a place to go in LA if you were a comic but you didn't tell standard jokes, or kept bombing at the Improv. In fact, it was kind of a migration. Comedians were arriving from clubs and improv theaters around the country to be in on the ground floor of this alternative comedy scene. Janeane was starting to hit big because of *The Ben Stiller Show* and *Reality Bites,* so everybody came to see her, which was great and made Hot Cup O' Talk an instant hit. But she also brought into the fold a lot of people who weren't really comedians—Chicago Second City guys like Bob Odenkirk and Andy Dick. David Cross was from an improv group in Boston, Tom Kenny—now the voice of SpongeBob—

Two not-at-all-bitter female comics.

came down from the San Francisco club scene. They loved the free-form nature of what we were doing. It's not like I auditioned comics for Hot Cup O' Talk. The pool of alternative comics was small enough that pretty much the same folks who did Un-Cabaret and any other alternative venues at that time—the Borders bookstore on La Cienega, a coffeehouse in Santa Monica, etc.—would rotate in and out of Hot Cup. And what I kept hearing over and over from people who came to see the show was, "Ugh, I normally hate going to see stand-up comedy, but this doesn't feel like stand-up. It feels like somebody just talking to me, like I was with friends and they were making me laugh."

Was it a coincidence that I gravitated toward the girl comics more than the boys? Or was it deliberate? A little bit of both. The girls were ten times more supportive—of me and each other—than the boys, for whatever reason. Obviously I could relate to the girls more, and one of the topics that came up—and still does to this day—is the raging, out-of-control, 1950s-style, backward, *Mad Men*-like-you-can't-believe-it level of sexism in stand-up comedy. It always pisses me off when I'm calling in to some Morning Zoo radio show to promote God-only-knows what—probably this book, so get ready, I'm comin'—when the DJ actually tries to convince me that there are as many female comics as male ones. Cue hypermasculine Morning Zoo Hacky McGee voice: "So Kath, I don't know what you chicks are always complaining about." To which I respond: "Really? Why don't you call your local comedy club and ask for the Saturday night lineup? I guarantee you the male to female ratio is going to be about nine to one. You dickwad."

It was organic, then, that I developed a camaraderie with my posse of female comics. We hung out together so much that we ended up on the same fucking menstrual cycle. I was starting to feel like part of a group, and even though some of them were my contemporaries, I was personally very starstruck by their talent.

Janeane and I spent many, many hours together talking and eating, and eating and talking, at a dining establishment called The Soup Plantation. (It's a plantation with soup.) The talk was gossip and boys and the history of comedy and who we liked and didn't like. Laura Kightlinger was this tall, beautiful model-looking girl who was really too hot to be a stand-up comedian. She rescued me after one of my worst breakups ever by forcing me to go to a screening of *Waiting to Exhale*. It was all I could do not to start a small car fire somewhere in Manhattan that night, à la Ms. Angela Bassett. Were I to then be asked by the hot, white fireman, "Did you know you're only supposed to set trash on fire, ma'am?" I would respond, "It *is* trasssshhhhhh." That movie did make me feel better. Margaret Cho, not one to be afraid of a torn pair of neon pink tights, saw me do stand-up the third time I ever tried it. She was instantly sweet, and took me under her wing. She gave me great advice that mirrored what Janeane, Laura, and Judy said: Don't change what you're doing. Just get better at it. It wasn't till later that I found out this sweet, semi-shy and, believe it or not, when off-stage quite soft-spoken woman had a day job where she worked at a sex toy shop, so she could reference this unique employment in her act, and not have to make anything up.

Also, these comedians all kept me on my toes. When comedians socialize, chances are we're not just talking to each other. We're talking, listening, and let's face it, always trying out new material. This is when my friends started interrupting a conversation with me if they laughed, and saying, "Are you just trying out your act now?" I'll be honest. Yes, I am.

We all hung out together almost every night, mostly at a house in Laurel Canyon shared by a talent manager named Dave Rath and a couple of comedians. It was the party house. Jay Mohr lived next door, and he was doing so well with movie parts and being a cast member on *Saturday Night Live* that we pretty much considered him a celebrity. I met Ben Stiller there. He was already well known because of his MTV show and Emmy-winning Fox sketch series *The Ben Stiller Show* that featured Janeane, Andy Dick, and Bob Odenkirk. Hanging out at that house was also how I met people like Judd Apatow (writer/director of *The 40 Year Old Virgin* and *Knocked Up*), Dave Attell (host of Comedy Central's *Insomniac*), Patton Oswalt (*The King of Queens* and the lead voice in *Ratatouille*), Mary Lynn Rajskub (*24*) and future late-night host Conan O'Brien. Seemingly every writer on network or cable television was there as well. This was also when Janeane introduced me to Sarah Silverman, whom I've known since the day she moved to LA. Sarah was—hell, *is*—gorgeous in her cut-off shorts and tank top, and she knew all the boy comics. I was so envious of that because I could never really get in with them. Janeane had the cool factor with the guys. Sarah was the one they all wanted to marry. And I was the pesky flea.

Then again, I was the one going up and talking about these guys in my act, commenting on them maybe a little too much. When you hang out with Andy Dick six nights a week, eventually one of those nights your set is going to be about the time you were making out with some guy in the bathroom and Andy bursts in and yells, "I want to fuck your boyfriend!"

Yeah, that's right, I school-of-rocked Jack Black's world.

Another example of getting flack from the boys is what happened when Jack Black dumped me. That's right. I fucked Jack Black. Okay, we went out only two or three times, but that's a relationship in my book. And by the way, this is my book.

I met Jack through this same crowd, too. Of course, I thought he was a weirdo, and was therefore instantly attracted to him. When we started dating, I took him home to meet the parents, and Mom said to me later, "OH! he's got those SERIAL KILLER eyes! I don't trust him. Did you see him in that *Bob Roberts* movie? He looked like a SERIAL KILLER!"

First Rod Serling, now this. "Well, yeah, Jack plays a stalker in it, Mom," I said.

She replied, "He plays that part so good, I think he's like that!"

Well, Jack and I pretty much were complete opposites. I was always kind of a neatnik, a stickler for rules, and Jack would smoke pot and play video games all day. But don't get me wrong, Jack is actually very hardworking, and knows his shit. He's very sweet and fun, and very driven. He only kind of acts like a rocker pothead dude. Compared to him, I was stuffy. I had a car that ran. He didn't. I had a clean apartment, and he lived in this filthy place, littered with video games and bongs. When Judy met him, she said to me, "Kitten, I can't believe you're dating Pig Pen from Peanuts. Every time he walks I see a cloud of dirt above his head."

One time, I spent the night at Jack's place. I got up the next morning to take a shower so I could leave. He stayed in bed. When I stepped out of the shower onto the towel on the floor, I couldn't find anything to dry myself with. "Jack, where are the towels?" I yelled out, dripping.

He said, "Um, I just have one that I use for a bathmat and a towel."

"What?" I said. "That *thing* on the floor? I'm supposed to pick it up and dry my body with it?"

"What's the problem?"

Oh, Pig Pen.

Even though the general population didn't know who Jack Black was at the time—this was when he and Kyle Gass's folk/metal parody act Tenacious D was just starting out, when *Bob Roberts* was his biggest role—he did get mad at me because I talked about him onstage. When our brief fling ended, I got up at Un-Cabaret and did a bit about how Jack dumped me for Andy Dick, because they had started hanging out and became their own mutual admiration society about each other's comedy. Well, even though there probably wasn't a single guy I knew who I hadn't gone up onstage and talked about, Jack and Andy were staring daggers at me after that set. I remember thinking, *I don't care. You broke up with me, Jack. And Andy, you're probably high.*

They got over it very quickly, and that was about the biggest dust-up I ever had in those days pertaining to anything I said onstage. That's because the crowds were small, the same two hundred people usually who were fans of the scene, and this was in the pre-blogging days, when what you said in your act didn't necessarily go anywhere, and someone like me could really get away with murder. What I said just died on the vine. I could go up and talk about what Winona Ryder ate when Janeane took me to her house to watch John Cassavetes movies—she was really more of a food picker, I never saw her have a whole meal, that's how she stays waif-y—and you certainly weren't going to read about it the next day on Perezhilton. But Jack and Andy's mini-snit probably foreshadowed how this kind of material might upset a famous person not accustomed to having their bullshit exposed. Not that I'm complaining here, but there's something about the safety of a theater. See me live these days, and you will get a much more eyebrow-raising act than anything you'd hear me say on a talk show or *The D-List*. In other words, if your name is Clay Aiken, you probably don't want to come to one of my stand-up shows. It may not go your way.

Nowadays when I see Jack, it's on the red carpet, and it's like high school all over again: as in he won't say hi to me. Maybe not out of any choice on his part. I don't think he's trying to be rude. I get it; the guy's a little busy these days. Huge movie star, wife and kids, the whole thing. Let's face it, he's an A-lister. I remember being at the Grammys and looking at him up on the podium as he presented an award and thinking, *That's so great. He's a giant movie star now.* It's the transient nature of show business friendships and relationships. It's a bittersweet thing.

There was a period when we all saw each other all the time. None of us had money to travel, but we could all hang out at someone's house. Inevitably, though, I started to lose friends to fame. I learned a lot about what happens when someone goes from not being famous to being famous very quickly. Janeane got so hot, she wasn't just well known: Girls wanted to *be* her and duplicate that Doc Martens-and-black-tights look of hers. I remember visiting Garofalo at one of the Chateau Marmont bungalows, and there were flowers everywhere from studio and network people. I was so happy for her, but also a little jealous. I wasn't getting flowers, not even from donut fryers. I mean donut *chefs*.

I went from seeing Molly Shannon all the time at Dave Rath's house, doing shows with her, to not seeing her for years after she got *Saturday Night Live.* I ran into Molly after her first year on the show. I was so happy to hear that she was having a great time. I distinctly remember her saying, "A year ago I was a hostess at Hugo's restaurant. I can't believe I get to do this now!"

That drift occurred with Cho, too. She had been doing Un-Cabaret and Hot Cup O' Talk constantly, and then all of the sudden she got her own ABC show, *All American Girl,* and none of us saw her anymore. I remember one of our mutual girlfriends saying, "Well, she's caught up in the machine now."

"What machine?" I said.

"You're on a television show," she said, "so you've got to lose the weight, get a trainer, take fen-phen, and you can't stay up till four in the morning because you've got to be at work at eight a.m. the next day."

It happened to Lisa Kudrow, as well. We were never best friends, but we spent a lot of time together because of the Groundlings and often auditioned for the same parts in sitcoms. My favorite story about Lisa is that when I was hanging with her, she had long black hair and real boobs. She got a few guest spot gigs, like on *Cheers,* but she felt like she wasn't getting any traction. So one day she said, "I'm gonna dye my hair blond, I'm gonna get a nose job, and I'm gonna get fake boobs." (I remember after she got the boob job, she was playfully knocking on them one day, and this girl walked by and said, "You might as well enjoy 'em, you bought 'em.")

Well, it helped change her career overnight. She got *Mad About You* right after that, and then *Friends*. Then her career just took off into the sky. I remember in the week or so after *Friends* premiered, we ran into each other at a mall. At Cinnabon, to be exact, a place Lisa referred to as "life-changing." During our chat she said to me, "You know, I think this show is gonna actually end up being pretty good." Well, if it had been a month later—after *Friends* hit the stratosphere—I doubt she'd have been able to be at that mall without a bodyguard. I remember thinking, *I'm not going to see Lisa for five years now.*

But then I started to get my own foothold in TV shows, from an HBO special to a few choice guest spots in well-known sitcoms, and I was finally on my way. I was only a few years away from becoming an overnight success.

8

I'M A STAR!
(OKAY,
A GUEST STAR)

So my luck with television shows started to improve after I became a stand-up, and it was about time. Obviously, my dazzling network debut *four years* earlier—on an episode of *The Fresh Prince of Bel-Air* during its first season—hadn't turned into the avalanche of offers I thought it would.

But *Fresh Prince* had been a pretty memorable experience. After doing student movies and training films—or "industrials"—for corporate entities, snagging a part on something that even my aunt Florence in Berwyn, Illinois, could watch was pretty exciting.

It was the fourth episode ever of *Fresh Prince,* and when I went to the table read of the script, the show hadn't even begun airing yet. This was the fall of 1990. As you might imagine, my heart was racing at having a small guest role on what was promising to be a hit show. Will Smith wasn't a big film star at that point, but he was still a giant figure in rap. Music legend Quincy Jones, who was there that day, was the executive producer, and then for some reason civil rights activist Andrew Young was also there. *Holy shit,* I thought. *This is fucking bigtime. This is not a normal gig. I'd better not trample on anyone's civil rights today.*

Left: George Clooney clearly has his hand on my ass, and Quentin Tarantino told him to put it there.

For those of you not in the biz, a table read is when the cast reads the script out loud for the first time, usually with all the writers and producers there as well. I had only a few lines, and I was trying to be casual by turning the page at the same time as everyone else, but all I wanted to do was flip to my page and read my part over and over. "Be in the moment, Kathy, you're playing a character," I had to tell myself.

And it was a real stretch, my character. I was the honky.

I remember looking at the writing staff, though, and seeing only one black guy. The two show runners were this white married couple, Andy and Susan Borowitz. What two New York, uptown Jews were doing writing a rap-themed show, I do not know. But I remember a couple of times during the read-through, Andy would say to Will, "Is that how you would say it?" Then Will would add some "flava." The consultation and correcting of lines was much more hilarious than the script itself.

When it came to my first line, I got a laugh. What was weird was, it wasn't a joke. And then when I read the joke line, I got a monster laugh. Believe me, not only was I not that funny, the line certainly wasn't. But that's when I first learned that table reads are notoriously uncomfortable situations because people laugh way too loud and way too often, especially writers responding to their own jokes.

Afterward, somebody asked the lead actors about their impressions of the script. This is the part I'll never forget, it was so clichéd and genius about actors. Janet Hubert, who played the aunt to Will Smith's character, said, "I think what's lacking is a scene where Will and I sit down one on one and we talk about what Aunt Viv went through when she went to college." Then the guy who played her husband said, "It seems to me there should be a scene where Will and his uncle go golfing to discuss things." The girl who played their daughter said, "Shouldn't there be a scene where Will and I go shopping?"

I'm listening to this thinking, *So what each of you is saying is, the script would be better if only you were in it a lot more.* They were all so unaware of how they sounded, too. I should have raised my hand and said, "I think the honky should talk more!"

Overall, though, my week on the set was a blast. I made friends with the woman who played the grandmother—a veteran actress by the name of Virginia Capers—with whom I shared a tiny dressing room. She would cook soul food and bring it every day, and I'd listen to her tell stories from her life in movies and television. Flavor Flav from Public Enemy showed up for no reason on the night we taped and got on the mike and the crowd went wild. There was a DJ, too, playing dance music as if it were a nightclub. As for Will, he didn't have time for me all week, which was understandable, but he was a different person on show night, bonding with the actors right before performing with them. It was very smart. Before my scene with him, we were dancing together and chatting, and he was extremely charming. Even though he was new to television, he clearly had a sense of knowing when to turn it on and with whom.

I was a nobody when I did *The Fresh Prince of Bel Air,* but by the time I filmed a guest spot on Ellen DeGeneres's sitcom, *Ellen,* in the mid-'90s, I was a little more known—somewhat from stand-up, but mostly from that Kenwood commercial on which I droningly recited "Play That Funky Music, White Boy," which had become hugely popular.

The table read for *Ellen* was tense. She ran that room with an iron fist, and you could tell people were nervous around her. If *she* laughed, *they* laughed, and if she didn't, nobody dared to. I remember I walked in, and Ellen seemed very friendly. She said, "Oh, you're the girl from that commercial!"

I was really excited that she recognized me, and I sort of felt a little bit famous, so I had fun with it. "Why yes, that's me!" I said.

Then in front of this whole room of actors, writers, producers, she commanded, "Do it."

I remember thinking at that moment, *Wow, the star just said "Jump," and now it's my "How high?" moment.* I'm the chick who's only going to be there four days, and it's an intimidating room of writers, and now I'm the dancing monkey. It's a power move, something only a celebrity or a corporate CEO would do. "You're the girl from that commercial. DO IT." It wasn't mean, but I certainly learned how much the tone of a show is set by the star, and it was clear that she set up a pretty tough energy. By the way, I did it. I reenacted that commercial. And then, as the week went on, I of course started fucking one of the production assistants. I showed her.

When I did the NBC sitcom *Mad About You,* I remember Paul Reiser being very fun and friendly, and Helen Hunt being . . . not. Then again, she really seemed like she had one foot out the door. And when you look at that show, she really did do the heavy lifting. She'd win Emmys for that series because Paul Reiser had all the funny lines while she rocked the acting when they'd do "a very special episode" about how her character couldn't get pregnant. So I got the impression that it had all gotten old for her, and that the show wasn't her thing anymore. She wanted movies, and sure enough, she won an Oscar not too long after for *As Good As It Gets.*

Another abrasive star I encountered was Thomas Haden Church, whom I worked with when I did an episode of *Ned & Stacey,* the short-lived sitcom he starred in with Debra Messing. Tom was coming off the long-running TV sitcom *Wings,* on which he made a name for himself as the dim-bulb mechanic, and to this day, he is one of the funniest people I've ever met, and certainly one of the most talented sitcom actors I've ever watched work. I've never seen a sitcom actor improvise as much as he did, and his improvised lines were all funny. It didn't surprise me at all that he went on to get an Oscar nomination years later for the film *Sideways.*

But Tom was extremely tough. He was hard on poor Debra Messing, because comedy didn't come naturally to her. Don't get me wrong, she's very good at comedy, but she's not a comedian. And he ran those writers ragged. I remember, at the end of the run-through, he had all the writers stand in a circle and he screamed at them. It was one of the first times I'd watched a star act in a temperamental way, but at the same time, I thought, *You know, he's right.* I could see why people on that staff bitched about him, but he was funnier than his writers. I've never seen anybody since improvise on a sitcom like him. I'm sure his behavior is the reason he doesn't have his own show now, but it got me thinking about how there's got to be a way to voice those same concerns but not completely piss people off.

Tom was sexy and good-looking in an offbeat way, and what was cool about him was that he treated me like a peer, not a girl. I completely interpreted it as that situation where guys are nicer to the girl when she isn't the hot chick. He just saw me as a human being—like a sister—and so it was "good ol' Kath" and a punch in the arm. Guys like that are not flirting with me, but at least they're not rude to me the way they might be to a girl who really turns them off. I'm in a solid middle category, where I'm safe enough to hang out with and joke with. I can keep up with these kinds of guys, and it's nice.

George Clooney was like that, too, when I did a guest stint on *ER*. I was playing a scout leader with a troop of sick kids. I was nervous to be in a scene with him and Anthony Edwards. But the handsome Clooney immediately put me at ease, joking and being an all-around charmer.

I'll digress for a moment to tell you just what a man among men Clooney is, ladies and gays. A few years after that *ER* episode, I got asked to do a table read for the Steven Soderbergh movie *Out of Sight*. It wasn't an audition, just one of these movie situations where the filmmakers want to hear their script read out loud. I don't know why they asked me at all, but the call came from my agent, and I quickly said, "Yes." It was going to be at Danny DeVito's house, since he was a producer on the film, and when I got there, they were very strict about where we could and couldn't go in the house, because of course I wanted a tour. Then the celebrities started showing up. Lolita Davidovich was there, reading the part that would go to Jennifer Lopez, and Don Cheadle, and big studio mucky-mucks. Of course, I didn't know anybody, and I was so nervous, clutching my script and trying to prepare, that when this nerdy guy came up to me and started making small talk, I thought, "I don't have time for your needs, mister," so I turned to him and said, "I don't mean to be rude, but I kind of need to be studying right now." That was Soderbergh. Oopsy!

But when Clooney came in, with the room full of people, he walked right up to me and said, "There's the sexiest girl in the room!" and sat right next to me. I will never forget that. He went out of his way just to be nice and make a fun joke, and I was much more relaxed from then on, and everyone in the room looked at me differently after that, which was nice. (I was reading a black woman's role, by the way, the one eventually played by Viola Davis in the movie. You'd think my experience on *Fresh Prince* working alongside Andrew Young would have helped me get that part, but alas, no.)

Anyway, aside from discovering how great Clooney was, that *ER* gig was special for me because at the time I was sort of seeing Quentin Tarantino, who directed the episode I was in. I met him through the Groundlings. Julia Sweeney had become friends with Quentin, and wrangled him for the night during the week when we had a guest star perform with the main company. *Reservoir Dogs* had just come out and was the biggest thing in movies. We all went to dinner after the Groundlings show and I sat across from this larger-than-life character shouting with passion and gesticulating wildly to make every point.

"Did you see *Reservoir Dogs?*" he asked.

I told him I hadn't yet. That set him off, but jokingly, and with no small amount of spastic confidence. "I can't believe it! You're the ONLY person in LA who hasn't seen it! It's genius! It's brilliant! It's a brilliant movie. Ask anyone here! There's this scene where Michael Madsen starts to freak out and slice a cop's ear! And then there's this other scene with Tim Roth where he's bleeding out of his stomach for hours!"

He just started describing the whole movie, and then stopped himself. "That's it! I'm gonna take you!"

I said, "Haven't you seen it a million times already?"

He said, "There's a screening next week with the whole cast, and I'm taking you!"

So he took me, I was his date, but beforehand we went to dinner with Steve Buscemi, Lawrence Tierney, Tim Roth, and Michael Madsen. I was like, "Holy shit. How did I get at the indie-film heavy-hitter serious-actor table?" I said to Madsen, "I understand you play a pretty brutal character. You don't hit any chicks or anything, right? Cause I can't handle that." An opener I've used many times with attractive men.

Michael started playing with my hair, and doing his whole brooding, mumbling, bad-boy sexy act, saying things like, "No, I would never hit a woman."

Movie actors are weird.

It was fun at dinner watching all the actors fawn all over their beloved Quentin. I was dazzled by him as well. He has a rapport with actors and movie stars that cuts through their Hollywood BS, and he's able to communicate with them as if he's talking to real human beings. He came from the fan-boy world, sure, but I felt like every star at that table knew they were in the presence of The Great Tarantino.

I went out with him only a couple of times, and I'm so glad I got to know him. He put me in small parts in several of his projects: *Pulp Fiction, Four Rooms,* and his episode of *ER.* But there is a dark side to Quentin Tarantino you haven't known about till now. I spent the night with him. That's right. The whole night. In bed. What we did is, um, a little hard for me to reveal. (Cue Barbara Walters.) Drum roll. We . . . *cuddled.* Yeah. Cuddled. Anybody could have fucked him. It takes a lot of balls to cuddle with Tarantino. He had come over to my studio apartment one night and we were joking around about whether or not he should stay the night. I made the point that I wouldn't be able to respect myself in the morning if I didn't fuck him. Because I didn't want to be one of those girls who did "that thing" with a guy. You know that thing, girls, where you decide you're not ready to sleep with someone, so you just want to cuddle for a night? Not on my watch, bitches. But Tarantino, being the persuasive cinematic artiste he was, was determined to see if I could go all night without fucking the shit out of him. So we did "the thing" instead. I've never felt so dirty.

Anyway, back to *ER.* This is how dorky I was about my day on that show. A little background first: With every TV or film job I got, I would make sure that I had a deal where my parents were allowed to come to the set. I wasn't a child actor. I was a woman in my thirties. And I took them to *everything.* I'd book the gig, and then add, "Oh, can I get a drive-on for John and Maggie Griffin?" My mother in her muumuu met nearly every giant star. When I did this low-budget indie comedy for Bobcat Goldthwait called *Shakes the Clown,* I made sure they came to the set the day Robin Williams was scheduled to film a cameo. Thankfully, Robin in his downtime didn't go hide out in his trailer. He was so restless he stayed in this communal room and

Me being a typical stage daughter, dragging her parents to a set.

performed all day. So my parents set up two chairs, like a small theater, and basically got to watch one of the biggest comedy stars of all time perform off and on all day. It was a complete treat for my dad, who was a huge fan.

So even though I was only working *one day* on *ER,* I brought my parents. To taping, lunch, everything. They had a set kit in the car—cooler, folding chairs, water for survival (although a box of wine was preferred)—for these very moments. I, of course, assumed everyone looked at me like I was a weirdo. In much the way I complain about people bringing their children to work, I am, it turns out, worse than any new parent. But the deal is, as those of you who watch *The D-List* know, Mom and Dad were so fucking charming that to this day no one has ever said to me, "You know, that was kind of strange when you brought your folks."

There we were on the Warner Bros. lot, with Mom pulling me aside in the cafeteria. "Look at that DARLING Julianna Marguiles!

She's a skinny young thing! You need to learn from that one! Look at how she keeps her figure! See how she has a salad? You shouldn't be having a hamburger, Kathleen! Look at the way she does her hair. Why don't you do your hair like that?" By the way, for years my mother tried to convince me that I could "train" my curly, kinky, frizzy hair to be straight. She actually believed that if I blew-dry my hair straight for long enough, that it would eventually grow in that way. This had to have come from one of those goddamn Rona Barrett magazines. A Myrna Loy tip, probably. In any case, she was focused, a mom-ager before there were mom-agers. Watch out, Dina Lohan.

Then there'd be Clooney in his scrubs playing basketball, and my father giving him shit. "You'll never be in the NBA, Clooney!" Then Clooney would walk toward the fence and gravitate toward my adorable parents, my mom fawning all over him. If you talk to my mom, she thinks they're best friends. But really, from minute one of my getting these types of gigs, I thought, *What good is this if I can't bring my parents?* It's cool I got the job, but way more fun that they got to meet Clooney and see Quentin work.

Perhaps the biggest deal for me during that time was winning a guest role on *Seinfeld*, the hottest show on TV. It was just one of those auditions that, after years, finally fucking went my way. Again, all the stand-up I was doing was probably what helped the most. The thing to remember is that, even if you've been doing characters for years in the Groundlings, when you go into an audition, you're kind of going as yourself. And the alternative stand-up comedy world had given me plenty of experience in that department.

That table read was mind-blowing, if only because you went in, and there was fucking Jerry, Elaine, George, and Kramer. Newman, too. The diner set. The living room set. The fake New York street. To be sitting in Jerry's living room was a thrill I was not prepared for. I asked about ten people to take my picture, thinking, *Who's gonna believe this if I don't have hard documentary evidence?* My part was that of George Costanza's fiancée's college roommate Sally Weaver, and during the actual reading, I was shaking, telling myself whatever happens, I *cannot* be the one who fucks up, because the other thing about table reads—it's where people get fired. You can have a good audition, but if you have a bad table read, you'll get the call a half hour later while you're in your trailer, and then before you know it, you're going home. The stakes are incredibly high.

Luckily the table read went well. Most of the cast, writers, and producers laughed. But Jerry was kind of an asshole. We were working early on a Sunday morning, which was unusual, but that was because the Golden Globes were that night. I was planning on going to a gay Golden Globes–watching party that night, so I went up to Jerry, thinking nothing of it, and asked if he'd sign something for me so that when we were watching the awards and his category came up, I could impress the gays. "Guess what, fuckers?" I imagined saying. "There's Seinfeld on TV, and I've got a fucking note from him!" I wanted him to write something like, "Dear Kathy's Golden Globe party, be rooting for me! Jerry Seinfeld." Or whatever.

Well, he wouldn't do it. "Grrr," was about all I got out of him. All day on the set he was like, "Ugh, are you still gonna bug me about writing your stupid note? Why do I have to write a note? I don't want to write a note. I don't even know you." I remember thinking, *Oh for God's sake, just write the fuckin' note!* What Jerry didn't realize at this point was that we were in a big fight, and I was officially not speaking to him anymore. He did not notice this, because he did not notice that I existed, and because he obviously had better things to do than tend to me and my needs. He finally, begrudgingly, wrote me that note for the gays telling them to root for him. But I think this was the first time I'd pissed off an A-lister to his or her face. Normally, as you know, I prefer to talk about people behind their backs.

Naturally, this experience had to go into the act. Beloved American treasure Jerry Seinfeld was an asshole. I thought it was funny. I felt wronged, and felt I had to blurt this out. It didn't occur to me to think, *Okay, Kathy, when you do stand-up in Los Angeles, there are going to be industry people there. Don't bash the number one sitcom star in the world.* But

Jerry Seinfeld with his comedy idol.

once I got laughs from it, I told that story in my act for three months. I couldn't tell it twice at Un-Cab or Hot Cup O' Talk, obviously, so it went into heavy rotation at all the clubs, alternative coffeehouses, and alternative donut shop performance spaces I could book myself in.

Then, around that time, I got my first HBO comedy special. It was a half hour, and I was one of eleven other people who got half hours. Maybe not as prestigious, but still pretty cool. Sure enough, HBO said to me, "Oh, that Seinfeld story is funny, you have to put it in." That's when I finally thought, *What if he sees it?*

Ever since the audition, I had become a little friendly with *Seinfeld* co-creator/executive producer Larry David, so I thought I'd feel him out. "How's Jerry going to take this?" I asked him. "I'm thinking about putting in this story about him."

Larry thought it was hysterical that I was giving Jerry shit. "I know Jerry," he assured me. "Jerry will NEVER see this. Never in a million YEARS. You're FINE, kid, you're good!"

Whew.

Meanwhile, *Suddenly Susan* was a-brewin'. After eight years or so of obscurity in the Groundlings, and a year of doing stand-up, I was up for a bunch of sitcom auditions. Casting directors and studio and network people were packing into Hot Cup O' Talk and Un-Cabaret, and I finally started to get a sense of inevitability. Granted, I was often the girl cast after somebody already hired didn't work out. But things were rolling. "You know what?" I would tell my friends, "eventually, they *have* to fucking put me on a TV show. They're going to run out of girls to play the secretary, and they'll have to come to me."

After paying my dues for more than ten years, I was *this* close to getting a regular sitcom gig. I really do believe I was the favorite for a part on *Caroline in the City*, that mid-'90s Lea Thompson sitcom where she played a New York cartoonist. But I blew it at the test for the NBC bigwigs. How? I lost my voice. I even got a huge laugh out of it when I turned to Jeff Zucker, the head of the network, and scratched out the words, "Sorry, I just got that chimp virus from the movie *Outbreak*." But they were starting production in two days, and they all just looked at each other, like, "She's not talking. How do we know she can do this role?" So they hired Amy Pietz, and she did that show for four years.

Actresses are pretty competitive when it comes to vying for those sidekick roles. Keep in mind, a studio or network may audition seventy-five girls for one part. So when *Suddenly Susan,* with Brooke Shields playing a San Francisco magazine columnist, was being put together in the spring of 1996, it just seemed weird that I wasn't in contention for the part of Vicki, Susan's wisecracking colleague. Sidekick girls were coming up to me at auditions and saying, "I didn't get *Sud-*

denly Susan. Are you up for it?" I'd have to say, "I don't know. They just haven't seen me."

They saw every goddamn girl in town. Megan Mullaly, Morwanna Banks, Jennifer Coolidge, Rachel True, Sarah Silverman, Jennifer Esposito, even Downtown Julie Brown. Casting director Tony Sepulveda said to me, "Nobody was sold on you to test for the role." Eventually for the pilot they cast Maggie Wheeler, that Fran Drescher–voiced actress who played Matthew Perry's ex-girlfriend Janice on *Friends*. The show got picked up, but as is often the case, the cast from the pilot changes, and for some reason it didn't work out with Maggie. Eventually it came down to the wire for the Vicki part. As in, the table read for the first episode of the first season's shooting was on a Monday, and the *Friday before* they finally agreed to let me audition. They still didn't even want to see me. But apparently Brooke wanted to look at other girls after that first audition, for whatever reason. The head of Warner Bros., the studio producing the show, wasn't sold, either. But somebody at NBC kept reminding them, "She's done guest spots for us, she's good." I'm positive the decision to hire me was out of desperation, because time was of the essence. A sort of "Fine, we'll take her" scenario.

But nothing beats that moment when you feel your life has changed. I knew it in the parking lot after the audition. The casting director rolled down the window of his car as he was driving out, and said, "Hello, VICKI." And no, he wasn't mistaking me for red-headed actress Vicki Lewis from *Newsradio*. He knew I was getting that part. When the news was official, I called my parents, hysterically crying.

I had a role on a series!

I was going to make $15,000 an episode!

I was going to turn this into even more work: voice-overs, bigger commercials, small parts in films!

I was going to get to know an icon of beauty and glamour whose movies I grew up with!

I was going to work closely with Judd Nelson, a star of *The Breakfast Club,* a movie I worshipped!

I was going to be a part of the hot-as-shit NBC comedy lineup, and get to see my old pals Phil Hartman and Andy Dick, now on *Newsradio,* at all the network events!

Oh SHIT, I was going to see Jerry Seinfeld!

It was only a matter of time. I heard later that Jerry had seen the HBO special. Perhaps Larry David had been fucking with me. One day, my agent called and said, "Jerry Seinfeld is sending you something."

Now, my imagination is such that if you don't spell out exactly what's happening, I'll just go to the worst possible scenario. I know it doesn't make sense, but I was convinced that Jerry Seinfeld was sending me a box of his own poo. Or he was going to send someone over to my house to break my thumbs. Okay, Kathy, snap out of it.

I remember saying to my agent, "Can he get me fired from *Suddenly Susan?*" And my agent was like, "I don't . . . think so. I don't know. He's pretty fucking powerful over there." Great. The biggest moment in my life, and maybe it was going to be taken away from me because of my big mouth.

Then the package came, and it was a box of Snackwell cookies. I was still terrified. What did this mean? Is this a comedy kingpin's version of a mafioso sending a fish wrapped in newspaper to someone targeted for execution? Kathy Griffin sleeps with the cookies?

There was a letter, too, and after reading it, I felt relieved. It was hysterically funny, as you can see. It was a little scary, but you could tell he thought the whole thing was funny. At the end, he wrote, "Enclosed, please find a box of Snackwells for you to enjoy with my compliments." Note the hilarious fake signature at the bottom of the letter, obviously scribbled by his assistant.

Later, I even found out from a friend of mine—okay, okay, some guy I was banging on the *Seinfeld* crew—that during tapings of *Seinfeld,* Jerry showed that bit from my HBO special to the audience while they would set up for the next scene. And after I went on the Conan O'Brien show to talk about getting that letter, Jerry added *that* clip to what he showed at tapings, too. Jerry not only got the joke, but he was growing my audience!

Seinfeld

October 31, 1996

Dear Ms. Griffin:

I was, up until your recent monologue on some obscure cable channel, unaware that you had ever appeared on my number one hit television series, that is named after me. I nonetheless, very much enjoyed your little skit. Although I obviously have no recollection of ever meeting you.

I was particularly amused at the "Fuck you Jerry Seinfeld" moment. I assume the point of it being how could anyone's opinion of me, no matter how slanderous, have any effect on my great empire in any way. How true and how delightfully funny.

Anyway, I wish you much good luck in whatever it is that you do and hope that you continue to enjoy my history making television program "Seinfeld" along with millions of other Americans and countless fans around the world.

Enclosed please find a box of Snackwells for you to enjoy with my compliments.

Best Regards,

Jerry Seinfeld

Want to know what happens when you make fun of A-listers? Every once in a while they get it.

Once again, just like when I bombed for two years after I got laughs the first time I tried stand-up, I was fooled into thinking, *Oh, celebrities are fine when you make fun of them! They all think it's funny! In fact, they send you funny gifts! And write you awesome letters that you can frame!*

To this day, Jerry Seinfeld leads the pack of A-listers who can take a fucking joke.

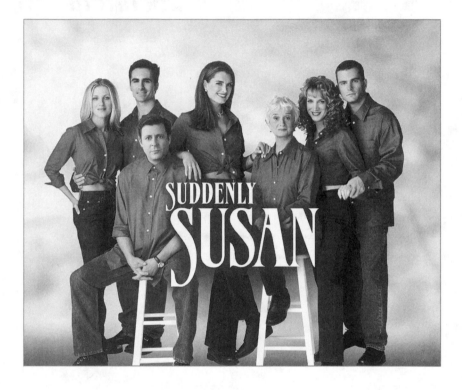

9

BROOKE SHIELDS, DON'T READ THIS

My first impression of Brooke Shields was that I'd never seen someone so beautiful that her face looks like it has makeup on when it doesn't. The color of her eyelids already looks like eye shadow, and the natural color of her lips looks like lipstick. My God, I thought, that's a whole other level of gorgeous.

Gracious hostess that she is, Brooke wanted to take the cast of *Suddenly Susan* out to lunch before the first table read. She wanted us all to hang out, and that's how I first met a lot of the other key cast members: Barbara Barrie, the *Breaking Away* actress who played Brooke's mom; the handsome Nestor Carbonell, who played the Cuban-tongued hunk Luis; David Strickland, the cute, funny guy who was the fictitious magazine's music critic; and Judd Nelson, the former Brat Packer who played the boss.

Brooke was very sweet, and I was impressed with her early on because she was very deferential to me when it came to the comedy. She would often turn to me that first season and say, "Ugh, help me make this funny. How would you do this line?" I'd think, *Wow, that's really cool of her.* It was also smart. It made me understand, no matter how

---

Left: From left: Andrea Bendewald, Nestor Carbonell, Judd Nelson, some ex-jeans model, Barbara Barrie, a future Emmy winner, and David Strickland (Photo: *Suddenly Susan* © Warner Bros. Television. All Rights Reserved.)

Brooke Shields seems flummoxed by my bad acting.
(Photo: *Suddenly Susan* © Warner Bros. Television.
All Rights Reserved.)

famous you are, don't ever be afraid to turn to somebody and ask for help. Don't ever feel above it.

Then she stopped doing it. Something happened, where the first time I got a really, really good review, and she got a bad one, that shit went out the window. Then there'd be tense moments when I would get laughs and she wouldn't. I was always blown away by that beautiful-girl syndrome. To me, Brooke had everything. She was gorgeous, success-ful, gracious, America's sweetheart, and yet there was this big part of her that resented that I got laughs. I just couldn't believe it. I wasn't trying to be a cover girl, for Chrissakes. I remember saying to her one time, "Isn't it enough that you're beautiful and perfect and wonderful and guys are in love with you and you're starring on a show and the head of the network is kissing your butt and you're rich and successful? I'd be happy to have *one* of those things. And on top of that, you want to get the laughs? Can't I just have this one thing?" She laughed at that reasoning, and thankfully it eased the tension.

The reality is, when you're the sidekick, you do the wisecracks. That's it. There was no very special Vicki episode in my future. And I didn't want that, anyway. But that always blew me away about pretty actresses and models. To this day, when I run into them, they'll be a little bitchy toward me if I get a laugh on a set. Really, gals? It's not enough that every statistic shows you can get a job easier than I can, that every guy wants you, and the world is easier for you in a multitude of ways?

I just want my dick jokes.

The truth is, I still feel like Brooke is my sister. There's something about working every day with someone for four years where you really get to know them well, and vice versa. And what's great about Brooke is that for as beautiful and perfect and iconic as she is, you could always break her down. I don't mean make her sob. What I mean by that is, if we were in a room alone, and the celebrity world of phone calls and photo shoot requests wasn't allowed to barge in for five minutes, she was just a regular person.

I was very cognizant of the weight of her celebrity, too. I saw many ups and downs of the limelight through her notoriety. She was my fame professor, really. Right off the bat, her marriage to Andre Agassi was like a spotlight times a hundred. It was my first prolonged exposure to a real celebrity power couple. The first week *Suddenly Susan* was set to air, we all came into work and Brooke said, "Guess what, everybody? Tonight we're all going to fly to Las Vegas, watch the episode, and fly home tonight on Andre's 747!" That 747 had a *bed* in it. That's how big it was. So we went to Andre Agassi's house, which I have to say was surprisingly lame for a guy with a $100 million Nike contract. It was a cookie-cutter McMansion, which just seemed odd. I expected

Brooke Shields and me on vacation looking a little gay for each other.

something a little more *Cribs*. But it didn't stop me from being inherently dazzled by where I was. I was in Andre Agassi's house. I'd look outside. There was his tennis court. Holy shit.

That was the first time I'd been around real wealth. One time during a rehearsal, Brooke said something that always stuck with me. "You know, with wealthy people there's a difference between money and real money. I have money. Andre has *real* money." That told me that in the celebrity world, the ceilings are different than anywhere else. Brooke had lived in New York for years, ran with a society crowd, worked in Hollywood since she was a child, and Andre's the one with *real* money? Maybe Andre is somewhere having that conversation about Warren Buffett. "You know Warren? I have money, but he's got *real* money." Again, holy shit. I had to start saving.

Brooke was a different person around Andre, though. She was a lot more fun and loose when she wasn't around him, and in his presence she would come off very wifey. One time she told me he didn't like cussing. "Don't be surprised if he snaps at you for swearing too much," she said.

"I'm a little old to have someone yelling at me for swearing," I said.

"I'm just saying, he's a Christian, and we go to church together, and he goes through phases where he gets really uncomfortable with swearing."

"Well, I go through phases where I might punch someone in the face who gives me shit about swearing," I joked.

I could tease Brooke like that, but I could never say that in front of Andre, because then she wouldn't laugh. It was like she had to dumb herself down for him. I want to give him his due about his tennis talent, but as far as personality goes, he was pretty humorless and kind of a pill. This was a period when he was taking a lot of heat for losing matches, and people were blaming Brooke, and that was rough on her. It's that world where as gorgeous and as famous as Brooke is, there was nothing like that Agassi cred. He was the guy who when he came to the set, everyone would freeze. Suddenly the heads of the network and studio were there, guys who rarely spoke to Brooke were suddenly stumbling over themselves and losing their shit, and bromances were sprouting all over the place. Men were practically crying. My straight guy friends who could barely remember the name of my TV show were asking me about him. I remember thinking, *Calm the fuck DOWN. He plays TENNIS. Brooke over here has worked with everybody! She's made movies! Survived an alcoholic mother! She models and acts! He does one fuckin' thing!*

Not only that, I remember a conversation Andre and I had when he said he didn't enjoy tennis anymore. Instead, he was golfing obsessively. "If it was up to me, I would just golf all the time," he said. I thought, *Well, you're not that good at it, apparently. There's a thing called a racquet you might want to pick up. You seem to be good with it.* It's a theme in my life. Go where you're welcome and wanted. I wasn't making it at the Improv, so I went toward Un-Cabaret. For a guy in his midtwenties, he seemed a little young to be bored with it all. And here was Brooke who mastered reinventing herself. When a movie of hers bombed she went on a date with the Sultan of Brunei, which resulted in tons of publicity. Later on when she was out of the spotlight, she did a naughty guest role on *Friends*. And that led to *Suddenly Susan*. She was expert at getting back in there some way, any way.

Much of this tenacity and knack for reinvention comes from Brooke's mom. Brooke and Teri Shields have a pretty well-entrenched public relationship. Teri is known as the drunken, overbearing stage mom, and Brooke is known as the beautiful, young, talented model/actress who was carted all over the world when she was twelve, who made something of her life. Brooke was certainly all those things, but her mom is also incredibly quick, witty, and smart. I got along great with Teri, because she's a hilarious, sarcastic drunk. Multiply her and you get my whole family. Those are the people I love. So I hit it off with Teri the minute I met her. Obviously I totally empathize with Brooke. It would be very difficult to have Teri as a mom. I understand that. Maggie Griffin certainly wasn't shoving me into a bikini when I was a preteen and flying me around the globe to be in movies. But I get Teri. She's clever, and has a true rapier wit.

One time Brooke started teasing me about how I get along with her mom better than she does. She pulled me aside and said, "I really like that you like my mom so much."

"We're not ganging up against you," I said, defensively.

"No, no," she said. "Sometimes when I get mad at my mom, I have to be reminded of the good things about her. I love that you get her and see the good stuff."

"Well," I explained, "she's not my mom. It's a completely different dynamic. Your mom is quick, funny, and biting, and those are my peeps."

I appreciated what Brooke had said, though. Especially because I couldn't help but giggle when Teri would say vicious things, like turning to Brooke periodically and barking, "It's not all about YOU!" Brooke would be so hurt, and I'd be like, "I thought everybody's relatives said that!"

My sister Brooke and I would fight, of course. It's testimony to how stupid our fights were that I can't remember what most of them were about. I borrowed her conditioner and didn't give it back, or something ridiculous like that. One time she stormed into her dressing room, and I heard her say, "I'm going to get her so fuckin' fired." I didn't think anything of it until I went up to David and Nestor and said, "Who was Brooke talking about?" And they said, "Um . . . you."

"Why?" I said.

"Because it's getting out that her marriage is falling apart, and Brooke thinks you're talking about it all over town."

Now, Brooke had come to my stand-up shows, and she was always very supportive of me, even as I told stories about *Suddenly Susan*. But this was ridiculous. She thought I was talking to *People* magazine about this guy who was hanging around the set all the time. His name was Chris Henchy, a comedy guy I'd known from those Dave Rath parties years ago. He was coming to the set twice a week, a set with fifty people around at any given time. How am I the only person who could have given out this info?

Brooke confronted me about it, and I said, "I didn't leak anything about your marriage, but your boyfriend is coming by constantly. And besides, I don't know people at *People*."

So we had a big blowup, and we tried not to talk to each other. Which is funny when you're acting in the same scenes, doing run-throughs together, and bumping into each other frequently. Every time one of us would try to be alone, we'd run into the other. If Brooke wanted five minutes to go get coffee somewhere off set, that's when I'd be walking out some other door to go to my car. Eventually, I went to this little diner to eat by myself, and sure enough, she shows up with her dog in tow. There was nobody but me at a table, and Brooke and her dog at the counter. I finally just turned to her and said, "I would like your dog to stop following me."

She laughed! And that's how we would make up. We'd have fights about nothing, then make up over nothing. I actually get a tickle out of remembering our fights, because they were the times when I got to see a real side of Brooke that wasn't a perfect ice princess model. We had a lot of good girl talk over those years, many heart-to-hearts, and I really miss that about her. I'm sure that she was relieved that I turned out to be more than a perfect ice princess model as well.

The ratings for *Suddenly Susan* were insane the first year, something like twenty million viewers a week. You don't get those kinds of ratings anymore, unless you're *American Idol.* We were part of a Thursday night lineup that included *Friends* and *Seinfeld,* so to some extent we were going to be golden for a while. But nobody was accusing us of being as good as those shows, that's for sure. I was perfectly happy, of course, doing my thing as a sitcom sidekick—my dream gig—but I had to take shit from people, too. Like from my former nemesis Jerry Seinfeld.

I went back to do another guest spot on *Seinfeld* as the same character I played in my first appearance—Sally Weaver—only this time the story line was taken from my experience with the real Seinfeld: In the episode, Sally becomes a stand-up comedian who makes her living ragging on Jerry. Oh yeah, inspiring an episode of *Seinfeld* is big-time. I remember walking on to that diner set having worked on *Suddenly Susan* all day, and there was Jerry all by himself sitting in one of the booths. I heard from across that stage, "Well, well, well! Look at Miss Famous!" I just thought, *All right, here we go.* I figured I could either be a submissive dog who would roll over, or I can act like a peer. So I just sat down in the booth and said, "You really were an asshole that day."

He laughed really hard. Whew.

It was actually an amazing conversation, because Jerry had just declared to the world that he was going to end the show and go back to stand-up. He'd been on the cover of *Time* magazine with his announcement. I really felt honored getting to spend time with him that week, this comedy icon who was closing up shop on America's favorite show. But boy, he would just be brutal to me about *Suddenly Susan.*

"So," he'd say in that uniquely Seinfeldian cadence of his, "are you having fun over there at *Suddenly Susan?*"

"Yes, Jerry," I'd reply, knowing full well where this was going.

"Is that a . . . is that a fun show to be on?"

"Not as funny as your show, of course, Jerry, but it's a fun show, yes. Brooke Shields is very nice."

"I'm just curious. I mean, you were just over there, and now you're here. What do you think makes that show different from this show?"

"Jerry . . ."

"Is it the scripts? Would you say it's the scripts? It's probably the scripts, right? Do you think it's the scripts?"

Then I would have to say "Yes, Jerry, the scripts are obviously better here. And you're fantastic and wildly funny, and everything is better here."

Larry David, meanwhile, was making these hilarious phone calls to me at the *Suddenly Susan* set, roping me into similar conversations, too.

"Um, Griffin," he'd say over the phone. "What, uh . . . what's going on over there this week on *Suddenly Susan*?"

I'd be like, "Larry, I don't want to do this now. It's taping day. I'm busy."

"No, no, I'm just calling . . ."

"You're going to make fun of me for being on this show."

"NO! NO! No, I'm not. I'm not. Just tell me what's going on! What's the uh . . . what's the 'A' story this week?" he'd say, referring to the primary story line of the episode.

"I'm not going to tell you."

"Aw, come on! Tell me! Tell me what they're writing over there."

I'd pause, then give in. "Well, this week we're going camping and I have an evil twin."

Then he'd let me have it: "Oh GOD, you've gotta get off that show! That's TERRIBLE! You're KIDDING me?!?! You CAN'T be doing a camping episode! You HAVE TO GET OFF THAT SHOW! Just leave! Get in your car! Get in your car and leave!"

But why would I leave? I really did have a dream job, and I was making good money. The first year of *Suddenly Susan* I made the same mistakes my friends did who went from earning $20,000 a year to $250,000. They'd get very loosey-goosey with money, buying things they couldn't afford, or just giving it away. So if somebody had a sob story, I wrote them a check. For tens of thousands of dollars. Insane amounts of money. I had a learning curve that first year, and then mom's voice of frugality rang out in my head.

The second year of *Suddenly Susan*, I decided that after years of renting and living in tiny spaces, I should own my own home. A big one. I always assumed I'd be doing something like this with a husband, but I was on a series, I was single, I hadn't met anybody, and I wanted to do something for myself. So I picked out a 3,300-square-foot house in the Hollywood hills, four bedrooms and three baths, big enough for me to have an office and a gym. (It's not the house you see on *The D-List*, but it was still pretty major.) The whole cast came over the day I closed escrow, and they all made fun of me. "Why the hell did you buy this big house?" they all wanted to know.

"Because I have the money *now*," I said. "If *Suddenly Susan* goes away, if I break both my legs, if I can't continue to make a living, I could live in this house forever. I'm not buying this for now. I'm buying it for when I'm eighty. This is a big box I can die in."

Looking back now, the size of the house for one person was a little ridiculous. Plus, I instantly embarked on a remodel, not knowing what the fuck I was doing. But I loved it, from the yearly formal Christmas parties I threw, to having celebrities as canyon neighbors. One night I was on the balcony talking on the phone, and across the ravine I could hear someone shouting, "I hear you, Kathy Griffin! Shut up!" It was none other than my goth-rocking neighbor Marilyn Manson.

That house marked me in the eyes of a lot of my alternative comedy peers as a sellout, especially among the guys who simply didn't have the same priorities as me, like David Cross. Then two years later David's star was on the rise because of the HBO series *Mr. Show with Bob and David*, and he says to me, "Who's your Realtor?"

"Really, David?" I said. "You're going to give in to The Man like that?"

Thanks to this sitcom I was on I was making good money, felt a sense of job security, and made some wonderful new friends. But another great thing about *Suddenly Susan* was the revolving door of guest stars I had the opportunity to work with and observe. Some, of course, weren't big when they were on and I don't remember them now. Dane Cook had a line once. Ali Larter from *Heroes* saw me at a party recently and a friend had to remind me she was on the show. Ali said, "I was the water girl."

"Let me guess," I responded. "You came in with the Sparkletts bottle, you were sexy, and Judd Nelson hit on you."

"Yeah!" she said.

The stunt casting, though—casting big names for a quick-and-easy ratings bump—yielded some choice experiences. It's how I got to know my friend Joan Rivers. She played my mom, and that was heaven. I had met her twice before, because her daughter, Melissa, was my student when I was a teacher at the Groundlings. But now we were working together, and we hit it off from the first day. She was complimentary toward me, and always had me laughing. She would improvise all the time, but the writers kept rejecting her lines. Their reasoning always had to do with things like camera placement and editing continuity, but I remember thinking, *That's a bad call. If Joan Rivers is making up jokes, why don't you just use them?*

Tommy Smothers was on once, too, but I admit I didn't know as much about him as I do now. He and his brother Dick were famous fighters against censorship when they had their groundbreaking variety show in the late '60s, and had I been aware of all that back then I would have tried to spend more time with him. He was very nice, though, and the last time I played in his neck of the woods in northern California, he sent me flowers and a gift.

Another legendary comedian we had on the show was Rodney Dangerfield. He liked me, too, but he was really loud and obnoxious. He would always yell, "You're a funny BITCH!" And I'd think, *You couldn't stop at "funny"?* But he was old school. Also, he'd sit in his dressing room in his bathrobe with his balls hanging out. He was flashing his crotch long before Paris and Britney. It wasn't on purpose or anything, but he'd have his boxers on and his man parts would just seep out. I'd walk by his dressing room and run into David and Nestor, who'd notice the look of shock and awe on my face, and say, "Aww, did you see Rodney's balls again?"

Sometimes what a guest star exposed was more personally surprising than anatomically disturbing. Hulk Hogan was on for at least two episodes. This was long before his reality show, so nobody knew what he'd be like. He showed up with an acting coach, which we all thought was weird. But at the table read, he seemed to have a lot of trouble reading. Maybe he's dyslexic, but Hulk would memorize his lines as quickly as possible and run through them with this guy. It reminded me of when I did this short-lived sketch show *Saturday Night Special* the year before *Suddenly Susan,* and Tupac Shakur was a guest, and he read in rehearsal like a first-grader. I kept thinking, *How could Tupac Shakur have made all that money, and he still can't read?*

Then there was Leif Garrett—and by the way it's pronounced "Lay-f" not "Leaf," and he *will* correct you—who showed up on the heels of his talked-about VH-1 *Behind the Music* episode in which we saw the extent of his drug abuse and how he's gotten his life back together. The story was about how Susan finds her wish list from high school and decides to relive it, and one of the wishes was to go on a date with Leif. Well, he was completely nasty to me, but more important, he really seemed under the influence every minute he was there. I'll never forget he had a ton of makeup on, which was a red flag, too. What are you covering up? Well, he told me that when he was jacked up on black tar heroin, he would scratch his face to the bone. He mimed it for me with his two forefingers, scratching either side of his face really fast like a chipmunk. I'll never forget him saying "to the bone." By the end of the week, he'd been such a prick that I used to call him "To the Bone" Garrett to his face. From what I understand, he went on to relapse several times after that.

All in all, *Suddenly Susan* was a very interesting work environment. For a show that was so sugary sweet and middle-of-the-road in quality, it actually had a backstage life that was very intense and biting. What was comical to me was how drama-filled it often was behind the

The wonderful David Strickland and I doing a scene together. I miss him.
(Photo: *Suddenly Susan* © Warner Bros. Television. All Rights Reserved.)

scenes, all while we were putting out this squeaky-clean show. Brooke went through a divorce, and would have to occasionally deal with her drink-addicted mom. Judd was struggling with his own demons and left the show before the end of its run. And worst of all, we lost David Strickland when he took his own life in 1999, during our third season. It doesn't get more intense than that.

I loved David dearly, from day one. He was funny on the show, but he was even funnier off camera, and easily one of the funniest people I've ever known. At first, I was unaware of the extent of his problems, and then one day he showed up with short sleeves and he had severe scars on his arm from trying to commit suicide. They weren't little slices, either. They were cuts that went lengthwise. It made me realize how often he wore long sleeves, something I hadn't picked up on previously.

We weren't close friends only at work; we also hung out off set. The fact that David was an addict rarely sank in with me because he was the unusual kind who even if he went missing on weekends—usually accompanied by a 2 a.m. phone call from Nestor saying, "David called me from a hotel in Hollywood, he's with somebody he doesn't know, and he's on crack"—still showed up for work on Monday morning. That's why I never thought his drug abuse would lead to any major consequences. He seemed to have a survival mechanism. I just thought he was one of those guys who goes on benders but has a part of him so driven and serious about his career that he's got to figure out a way to get his ass to that table read at 8 a.m. on Monday, which he always did.

Looking back, I have a lot of guilt about one incident that showed how much I truly didn't understand how bad his addiction was. It was a Friday night, I was bored, and I called him and said, "Do you want to go to Vegas tonight?" We were both single, so we got cash out of the ATM—"hundies" in our running-joke terminology—looked up the latest flight from LA, and got to the airport and ran down the terminal, David making me laugh as he yelled out, "Wait! Wait for us! We have hundies!"

When we got to Vegas, we had a plan. It was going to be an eight-hour trip, in total. We'd land, I'd go play my beloved slots, he'd go play blackjack, and we'd meet up in a couple of hours to take the earliest Saturday morning flight home. But since I'm not a drinking/drugging person, it didn't occur to me that that might be the last I saw of him for the entire weekend.

So as discussed, I'm waiting for him at Bally's at the appointed time, and he's not there. I'm calling and calling and calling, and now I have to go to the airport and fly back home by myself at six in the morning. I was pissed. I called his mom, and called Nestor, "We lost him again. I don't know where he is." Well, sure enough, he fucking got his ass to work Monday morning. I was yelling at him, telling him not to ever do that to me again. He was repentant. Then he'd be fine for a while, go to AA, have a sponsor, and I'd be optimistic all over again. Surely, I tried to convince myself about David, "He can get it together at twenty-eight. He's got his whole life ahead of him."

One day, though, about a month before he took his life, he pulled me aside really close during rehearsal and said, "I don't think I can ever quit drugs and alcohol." He said it so matter-of-factly. I said, "Oh

David, yes you can. Keep going to your meetings!" But in truth, he and I never talked about his problem very seriously. If I got mad at him about one of his benders, I might not talk to him for a while, but looking back I wish I'd taken it more seriously. Because he could function at work, the fact that he seemed so good with finances, that he was dating Tiffani Amber-Thiessen from *Beverly Hills 90210* and madly in love with her, and that he had a big movie with Ben Affleck and Sandra Bullock coming out, it always seemed to me that the sensible side of him would win out.

It was a Monday when I learned what had happened. Steve Peterman, the creator of *Suddenly Susan,* called me in to Brooke's dressing room, where she was crying. Even then I thought, *Maybe David's in the hospital again,* because he had spent time in a psych ward once. That's when they told me he had taken his life. I don't remember physically what happened next. I couldn't tell you if I was sitting on a couch or what, but I remember instantly wanting to know everything about how it happened. I thought if I knew how he did it, it would give me insight into his state of mind. They told me he'd hung himself. That hit me like a ton of bricks. It was such a message, such a visual picture, the suicide method that has the most despair. It broke my heart more than if he'd chosen another more passive way. As if he were saying, "I'm so sad, I'm so despondent that I'm going to pick the most premeditative method possible so you know how much I really wanted to do it."

Since then I've talked to a lot of people who have known relatives or loved ones who've committed suicide, and they always talk about getting angry at the person. I've never been able to get angry with David. I understand those feelings, because it leaves people without parents, without children. But more than anything I'm just incredibly sad about it all. I saw him try. I saw him go to AA meetings. I saw him with his sponsors. I don't think he was cavalier about it. He showed up for work, knew his lines, was funny and smart. I can only think about how tragic it is that he was so sad that he felt like this was his only option. I'll always want to know more about that night, and to this day I have friends who think it's despicable that I even talk to Andy Dick, who was with David in Vegas his last night partying together before David went to a motel and took his life. But I'll never stop asking Andy about that night. Maybe I'll get one more piece of information about what happened. David's mother once said to me, "Even if he had left a note, it wouldn't have answered anything." It's true, of course. What could he put in a note that would justify it?

Back at work, David's suicide was a very divisive issue for the cast. I completely understand now why married couples get divorced after losing a kid. I used to think, *Wouldn't that make a couple closer?* But how you grieve is a really touchy thing. Barbara Barrie was like a second mom to me, but she was angry with David, almost flippant about his death, and for some reason I couldn't handle that, and it irreparably fractured my friendship with her. When Brooke did interviews about his suicide, there were those in the cast who resented her. She, on the other hand, saw it as a chance to communicate with people about this issue. I make no judgment calls, but I can say it's a weird thing to reconcile the way others grieve. We shot a good-bye–David episode, which at the time I didn't like at all and thought was tacky— we were going back to work too soon, I believed—but recently I caught a rerun of it late at night and it's actually a well-done, tasteful episode. I was sobbing. Although I remember the producers wanted to end the show with five minutes of David clips, and somehow via the network or studio it got negotiated down to a lot less. All I could think was, *That's* fucking cold.

I was with David nearly every day for four years. I really loved that guy. Although I've got a big enough family that I've had various older relatives pass away, I consider David my first loss. I still keep a picture of him in my room, and I miss him every single day.

10
TALK SHOWS: LET THE BANNING BEGIN

Among the many perks *Suddenly Susan* provided, getting to be on talk shows was a big one. Let's face it, if I could be a professional talk show guest, I'd do it. By entering that world, I was allowed a chance to meet people I never dreamed I'd get to, and then during the commercial break, hear all the crazy things celebrities sitting in your vicinity would say. I would soon learn who was cool, who wasn't, who got me, who didn't, and—of course—how easy it was to get on someone's shit list.

When I started going on talk shows, it was a dream of mine to eventually be sitting next to somebody I'd idolized. But sometimes your heroes turn out to be something completely different when you meet them. I found this out the hard way, and with hundreds of thousands of viewers watching.

Back in the late '90s, Martin Short had a late night-talk show, and I got to be a guest on the second night it aired. Marty wasn't the problem, though. I love him, and think he's hysterical. The honor of being the biggest asshole would go to lead guest Steve Martin. I'd heard he was kind of cold, and not someone who was naturally, off-the-cuff funny. But I was still excited to meet the best host *Saturday Night Live*

---

has ever had, and a guy whose longevity in comedy—from albums to TV to movies—I always admired. I mean, come on, this guy is a legend in the comedy world.

Well, let me tell you, he was a douche bag. He was such a douche bag it was like he was a caricature of a douche bag.

It always rubs me the wrong way when comedians are serious all the time. It just seems disingenuous to me. I understand that not everybody wants to be "on" all the time, but when you're suddenly an art expert, or writing plays like that piece of shit *Picasso at the Lapin Agile,* it seems you're making a conscious choice to be anything other than what made you a success. Martin Short, on the other hand, is so brilliant and quick and funny. I'm a big fan, and he's obviously completely comfortable as an entertainer.

It started with Steve Martin doing his bit, and all the while Marty talked to him like he was a head of state, taking every opportunity to defer to him. Then I came out. Steve wouldn't look at me or talk to me directly. Marty would say, "How's it going?" I'd say, "Oh, this funny thing happened the other day . . ." and then I'd just be chatting with him. But then Marty would lean over my lap and say to Steve, "Kathy is a stand-up comedian." Steve in his fucking Armani suit and crossed legs would nod, and add an "Ah" in an achingly bored tone.

I'd continue talking to Marty, and then Marty would lean over again, and say, "She does this really great thing where she doesn't really tell jokes, she kind of just gets up there and is free form. You feel like you're just having conversation."

Steve: "Ah."

I thought, *You're shitting me.*

I even turned to The Right Honorable Steve Martin and, doing my best not to gush, told him I was a fan and thought he was great. But he literally did not say a word to me or look at me, and the whole thing was just uncomfortable. For me, for Marty, and for everyone watching the show. Every time Marty did the lean-over to say something quietly to Steve, I wanted to say, "Why are you translating for him like he doesn't speak English?" The whole exchange felt like Marty was essentially saying, "What this horrible wild animal really means, Steve, is that she went onstage last night at eight-thirty." He was working over-time to placate Steve. I know they're old friends, but Steve's "do I really have to be here?" act was just weird. I should have said, "I'm sorry you're not in your gallery wondering where Picasso went next, ass-hole." He is simply not pleasant. You would be hard-pressed to find five people who'd say, "He is a PISTOL at a party! Fun, warm, sweet, and just HILARIOUS!" I'm telling you, it can be tough to meet your idols.

The Reverend Al Sharpton, on the other hand, whom I met while taping Bill Maher's *Politically Incorrect* television show, was just the op-posite. I'd heard a lot of rumors about what a publicity seeker he was, and I'll admit I only knew him from the pink sponge curlers and the Tawana Brawley scandal, but when I sat next to him on *PI*, he was so friendly. Out of the blue, he said, "Where do you do stand-up?"

"When I'm in New York I usually do Caroline's."

"I'd really like to come see you sometime," he said. I thought that was pretty cool. It seemed really open-minded of him to acknowledge what I do and offer to check out my act sometime. He's somebody I admire because, like Ted Kennedy, he's spent his time working his way back from a negative image to try to turn himself into somebody respectable and influential. I wouldn't see him again until several years later when he graciously agreed to be a guest on season five of *My Life on the D-List*. When I decided to do a stand-up set at the legendary Apollo Theater in Harlem, Reverend Al said he'd introduce me on-stage. I spent the day with him, went to one of his speaking engage-ments at Medgar Evers College, and was a guest on his radio show. That night at the Apollo he rocked my introduction, warning the au-dience that I sometimes went too far, but that I was funny. It was the ultimate stamp of approval for me, and I think he is a man among men. I've been keeping an eye on you, Reverend Al. I take extra special notice of people who make controversial statements and take a stand. (And, of course, get called out for publicity garnering.)

As for the host of that show, I'm pretty sure Bill Maher is of that boys' club mentality that doesn't think chicks are funny, aside from maybe Sarah Silverman, but he's been supportive of me to a degree.

Bill Maher and me backstage at the Larry King anniversary special.

He's kind of a prick—if I run into Bill at a party, even though I've known him all these years, it's no guarantee he'll stop and chat with me—but I like him, and I love his shows, *Politically Incorrect* being one of my favorite experiences. I was on half a dozen times at least. One time rock singer and ex–Van Halen frontman Sammy Hagar was on with me, and during the commercial break, he started to talk to Bill about how aliens had downloaded material into his head. Oh yes. Watching Bill try to have a semiserious conversation about this—"Oh really? What was that like?"—was priceless. I don't think that kind of shit happens in conference rooms in corporate America.

Bill's show was solid training ground for how to act with celebrities I'm nervous around. My m.o. was, I'll try to get things rolling by making a ballsy joke, because instead of small talk, I think these celebrity situations demand an icebreaker, and Hollywood has a pretty thick sheet of ice. Like Bill O'Reilly, America, I'm always looking out for you. Besides, I usually want information from that celebrity: it could go into the act, right? Of course, 90 percent of the time saying something ballsy doesn't go my way. But I'm sticking to my plan! When I was on *PI* with Michael Bolton, for instance, I turned to him and blurted out, "Bolton, you've got to lose that ridiculous hair, seriously. What are you thinking with that hair?"

Every time I say something like that, the pause afterward can seem excruciating, even if it's only a nanosecond: Are they going to laugh? Flee? Threaten me? Or ban me from their own future talk show? Well, thankfully, Bolton laughed. I ran with it. "I can get a clipper here in ten seconds. Do you want to make a commitment to me right now? You're talented and wealthy, but you can't pay someone to cut that?"

Really, in a situation like that, that's all I can do. God love him for laughing, but was I going to have a serious conversation with Michael Bolton? What the fuck am I going to talk with that guy about? Time, love, and tenderness? So I try to make the celebrities I encounter laugh. That time it went my way.

Then there are the times laughter can mislead. When HBO gave me an hour-long special during my time on *Suddenly Susan*, I got to promote it on David Letterman's show. That was a major get for me. In the world of comedians, Letterman's show is worshipped because he's had the ultimate career, from his stand-up days to his great *Tonight Show* guest-hosting, to his brief, ill-fated, but brilliant morning talk show and obviously his groundbreaking late-night show on NBC. But even though appearing on his show was a major get, it's not like I had anyone telling me how to do it. No makeup or hair people. No stylist. No publicist. Just me in New York the day before going to a mall store and buying an outfit thinking, *This will look good on Letterman!* It was the most preposterous outfit you've ever seen: black midriff top, and black matching pants, made out of stretch polyester, with flares. It was awful. I'm thirty-six and sporting a midriff top like Mary Ann from *Gilligan's Island*. Someone should have had me arrested.

In terms of the actual appearance, there were a lot of rules. The segment producers said, "Whatever you do, don't talk to Dave during the commercial break, and don't hug him when you make your entrance because he's tall and has a bad back so he can't bend over to hug you.

And whatever you do, don't go off the cards." The cards are what the host has that include all the things you said in the preinterview, so all the host has to do to facilitate a good story on air is reference the card in front of him. Well, my main story was about meeting Jerry Springer, and as I'm telling it on camera with Dave I swore. I said "shit" and got a rim shot from the drummer. Dave turned his attention from me to the audience. Uh-oh. I turned to him trying to act all innocent and said, "What did I say?"

He said, "Well, I thought you were gonna say 'damn' or 'hell' and what you said is really a whole other category."

"I said 'shit'?" The audience laughed.

He said, "Yes." More daggers.

"Well, you know, Dave, you can't shit a shitter." More audience laughter.

When it was all over, I went back to my hotel, and then the next day I got flowers from the show, with a card from the segment producer that said, "You were so funny, it was so effortless. Consider yourself a friend of the show!"

I have never been asked to be on again. I mean, I thought I nailed it! I thought I'd made it so easy on Dave, me being a potty mouth and him just sitting there and mugging at the camera. Looking back now, that swearing episode probably led to my downfall. Dave doesn't like swearing, which means I'm obviously not his cup of tea. It was my first banning. Of course, you don't know that kind of thing initially. For the longest time they just kept telling my publicist, "Oh, we're just booked, we don't have the slot." But after ten years? Two Emmys? Finally executive producer Rob Burnett denied/confirmed it to *Entertainment Weekly* when the magazine did a story trying to fact-check my claims of banishment. He told *EW*, "She is not banned. We simply don't feel she warrants a booking at this time."

Gotcha! You thought perhaps this book had gone to press before my magical return to Dave's show in the summer of 2009? Well, here's the deal. I may pride myself on the street cred that comes with getting banned from so many shows and pissing people off. But look, when these shows call me to dangle a reappearance carrot—and you know me, I hate vegetables—no matter how D-list, I'm more than happy to eat shit (my term for vegetables) and grovel back on my hands and knees. So you can imagine my thrill and surprise when after twelve years of being banned from *The Late Show with David Letterman,* on Monday, June 8, 2009—after season five of *My Life on the D-List* debuted to its highest ratings ever—I got a call in my hotel room in New York asking if I would do the show that Wednesday as one of their guests had dropped out at the last minute.

It was a dream come true. Dave was in the middle of his Sarah Palin joke scandal, where the Alaska governor felt he'd made inappropriate remarks about her daughter, so it was heaven for me to be there that day and feel a special shitstorm kinship with him. I remembered not to curse, too. I never said "cunt" or referenced anal leakage, or invited any deities to suck it, and at the end of the interview Dave gave me the Letterman hand kiss! I don't know if I'm back in for good, but as life on the D-list goes, I was back in for a day.

I don't feel as good about the situation with Regis Philbin's morning show, though. Back when Kathie Lee Gifford was co-host, I had been a guest on the show. All had gone well, and they even asked me if I wanted to guest host for a couple days while Kathie Lee was away. *Suddenly Susan* and being on the road was really knocking me out, so I remember balking at the fact that they weren't going to pay anything. But the folks at Warner Bros. said "No, no, this is a good thing. You should do this with Regis." So I agreed. They gave me Kathie Lee's dressing room while she was gone, which I thought was strange. I mean, I wouldn't want my dressing room being handed out to anyone else in my absence. So there I was surrounded by all the Kathie Lee-ness, the shoes and the wacky neon lime green suits and a few Bibles.

Well, it was pretty fun. I love Regis. He's an absolute gem. You won't find a guy who's funnier, more low maintenance, and easygoing. I ended up speaking gay (I'm bilingual) to his executive producer, Michael Gelman, until I met his female fiancée, so that was awkward. But Gelman and the fiancée came to see me at Caroline's, which I thought was cool. So on one of my guest-host days I made a joke on air that Gelman was Regis's bitch. Regis laughed. The audience laughed. You know the rest. I was never asked on again. To this day. For a while I entertained the thought that it was maybe coming from Kathie Lee. But after Kelly Ripa came on, still no booking.

It was Joy Behar who nailed the episode. She asked me in the makeup room at *The View* once, "Did you ever get asked back to *Regis* after you said Gelman was Regis's bitch?"

"No, but I don't think it's a problem," I said. "I'm sure I'll be on again!"

"Really?" she answered, with one eyebrow raised. Hmmm.

One time I ran into Regis at Carson Daly's talk show, and we had a great conversation. He was being so nice, saying, "KATH-y GRIF-FIN! You're on FYE-UH! You're on FYE-UH!"

I told him how glad I was that things were going so well for him, and that nobody deserved it more than he did, because he'd worked so hard. Then I brought it back to me. "Rege, I feel bad about my ban for life from Gelman. Really? Gelman's the all-powerful?"

"Well, you know, he holds grudges," he said.

Then Regis suggested I make a surprise appearance the next time I was planning on being in New York. Just walk out onto the set during the show—"Don't even plan it! Be a surprise guest!"

It was sweet that he thought I was A-list enough to pull off a stunt like that. But I'm no Don Rickles and this wasn't *The Tonight Show*. I doubt I'd make it past security. And if I did, I told him, "Then I'm just Sean Young trying to get the role of Catwoman." Meow.

If you're wondering whether I watch a show that I've been banned from, I do. Why wouldn't I?

Here's the lowdown on banning: it's not like anybody makes a declaration outright that you've been banned. You find out by not getting booked on the show anymore. The reasoning can sometimes be elusive. I appeared on *Late Night with Conan O'Brien* a few times during *Suddenly Susan* and then I went ten years, *ten years*—until early in 2009— before being asked back. Even though Conan and I go way back.

When I was in the Groundlings, one of the girls there said to me one day, "Hey, there's this guy named Conan who writes for *The Simpsons*, and I think you should go out with him. He's really funny and smart." He was taking classes at the time, and I was actually in the main company, so I'd be "marrying down," as the phrase goes, but I figured, why not? We met, but he didn't ask me out. So I came up with a scheme to get him to date me. I suggested we go for a pizza and write a sketch together. He said yes. I really thought I could turn this writing session into a legitimate date.

We went to this old-school place on Fairfax called Damiano's, ordered a pizza, and though I was being all flirty, I think we actually did write a sketch. At the end of the night, the check came, and we split it. *Well, that's a bad sign,* I thought. I don't think it's a date when the guy says, "Okay, you had *two* diet Cokes, so it's an extra dollar for you." Ouch.

Conan and I were both attending the wedding a couple of weeks later of a mutual friend who was also an old boyfriend. More date potential. So I said to him that night, "I can't bear to go to that wedding without a date. Will you go with me? I'm not saying this has to be some boyfriend/girlfriend situation," I said, clearly trying to manipulate him into thinking of it as a romantic and sexual date. He shrugged his shoulders and said, "Sure."

Well, he called me the day of the wedding and basically stood me up, telling me he was sick. I was humiliated and went to the wedding by myself, and wouldn't you know it, at the end of the reception, in walks Conan. "Hi, feeling better?" I said to him. I think he thought he could wait me out. But of course, I'm the last to leave any party, so I was there for his secret appearance.

Clearly we were never going to be a Groundling power couple, of which we would have been the first. But I was starting to see Conan fairly regularly in that Dave Rath pizza party crowd, or he'd be one of twenty when we were all going to dinner somewhere, becoming somewhat of a fixture in my comedy orbit. When he got his talk show, I remember calling him and congratulating him, thinking he really deserved that break, because he was often the funniest guy in the room. I thought it was really cool that this hysterically witty "kid"

From my return to Conan O'Brien's late-night show before he moved to the *Tonight Show* spot in the summer of 2009 (Photo: Dana Edelson/Bravo/NBCU Photo Bank)

whom people didn't know was about to be introduced to the whole country on a big national stage.

So I went on *Late Night with Conan O'Brien* those few times during the *Suddenly Susan* years—we'd chat during the commercial breaks ("Have you seen Janeane lately?" he'd ask, "How do you like living in New York?" I'd ask) and nothing seemed awkward between us—and then all of a sudden I wasn't asked back. Specials coming and going, no Conan. Emmy win, no Conan. Second Emmy win, no Conan.

Since he'd had me on the show initially, my guess is when he was a newcomer, NBC probably said, "You're going to have her on." But when *Suddenly Susan* ended, at which point Conan had come into his own, he had bigger sway with who made the cut. So I spent ten years thinking, *He can't stand me, and I guess that's the way it's going to be.*

Then in late 2008 we ran into each other in the hallway of the ill-fated-but-fun-to-be-at Rosie O'Donnell variety special *Rosie Live.* It was right before the show, and for some reason he was completely nice to me. Well, he did just have a pie thrown in his face onstage. Maybe there's something about being covered in whipped cream and standing in the hallway of a sweaty off-Broadway theater that just makes you happy to see an old friend.

It was after this exchange that I went on *Late Night* in February 2009 for the first time in ten years, just in time for Conan to close out that show and get ready to segue into *The Tonight Show* in LA. We had a good conversation on his show, and it felt great to be back. It was really easy-breezy and he laughed at my jokes, and overall it was really fun. (Note to Oprah: When a comedian is on your show and makes a joke, you might want to laugh at them instead of giving a death stare. Jokes are their job. Just like your job is to be omnipotent.) He didn't bring up my long absence from his late-night show, or any possible ill feelings. Probably because he doesn't even remember what they might have been. I certainly didn't bring it up. We talked about old friends, and it was wonderful. I just hate having a frost with anyone from that era, because it was such a good time, and I'm so glad he's doing well.

Then he said, "Well, when I go to LA, you've got to do the show." I was so thrilled! But I think I'm going to make him attend at least one wedding with me first.

A few of the guy hosts, like Craig Kilborn when he had *The Daily Show* and his own late-night talk show on CBS, have always been in my camp, and one in particular you wouldn't necessarily think of has definitely supported me. Howard Stern. Total mensch. People had warned me about going on Stern. "Don't do it, he'll eat you alive." And from the first time I went on Howard, during the *Suddenly Susan* years, before he was on Sirius satellite, we had the funnest conversations during those twenty-minute-long commercial breaks. He showed a softer and gentler side that his listeners don't get to see much of.

On air, however, he absolutely gave me and continues to give me shit. And the call-ins are brutal.

"You horrible old hag/cunt/bitch. Nobody would ever fuck you in a million years. You are awful, you should die now," someone will say.

You can't show weakness on Howard; you just have to wait for it to be over and hope the next caller is a gay guy saying, "We love you, diva."

And Howard, being the expert ringleader that he is, plays along. "Now come on, cut that out," he'll say, but lets the call go on, of course. But you know that's the gig going in. During my divorce, I would have a conversation with him during the commercial break where he'd compassionately ask, "How are you doing?" But when we were back on the air, it's "What'd that guy do, steal all your money?"

I really respect Howard, and think he's genuinely comedian-funny, not just witty. There's a thing he does that's very smart with women in my category, meaning those of us who remain fully dressed while on air. He'll strike a nice balance between giving us complete shit and then adding, "You're hot. I think you're totally hot. I'd totally bang ya." First of all, it's a treat, because it never happens. And for his audience, it's a stamp of approval. I know it sounds weird, and it requires an adjustment in recognizing what, exactly, a compliment is, but the funny thing about going on Howard is, when you're me, the nicest thing he can do is say, "I want to bend you over and buttfuck you cause you're so hot." Oh Howard, you softie.

What I learned early on from doing that show is, the way to survive is full disclosure. If you go on Howard's show and try to be coy or not answer, he's going to have you for breakfast, lunch, and dinner. During my first appearance on Howard, I was having a little fling with one of the guys from 'NSYNC, which, yeah, is really sleazy because I was way too old for him. (I told him I was twenty-seven and my real age hadn't had a two in front of it for nearly a decade.) And when I say fling, by the way, I think I made out with this 'NSYNC-er twice. (Hope you're sitting down, Oprah. It was NOT golden-haired hottie Lance Bass. I know, I know, the sexual chemistry between him and me can be electric, but he must have been reading your favorite book *The Secret*, because I think he had one!) Anyway, I talked about it on Howard—I thought it was funny, he thought it was funny—and he wanted to know every single detail. So I told him. If I had gone on and said, "I made out with someone from 'NSYNC!" and then said, "I'm not telling you any more, Howard!" that would have been disastrous.

So I had to go, "Okay, he touched my boob over here, and I was wearing this." When Howard says, "What do you want to do with him?" it means you say, "Well, I want to do missionary, and I want to do doggie-style, and . . ." It's all about how explicit you can be. And in return, he always plugged the hell out of my shows.

The environment at Howard's studio was heaven for me, too. His green room was a show in itself. And it made for instant material when I'd have to go play Caroline's that night. One time when I was there, I was sharing the room with a couple of Scores girls (Scores being an infamous New York strip club), who were on the show to do one of Howard's crazy games involving strippers. I'm wearing jeans and a sweater and heels, and they're in silver lamé bikinis with tassels covering their fake tits. One girl said, "I think I'm gonna win cause I'm mohonia."

I'm thinking, *What? Is that an affliction?*

Then it hit me. She's *more hornier.* I didn't know what game they were about to play, but I should have gotten some prize for deciphering their code.

I loved Howard's whole gang, too. Howard really defers to Robin, and he truly feels he can't do the show without her. I think she's wonderful, too, and I adore them as a pair. I have a total crush on Fred, and Baba Booey enjoys the celebrity dish as much as I do. The first time I did the show with Artie Lange, I really thought he was gonna go after me. The guys' guy comics don't always dig me, because let's face it, a lot of people, and especially boy comedians, don't think chicks are as funny, and can only think of women in terms of whether they'd want to fuck them or not. I totally expected the "Ugh, she's ugly, who'd want to go near that" treatment. But I'll never forget how nice Artie was to me. From day one. He was quiet during my interview, and then afterward said I was really funny. Strange as it sounds, I really felt respected and welcomed by the whole Howard crew.

Plus, Howard single-handedly broadened my demographic. The first time I did his show, I walked down the street ten minutes later and every cop and construction worker said hi to me. Basically, every straight guy. I can perform for 7,000 people, and all that the straight guys there know me from is *Seinfeld* and Howard Stern. They don't know the stand-up specials, they don't know *D-List* or *Suddenly Susan*. And overseas, when I performed for the troops in Iraq and Afghanistan, all those guys were saying, "Oh, you're the girl from Howard!" To which I say, "Thank God."

So that's why I do it, why I've been on at least a dozen times. It's why I take the licks. I never know how it's going to go—brutal calls and nice Howard, or brutal calls and brutal Howard—and it's something that can rub my female friends the wrong way. Jenny McCarthy said to me one time, "I told Howard I can't do it anymore. Those calls are too mean." During *Suddenly Susan*, Brooke got mad at me once because she felt I didn't stick up for her when Howard started baiting me about her. I never threw her under the bus, but I couldn't spend my entire forty-five minutes on Howard saying that Brooke Shields was a comedic genius. My first job is to be funny.

Going on Howard was a great learning curve for me, and overall I've gotten a lot from it. At the end of the day, from being on his show, there's going to be five more straight guys who'd never heard of me thinking, "Oh, well, if she's cool enough to be on Howard . . ."

That's all I have to say about talk show hosts for now. In the world of celebrity, what makes talk show hosts unique in terms of whom I would put in my act (or my book), is that they're probably the one area I occasionally have to hold back on. I can make fun of the president and it wouldn't do anything, but I need talk show hosts more than I need my own boss at the network. Network CEOs come and go, but some of these fuckin' talk show hosts seem like they're never going to die.

11
FROM WORCESTER, MA, TO DICK: STORIES FROM THE ROAD

Could I hit the road and make it work? Or would I be roadkill?

That's what I wondered when I started getting real stand-up offers, as in headlining gigs at places around the country. Even though I was raised in the alternative scene, being a fixture on television meant offers from spots like Caroline's in New York and all the Improv clubs nationwide.

But would I be able to get laughs anywhere besides coffeehouses and "alternative" showcases? Remember, I hadn't had such good luck at the Improvs and places like that in the past, whose audiences expected more traditional joke/punchline comedy. Luckily for me, Margaret Cho continued to reassure me that I could do it. It just required adjustments. Change up the material faster. Don't spend twenty minutes on one story when half the audience is drunk or on a date or trying to impress their boss. Move it along, people.

I was getting asked to play colleges now, too, which was always a good and lucrative gig. I was in my midthirties but a pop culture sponge, so I was still young enough to be able to talk to the eighteen-to-twenty-two-year-olds, for one thing. I remember once going to the MTV awards, and that experience made for great material at a college gig. I could talk about running into Christina Aguilera (teen diva), see-

---

Left: Andy Dick having boundary issues with me and Sharon Osbourne.

ing Whitney (all "sweaty") and Mariah (hi, crazy!). Margaret was right. It was about knowing what subjects fit with which audience.

So I was now the headlining act, and the stakes were higher. Bombing is a whole different animal when you're the marquee name who people have paid money to see. In the days when I was the only girl in a lineup of ten comedians at a club, following the prop comic with the bad jokes about hating his wife gives you a little cushion of lowered expectations. And when I was in the Groundlings company and we had a crappy show, we could sit around backstage afterward and commiserate about it and laugh. But as the headliner, a bad night means bombing alone. The blame can't be shared. I don't mean to put myself on a watch list, but I became a una-bomber. If only I'd had the hood and sunglasses to hide in. Anyway, my greatest headliner bombing story is as follows:

Year one of *Suddenly Susan* I got a call from my stand-up agent. He said, "You have an offer for a club in Boston. It's called the Comedy Stop."

Boston! I'd never played there before. A city full of drunken micks? I'm gonna kill!

"Or . . ." he said, "the alternative is this other club in Worcester, Massachusetts, about an hour from Boston, called the Comedy Palace. You'd have to do a show there Thursday, two on Friday, two on Saturday, and one on Sunday. The catch is, they have a sister club that's a forty-five-minute drive from Worcester, so on Saturday you'd do the early show in Worcester, get in a car, and then you'd be driven to the sister club, perform there, go to bed, then come back on Sunday. But it's more money."

It was a heavy workload, and during my week off from *Suddenly Susan* to boot, but thinking like my mom, I said, "Well, screw Boston's Comedy Stop. I want to make more money." We were talking a difference of maybe $2,000 between the Boston club gig and the Worcester venues. But I was the girl who'd happily take that $15,000 to do a horrible corporate gig, knowing full well I was going to bomb, because, you know, how can you turn down money?

Well, it turns out that there were some big differences between a

Boston institution like the Comedy Stop, and a Worcester noninstitution like the Comedy Palace.

I showed up at the Comedy Palace alone, which right off the bat was just a stupid thing to do. I mean, I wasn't famous, but I was on an NBC show in a big Thursday night lineup, and I just shouldn't have been traveling by myself. I should have dragged a friend with me. Thinking cheap and convenient, I booked myself into a Days Inn a block from the Comedy Palace and headed over to the club. The guy running the club was like a Jewish goombah, with a really big, boisterous personality. The tickets were going fast because people knew me from television, so that seemed to bode well. I went onstage, and the crowd was *tough*. We're talking crispy bangs, mall perms, hardcore eyeliner. That kind of crowd. They looked like they weren't even there to laugh, but instead were waiting to be provoked.

I did my act, stories about Andre Agassi's house, an episode of *Frontline* I found particularly amusing, and I closed with an *hil-a-a-arious* anecdote about how I had attended the trial of a serial killer and accidentally spoke to one of the jurors. Silence. Deafening silence. My opening act, a local comedian, had killed. And now me, the headliner, was bombing badly. This was a club where the front row is three feet from you, and the bachelorette party of twelve with their cardboard tiaras weren't having my la-di-da tennis player/PBS show/courtroom shit for one second. There was no air-conditioning, either, so I've got the ass-crack sweat and the flopsweat and all I can do is think, the contract says an hour and ten minutes. I don't get paid unless I do my time, so even if I just stand there and read the phone book, I've got to do my contractual time.

Meanwhile, the girls in the audience are vicious. "HEY, AW THERE ANY JOKES IN THEAH?" "YOAH NAWT EVEN FUNNY!" "WHERE'S THE PAHT WHERE I STAHT LAUGHIN'?"

After the show, however, the oddest thing happened. I was trying to slink out the side door without being noticed, like a criminal, but in fact my crispy-banged hecklers were now crowding around me. Was I gonna get jumped now? Girlfight-style? Should I have brought my shiv?

When you're doing clubs, it's two shows a night, sometimes three.

No, they were actually standing in a line. "TAKE A PICK-SHUH! TAKE A PICK-SHUH!" That was surreal, the notion that these people wanted snapshots of themselves with anybody from TV, even somebody they'd just finished razzing for giving them a shitty night out.

The next night, I bombed again. *Bombed.* Not even with the same material. I changed my act as much as possible trying to figure out what they were into. You know what they were into? Heckling, and then having their photos taken. Then I had to get in a car and drive forty-five minutes to the sister club in Saugus, which—no joke—was a Chinese restaurant that one night a week put a cardboard sign that said COMEDY PALACE in its banquet room. I'm on a riser with a microphone with another hour and ten to get through, and I am *bombing.* The set ends, and I go back to the Days Inn to recover and lick my wounds. But instead the phone in my room rings constantly with harassing "fans" calling me, saying, "Are you Kathy Griffin from TV?" I can't even get a minute's peace at the fucking Days Inn, and now I'm sobbing hysterically because I have one more night of this misery.

To top everything off, the owner of the club calls me and says, "I want you to give some of the money back. That's how bad you were."

So I head to his office, thinking, if nothing else, I am not giving any goddamn money back. And I tell him this, all while trying not to cry in front of him. I mean, I took a picture with every single person in that line after those shows.

If you're going to try to get my money, I thought, *you better have a fucking gun, pal.*

At the time, I knew one person in Boston: Jonathan Katz, a wonderful, droll comic and writer who did the hilarious Comedy Central show *Dr. Katz: Professional Therapist,* which featured funny recorded exchanges between Jonathan and comedians playing themselves, that were then animated. I was a giant fan of that series, and he had always wanted me to do the show, but the only way you could do it in those days was go to Boston, where Jonathan lives. Somehow I got his number, and because I desperately needed a friend, I called him. And I barely knew the guy.

Through a wall of tears I told him what was going on. "I'm playing at this place called the Comedy Palace . . . [sob] . . . and I'm bombing every night . . . [sniffle] . . . and the guy yelled at me in his office . . . [sniffle, sob] . . . and he wants his money back . . . [sob, sniffle] . . . and I have to take pictures with people who are heckling me . . ."

There's this pause, and Jonathan says, completely deadpan, "Well, first of all, I could have told you, it's not an actual palace."

I laughed, for the first time all weekend. It felt great.

"You shouldn't be staying in Worcester, you should be staying in Boston," he continued. "So here's what I'm going to do. I'm going to send a car for you, you're going to come to my house, we're going to record an episode of *Dr. Katz,* I'm going to make you laugh, we're going to have fun, you'll have a nice meal, I'm going to book you into a hotel in Boston, you're going to do your show, and then you're going to get a good night's sleep."

He was absolutely my Prince Charming. He had a car come get me, we went to his studio and recorded the *Dr. Katz,* and then he picked out a nice hotel for me, asking me if I could afford it, and I said

Performing at the state pen. I love a captive audience! (Photo: Jake Johnson/
Bravo/NBCU Photo Bank)

yes. Because it never occurred to me that if I'm doing stand-up far
from home—with bombing being a distinct possibility—I should
make sure I'm as comfortable as possible. As far as the club owner
wanting his money back goes, they sold tickets, and they sold drinks.
So why would I need to give money back? Fuck him.

Well, I'd been such a disaster that the Comedy Palace club owner
bumped me out of the main room for the last night. My replacement?
A woman called "The R-Rated Hypnotist." Her big closer was hypno-
tizing a guy to give a blow job to a banana. Naturally, it killed. And
like a kid sent to the corner in class, the owner told me I had to do my
final Sunday show in the diner next to the club. *Fine,* I thought. *I'll
play in the fucking hallway to get the fuck away from you.*

But wouldn't you know it, even though that diner had maybe fifty
seats, the people who showed up came to see *me.* Worcester's gays were
there in force, the setting was intimate, and it was like doing my thing
at the coffeehouse. No two-drink minimum, nobody screaming, just

me telling my little stories and making jokes about people getting comedy with their tuna melts.

Thank you, Worcester, Massachusetts, for making the tuna melt my favorite sandwich.

My best college gig story is really an Andy Dick story.

The University of North Florida in Jacksonville wanted me and Andy as a double bill for a show in early 1999. They probably wanted us together because we were both on NBC sitcoms, and although I'd performed with Andy many, many times on the alternative circuit—where we both had fifteen minutes in a lineup of a half dozen comedians and performance artists—we'd never double-billed a college. This was a high-paying gig. Plus, the college said to me, "We'd like you to go second, because we consider you to be the headliner."

"I'm flattered," I told them, "but I will not follow Andy Dick, because you never know if that crazy crackhead is going to show up or not." FYI, I have a no–Macy Gray policy as well. Check my rider. One time I was supposed to open for her at a charity event, and I got a call from someone saying Macy was missing and they couldn't get ahold of her. I said, "I'll wait for somebody who's stuck in traffic, but not somebody who's just missing." That's just a recipe for me doing four hours of stand-up in a row.

Everybody in the comedy world who knew Andy knew he fought his demons. I've seen him do brilliant sets, and sets where he was so messed up on drugs I felt it was the last day I'd ever see him alive. We're talking an admitted serious, serious drug addict and alcoholic.

Also, content-wise, I knew what Jacksonville might be in for, and it's not an easy thing to follow. If I'm inappropriate for colleges, Andy is Larry Flynt at a Cub Scout meeting. At the time Andy would travel with his band The Bitches of the Century, and they'd play ironic songs and do bits that were really, really out there. For example, they sang one song called "Little Brown Ring," about licking assholes. Andy sings it in a kind of falsetto voice, over and over and over, about his little brown ring. Or your little brown ring. I'm not sure whose little brown ring anymore, but he's very fixated on someone's little brown ring.

So I fly into Jacksonville a day early, because I'm always too nervous to fly the day of a gig, and as colleges usually do, they make a student my babysitter. I love that—some kid from the drama department coming out to get you and drive you to the hotel. I can't tell you how many young men have outed themselves to me on that ride from the airport. There's also usually an excited offer to take you to dinner, which is hard for me because I don't drink and I would find myself inevitably stuck at a Señor Frog's at two in the morning hoping for more fried zucchini zircles. College gigs are quirky that way.

Well, for some reason, the college had hired two stretch limos for us. I'm not really a stretch limo gal, but there it was the day of the show waiting outside my hotel, and when I got to the university, I asked, "So how's Andy doing?" I never say, "Where's Andy?" I just start in with a broad question about his state of mind.

"Well, we don't know if he's here yet," the college rep said.

"At the school?" I said.

"No, we don't even know if he's in Florida yet."

It's now 7 p.m., and the show starts at 8 p.m.

"Well, do you have any hints that he's left California?" I said.

"We don't know anything."

I felt a little psychic. So I said, "If Andy doesn't come at all, no matter what, I'll go out there and give it my best, and hey, maybe he'll show up! Stay positive!" I knew, though, there was probably a 50/50 chance that he'd show up. Those aren't *terrible* odds.

The gig was set up in the basketball court, a common venue at colleges. It can be great for music, but not for stand-up, because acoustically those spaces are better for accommodating loud noises, like a concert. And instead of nice theater seating, you're dealing with metal risers on the side and metal folding chairs taking up the court itself. What's fun about it, though, is you get a big audience, and for me, that was a huge audience. Something like 1,800 kids and, it turned out, adults, since it was homecoming weekend. Oh yeah. It wasn't just eighteen-year-olds on their way to keggers afterward. It was alumni, the dean, and university staff.

So I'm out there trying to keep in mind the youth contingent—the MTV music awards, Britney and Justin, and any frickin' young celebrity I could think of that I'd had a run-in with. Jokes about my seventy-something mom just weren't going to be relatable. Anyway, the crowd was nice, and at the end I yelled out, "Thank you, everybody, get ready for Andy Dick! Good night!" and walked off. Meeting me halfway from the wings is a mousy unibrow-sporting girl from the audio/visual department who had squeaked out a shaky-voiced intro calling me "Kathy Griffith," and now she's trembling even more. "Um . . . Andy's not here yet," she tells me. "Can . . . you . . . keep talking?"

"Fuck no," I said, and just walked away from her. Later I realized that was kind of rude—sorry, Unibrow Girl, if you're reading this now—but we were sort of in the middle of the stage, and in my head I'm thinking, *I'm saying no because I know Andy, and he might not be coming for a very long time.* He's not just parking the car or finishing up his costume, surely.

So Unibrow Girl quiveringly tells the crowd, "Give it up . . . ladies and gentlemen . . . for Kathy Griffith. We're . . . waiting for Andy Dick . . . who's not quite here yet . . ."

And just then from the side of the stage comes Andy's distinctively flamboyant roar: "I'm HE-E-E-E-A-A-RRRGGGH!"

The A/V girl's pleasantly surprised that he arrived. And me? Well, with just those two words, I know he is *Fucked. Up.*

Andy walks out in a suit, and he brings his band out with him. He starts by saying, "You guys all think I'm gonna be Matthew from *Newsradio,* don't you?" His words are slurry, that sibilant meow of a voice is kind of trailing off. "But like, I don't really have an act. Kathy's got her stories, but like . . . I don't really . . . *have* anything. I didn't really . . . *prepare* anything. For you guys. So . . ."

And I'm like, "O-h-h shitballs." The audience is confused, they're not sure if it's part of the shtick or not, and they're just looking at him. He's not giving in, either. "S-s-s-s-seriously, I don't . . . have anything.

I didn't . . . *do* anything." And then, out of the blue, "You guys are all looking at me like I'm a FAGGOT."

Pause. "You think I'm a FAGGOT?"

Nervous laughter, signs of discomfort are emanating from the crowd. Maybe it's a bit, they're thinking. But . . . maybe it's not a bit. Is he supposed to say the word "faggot"? Those kids are there for a show, and to be able to laugh and blow off steam. And here's this guy saying over and over, more belligerently each time, "Quit lookin' at me like I'm a FAGGAHT! YOU'RE THE FAGGAHT, FA-A-A-GG-A-A-AHTS!"

Whatever I do or don't know about Jacksonville, Florida, I'm pretty sure eighteen-year-old guys there don't like being called "faggot" over and over on a microphone when they're at a comedy show. Maybe there are audiences out there that would enjoy the on-the-ledge aspect of this brand of humor, but when it's guys who will be piling into pickups to go to the Outback steakhouse afterward or a frat house to drink cheap beer, they probably don't want the word "faggots" ringing in their ears on the way there. No surprise, the crowd starts to turn, and one guy gets the nerve to respond, "Yer the faggut!"—which of course Andy in his Andy Kaufmanesque way loves.

Cue a louder, even more aggressive Andy: "DID YOU CALL ME A FAAAGGGAATT?? *YOU'RE* THE *FAAAAGGAAAHT*!!!"

At this point those nice audio/visual department kids come up to me with crisis-management looks in their eyes, as one of them says, "Ms. Griffin, would you like us to take you out of here?"

"No," I blurted. "Get me a folding chair, a cheese platter, and a Diet Coke." Who would want to miss this?

I park myself in the back of that theater in a little protected area offstage where I could see Andy but he couldn't see me—thank God—and settle in for the train wreck. Now, a tiny part of me is thinking maybe I can help in some way if Andy really goes too far. I've known him long enough that if I had to (and I never have), I could play bouncer and go grab him by the seat of the pants and pull him off the stage. I'm sort of on standby, I realize. But really, I wouldn't have left that spot for all the money in the world.

Suddenly, without warning, Andy's off the stage and out in the audience. It's pitch-black out there, so there was really no way to tell who had yelled back at Andy. The sound is bouncing. But he picks some nearby random audience member—there was no way it was the guy who actually heckled him—and says, "I'll show you who's the fag now, FAG!" And with that, Andy pulls down his pants, revealing his lack of underwear, and starts grinding on some poor guy's lap. It really was like one of those Abu Ghraib prison photos. The look on the audience member's face was like, "All I wanted to do was come to a comedy show and now I'm being called a 'faggot' and getting Andy Dick's bare ass rubbed on me!"

This whole episode happened at lightning speed. Andy is stealth. He was back on that stage as if it had never even happened. The audience was traumatized, like they'd been given a roofie. The vibe from the crowd had turned as well. "I think something really bad just happened. It was over fast, but I don't feel right. I don't feel good about myself. I feel dirty."

Andy, meanwhile, is on to the next thing. "Oh, you guys, this is my band, and I'm gonna do a song!" he cheerily announces.

"I gotta go change, there's gonna be a few minutes where you guys are gonna be looking at nothing. Does anybody *sing* or *dance*? DO YOU GUYS DO *ANYTHING*?"

People are genuinely looking at each other like, "Oh God, now I have to perform? I just got over the guy getting a bare-assed lap dance." There was lots of murmuring of the "Do you do something? I could do card tricks, I guess?" variety.

Sure enough, one guy raises his hand, a big man with long, straight brown hair in a ponytail and a beard, and he says in this southern drawl, "Well, ah could SANG."

"Where are you from?" Andy asks.

"Ah'm from right here in Jacksonville," he says.

The minute I saw this guy, I recognized him. His nickname is Big Fat Paul. I know him because he travels with Andy and he does bits with him. They do the kind of bits at clubs that end with them bloodying each other, or one of them puking. These are committed guys. So

I am now the only person outside of Andy's group who knows this man is a plant. Everyone there thinks he's an audience member. Everyone there thinks he's a local. Everyone there, I begin to think, is fucked.

Andy prodded everyone to give it up for one of their own. "CLAP, you guys! CLAP! He's gonna come up! BE NICE!"

Big Fat Paul had some story about how he was a town florist or something, and when he gets onstage he acts as if he's unfamiliar with the mic. He turns to the band and says, *Well, ah mean, ah don't know what songs y'all have, but ah mean, I wrote a song, and if y'all want to follow me, that'd be fine.*

At this moment, the audience is almost a little calm, because they're probably thinking, *Well, at least Andy isn't out here calling us "faggots" repeatedly. Maybe one of our own is going to rescue this.*

I got a second Diet Coke.

Paul starts singing a made-up song called "Hey Go-Go Girl," in this surprisingly sweet, Sinatra-style crooner voice.

After a little while, Andy reenters in full drag, dressed as a go-go girl. I mean, white-fringe minidress, white platform stripper boots, white fishnets, huge blond wig, and drag makeup he's obviously slathered on very quickly. Paul picks up the pace, and Andy starts doing some very funny go-go dancing, like something out of *Laugh In*. Real Goldie Hawn-in-the-cage stuff.

As Paul is singing "Dance, go-go girl! Dance!" Andy's dancing gets more frenetic. Then Big Fat Paul in character starts to act like he's so sexually attracted to Andy's go-go girl persona that he can't stop himself. As he sings faster, he moves toward Andy and starts gently grinding up against Andy's butt. Andy affects a look on his face like, "Who the fuck is this guy?" Andy tries to wrest himself away, making hand gestures as if attempting to keep Paul from touching him.

What happens next takes place in a flash. Paul, who's 300 pounds, grabs Andy and pulls his dress up, and sure enough, Andy is wearing nothing underneath. You just see his dick flapping in the wind. Paul throws Andy on his stomach and proceeds to act as if he's *ass-raping him*. This happens for maybe four seconds, after which Paul makes his exit, running into the audience like he's filled with shame.

Remember who's watching all this: not just students, but storied alumni wondering what in God's name had become of the glorious educational institution they once attended.

Overall, the audience at this point looks like those see-no-evil, hear-no-evil, speak-no-evil monkeys. There's a smattering of traumatized gasps, appalled outbursts, nervous laughter, and then walkouts. Those metal risers echoed in a symphony of disgust: CLUNK, CLUNK, CLUNK, with plenty of shouts along the lines of "I'm fucking outta here!"

As if that weren't enough, Andy is back on the mic, and with full commitment starts screeching, "I WAS JUST *RAPED!* AND YOU DID *NOTHING!*" Now, there was an element of the audience that you could tell was genuinely thinking for one second, "Oh my God, did I really watch this poor little one-hundred-seven-pound comedian get violated by some freak?"

But it's mostly a lot of walkouts, a controlled chaos as people can't get out of there fast enough. And then, the one truly unplanned thing happened: Somebody hit the fire alarm.

BOOOWUP BOOOWUP BOOOWUP BOOOWUP.

It's now a melee. All you hear are people flinging themselves off the risers, out of folding chairs, trying to find the exit, going every which way, holding hands buddy-system-style. As the fire alarm keeps sounding, Andy looks pissed because his bit ended too soon. He looks bored, and barely even cognizant of the fact that 1,800 people are basically running amok. "Fuck it," he says, drops the mic, and walks offstage.

I was there to meet him, and so was a reporter from the city paper, with a tape recorder. Right away, I knew this was not good. Remember, Andy had fully exposed himself. Now, I'm sorry, but Andy is *my* junkie. I have a theory that everyone has a relative in prison, and everyone has a junkie. Think about it. Look at all your friends and relatives, and I'll bet you have a junkie. It doesn't mean you own them, or clean up after them, but they're a presence in your life. Well, Andy had been my junkie for a while, and a little part of me thought, *I don't want Andy to go to jail for this.*

The reporter starts right in, "Did you expose yourself? It looked like you exposed yourself."

"I don't know what happened!" Andy replied in a woozy tone, clearly sensing a chance to continue his bit for the benefit of the press. "I took my . . . I think I was RAPED out there!"

I jump in, "Sorry, Andy's not doing any interviews!"

"Oh, can we talk to him for a—"

"No, Andy's not doing any interviews!" I yell as I pull him away.

As we get some distance on the reporter, Andy turns and says, "Are we gonna go eat something?" We had plans to eat after the show, but in an attempt to keep his ass out of jail, I laid down the law and said, "Yes, Andy, but at a restaurant, not a bar. We're going now. We're getting a meal, and you need to stay away from any reporters."

"I have to come in your car," he says. "I lost my limo."

I'm dumbfounded. "How did you lose your limo in Jacksonville, Florida?"

"I DON'T KNOW!" he cried out. "GA-A-AHD!"

"Fine. We're going to a restaurant, but it's just you and me. No boys." Andy has a penchant for eighteen-year-old boys. As well as girls. He can't decide. "No eighteen-year-old boys. I'm not gonna get pulled over in fucking Jacksonville, Florida, with you and some fucking teenager."

"All RIGHT, *GRANDMA*!" he screams.

So I'm waiting in the limo, and when Andy hops in he goes, "Let's go eat!" He's acting like nothing's happened. Sure enough, three college boys get in. I say, "You're fucking kidding me. I might be codependent, but I am not going to jail for this shit."

Andy closes the door, and as the car was pulling away, I turned to all three boys.

"You guys all know you have to blow Andy, right?"

Two of them instantly hop out of the moving vehicle.

The other one shrugged, and stayed.

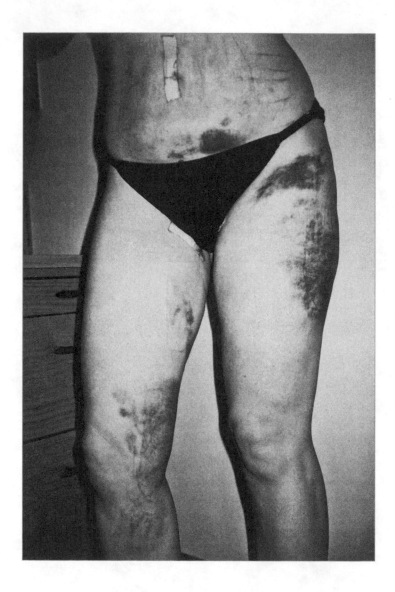

12

NIP/
FUCKED

Trust me, if you're watching TV or a movie and you see a pretty lady over the age of seventeen, she's had some shit done. (Not you, Miley. You've got at least six months before Daddy signs you up.) I would estimate that a lot more women and men in show business have had plastic surgery than not.

But this is *my* chapter about plastic surgery, so I'm not implying in any way that these experiences reflect any of the plastic surgery that, oh gosh, *may* have played a part in the lives of, say, if I were to pull names out of thin air, Mickey Rourke, the cast of *Desperate Housewives,* Al Pacino, Nicole Kidman, and the Octomom.

It's still a taboo topic to talk about and admit to, so let's get to it, shall we?

I got my first nose job when I was twenty-six. This was in the '80s, when face-lifts and boob jobs weren't as common, but nose jobs were everywhere, and altering my nose—one of my more Griffinesque features if you look at the rest of my family—was a no-brainer, especially after I'd meet with prospective agents, who would just be brutal about this kind of stuff. I'll never forget one agent who said to me, "You could be pretty if it weren't for that awful nose." But he said it as casually as if he'd said, "Would you like some water?"

Left: Do I look thinner?

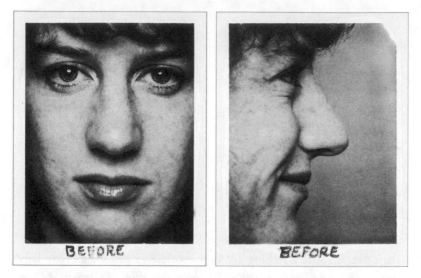

These are my nose job "before" pictures. I had a deviated septum. Really.

When you're an actress, you're expected not to react to something like that. These people are supposedly trying to help you, albeit without any tact or compassion. You can't get indignant—"Who the fuck do you think you are?"—and you can't cry (because then in my case my freakishly deformed, gigantic nose would run), and you can't argue with them: "Well, I'm beautiful!" They're just going to say, "Really? Have you seen JAMI GERTZ?" If I may pull out of my memory an '80s paragon of beauty for you.

I constantly heard from agents and casting directors that my nose was keeping me from being successful as an actress. And if you look at the lovely pictures I've provided, you can see that it's not like I had a big bump or that it was crooked. It was just bigger. A little bigger. Not even a lot bigger. I wasn't Streisand, where my nose was my most prominent feature and what everyone was talking about. It just . . . had a little character to it. And yet, this was what I needed, supposedly, so I arranged to get a nose job. I didn't even think of it as surgery. If my philosophy was to do whatever it took to be on television, it seemed like a small price to pay.

It wasn't a small price to pay for my parents, because they actually paid for it. Their attitude was matter-of-fact, too. If this is what show business requires, this is what you will do, they said. Nobody in my life for one second countered with, "Be who you are! Don't let them get you down!" It was, "Start saving money because insurance doesn't cover it."

As for the surgery itself, it was insanely painful. I hate when people say, "Oh, it wasn't that bad." Let me tell you, it fucking hurts. First off, they break your nose when you're under. I woke up during that part, by the way, because while they always have to be careful not to over-anesthetize you—it's routinely considered the most dangerous thing about surgery, making sure you're completely under but never *so* under that you stop breathing or anything—they sometimes can't prevent you from opening your eyes for the "ick" moments. There I was, emerging from being knocked out, and seeing a little hammer and chisel as they broke my nose with an excruciatingly audible *CLINK*. They'd said to me earlier, "Squeeze the hand of the anesthesiologist when you are awake." So I woke up, *CLINK*, and then crushed that person's fingers as hard as I could.

That's all I remember. When the whole thing was over, my face was completely swollen with two shiners. This was followed by a setting period, when they pack your nose with gauze, and because it's broken they put a cast on it. Like it's a fractured arm. And don't think you can get any sleep with something like that on, either. This is all followed by the real express train to agony, when they have to pull the gauze out of both your nasal passages a few days later. "Okay, get ready, this won't take long!" they said, and *oh fuckChristholyshit* did that hurt. To this day, it was the most intense physical pain I've ever experienced. I remember tears just springing from my eyes, like they were sprinklers. *Why couldn't they just novocaine my entire fucking head?* I thought.

The nose job was a bitch, but I was pretty much fully recovered after a few weeks. Once the swelling and bruising had gone down, I looked at myself and felt a little bit better. This was what I had to do, after all. I had no regrets. Now it was back to auditioning, where the parts would be mine for the taking!

And that's the story of the nose job that didn't improve my life or career. At all.

I wish I could say I went on to become a very prominent nose model, but the phone didn't ring. The offers weren't coming in, or maybe I just couldn't smell them, because of my puny nasal passages.

The irony is that, as you get older, your nose and your ears grow. My nose had changed form again, so in 2002—wait for it—I got *another* nose job. My problem with the second nose job was this: I still don't think enough got sliced away. Yeah, that's right. He was way too subtle. Fuck that. I wanted the full Naomi Judd. I say that because I worked with her one time, and I stared at her tiny nose and thought, *Holy shit, it looks like somebody hacked the shit out of that thing. She'll never have to get a second one like I did. I love it!*

So after all that, I actually believe that my current nose is my original nose. I've just grown it back.

We'll now move on to other battleground areas of my body, namely a war I almost lost—literally, as in nearly dying—to liposuction.

First, though, a quick update on my weight battles. A few years of off-and-on Overeaters Anonymous meetings in my twenties—introduced to me by the ever-supportive Judy Toll—helped me come to grips with the fact that other people had experiences similar to mine. For somebody who believed she looked like Meat Loaf—the old Meat Loaf—coming to a safe gathering place and seeing everybody from anorexics who were truly at death's door to people who looked like me—in other words, not really overweight, but obsessed with the notion that we were—was a helpful breakthrough. After years of looking for what I thought was the Big Solution, the thing that was going to make me never want cake again, it helped me realize that there was no magic pill, just hard work and awareness.

Therapy helped, too. One time after a bad binge—stomach distended, hating myself, the whole nine yards—I went to a session with a therapist and she said this great thing that really stuck with me. I was talking about some audition coming up, and I kept saying, "I have to

Joyce looks like that because she's pissed I won't share the cake with her.

get down to one hundred ten! I have to get down to one hundred ten!" In other words, my weight when I was a freshman at Oak Park High.

She just said, "Well, what if your goal weight was one hundred twenty-five?" As in, get rid of this stupid, unrealistic number in your head, and substitute another number. Suddenly, being 135 didn't seem so bad, or so far away from a reasonable goal.

When you're in this image-conscious business, though, the challenges to your perceptions come fast and furious. When I was on *Suddenly Susan*, I'd have to go in for fittings with the wardrobe people twice a week, and I have to say, those sessions were just awful. Here I was, a supposedly integral part of a big network comedy—there to make people laugh, not turn heads with my figure—and yet two times a week I'd be made to feel as if I was an anatomical freak. Really, the wardrobe people would just act as if the size 6 didn't exist, or refer to it like old Jewish women whispering about someone's cancer. And forget about it if you're an 8. Then you're twice the size of Style Network's reality star Ruby. You know, before she lost the weight.

Well, I'd been hearing about this magical process called liposuction. It apparently wasn't just about sucking the fat out. The word was they could sculpt your body at the same time. Actresses everywhere were doing it and saying it changed their life. "I went down two pant sizes!" you'd hear. So in between seasons of *Suddenly Susan* I had a meeting with a big-time celebrity plastic surgeon. I had heard hush-hush rumors that he had done Michelle Pfeiffer's eyes, and whether that was true or not, who doesn't want to look like Michelle Pfeiffer? I'm telling you—like talking about your body with an agent—those sessions with plastic surgeons are fucking brutal. It's very much like the way you see it on *Nip/Tuck*: "Tell me what you don't like about yourself." Suddenly you're discussing your "problem areas," and then they take a Sharpie and write all over your body in the most humiliating fashion, reminiscent of the iconic scene in *Billy Jack* where the townies throw powder in the face of the "injuns."

What happens is these plastic surgeons start laying on other shit you'd never even considered. My "problem areas," you wonder? The biggest one was my brain. Get a load of the crazy shit I wanted to do to my body. As soon as I mentioned that I wanted to be able to stand so that when I touched my ankles together there'd be space between my knees, like you see on models in swimsuits, this guy said, "Oh, we could do that."

"Really?" I said. "You can *change the shape of my knees*?"

"Yes, we can!" he said. Way before Obama.

I showed him a picture of Jennifer Aniston. "I can have Aniston's lower body?"

"Yes!"

So the next thing I know, we're scheduled to do my stomach, my inner thighs, my outer thighs, and my fucking *knees*, all in one long surgery that went on for well over four hours.

I didn't really know what I was getting myself into. I thought I'd just go to sleep and wake up skinny. I knew it was some sort of vacuuming situation, but what really happens is first they take a hollow knitting needle vacuum—it really does look like a mini-Hoover—and stab a bunch of holes in you. I really question whether or not these doctors just hated their mothers and felt like taking it out on me. Then they remove the fat cells, and also a lot of your bodily fluids as well. The next part—the juiciest, really—is that for a long time afterward you have to wear a medieval girdle, night and day, except when you're showering. And there's a hole in it to pee through. This is because they actually think that after they've abused your body, as long as you wear this elasticized gauze twenty-four hours a day, it will mold your body into shape. I'm pretty sure people don't get six-pack abs from wrapping their bellies for a month. It's crazy logic. It would be like taking a stacked woman, wrapping her breasts, then telling her, "In a month, you'll be flat-chested!" It makes no sense. Wait a minute, it would be like someone's Irish-Catholic box-of-wine-drinking mother telling their frizzy-haired daughter that if they blew dry their hair enough, it could be "trained" to be straight. Oh crap, I'm repeating myself.

Another ridiculous thing they said was, "Now, once we suck out the fat in these areas, if you're not careful with diet and exercise, you'll gain it back in other areas of your body." This should have been the tip-off that diet and exercise were what I should have been doing all along to lose weight—that the whole operation was a scam. So according to the doctors, the fat stays out of my belly, but eat too much and it'll go to my arms? That made no sense, either. But when you're in that office, you want to believe. I was an idiot.

Something else I didn't know at the time was that a plastic surgeon isn't necessarily someone who's trained for years and years. It might be an EMT who went on a weekend retreat and then opened up shop as a way to double-dip. You might be having this very serious, potentially dangerous surgery done in a place that looks like it's in a hospital—cause it has the gurney, the equipment, the lights—but it's just a broom closet some doctor has converted next to the room they do checkups in.

In any case, I was sold on surgically slimming myself down, so I went through with this painful liposuction surgery. The first indica-

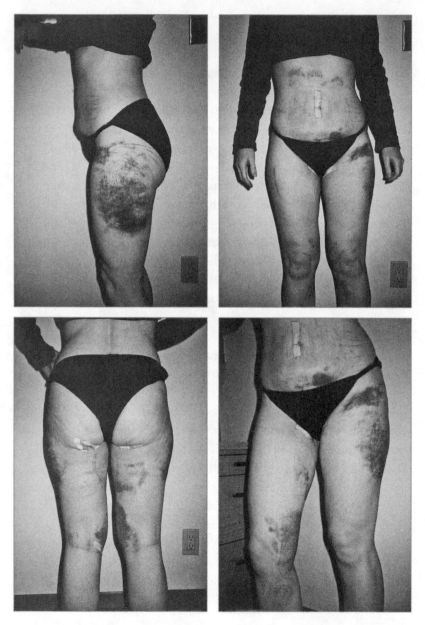

My post-op lipo photos? Or first date with Chris Brown?

tion that something was wrong—with their protocol and my recovery—was that I wasn't peeing. Nobody told me that I shouldn't go home from the procedure until I'd peed, or voided, as they say in doctor lingo. I didn't know it was a big deal if you didn't pee. So they sent me home, I went to bed, and I was bleeding from the incisions. Bleeding all over the bed. The pain was unbearable. Finally I got the surgeon on the phone late that night and he said, "Have you voided?" I said, "No, I can't seem to pee." It felt like I had to pee, but I couldn't, and now I could barely move or walk.

He said, "I'm sending a nurse over to your house, and she's going to put a catheter in you." Great. A plastic tube stuck up my vagina. I was so distracted by the pain that I just said, "Okay."

The nurse came over, and said, "Well, I'm glad I had my beeper with me when the doctor called, because I was at dinner having a glass of wine."

With Maggie Griffin, perhaps? What an odd thing to admit. I'm pretty sure this is probably considered to be a highly inappropriate thing to say if you're in the medical profession. Did she really have a glass of wine and some crystal meth, but decide the crystal meth part was inappropriate to tell me? They didn't have anybody who wasn't drunk that they could send? Oh well, it was late and I was in hellish pain.

As I'm sure you can imagine—even those of you without vaginas (that's you, gays)—that catheter in my poor little peesh hurt like hell, especially the trial and error it took to find where it went. But I have to say, once it was in place, I did feel relief. The doctor had said whatever was causing my lack of peeing would be gone by tomorrow, so after the nurse cathed and then uncathed me—ouch—she took the bag of pee and left.

Next day comes and I still can't pee.

I call the doctor again. "What should I do?"

"Well, come into my office. We're going to cath you again."

Get ready: I went to his office for *five straight fucking days* to get cathed.

Each day it was, "Well, this time we'll cath you and you'll be fine tomorrow."

By the fifth day, I wasn't going through the lobby anymore. They had me entering through the side door. Gee, I wonder why. Bad for business to see a lipo patient returning over and over again in excruciating agony?

On that fifth day I walked into the office, doubled over in pain. I'm barfing and sweating. I actually think I had dementia. I truly wasn't thinking straight. Suddenly, this guy on a gurney nearby, who must have been there to get a facial done because he had the shower cap on and looked like he had been freshly lasered, looked at me and said, "Oh my God, what happened to you?"

"I got liposuction and I can't pee."

Then, like a scene out of some movie, he bolted up, tore his shower cap off, and started yelling for a doctor. He said to me with no small amount of urgency, "You have to go to a hospital *right now!*"

"What?" I said.

When my doctor showed up, this guy started screaming at him: "You'd better take her personally to the ER right now! I'm calling the hospital. What the fuck did you do to this girl? *What did you do to this girl?*"

Get this: My hero was a physician who indeed was there to get a facial. One look at the color of my skin, and he knew it was bad. So the lipo doctor took me in his car to Cedars Sinai Hospital, where they rushed me into the ER, and what they discovered was that because my urine wasn't exiting my body, it was going through my organs and up into my back. My kidneys were close to being permanently damaged. The ER doctors were seriously freaked out, and so was my lipo doctor, who I'm sure cared only about the fact that I was surely going to sue him.

What I remember the most from this whole episode is that they had to cath me *again*. I was crying at this point, murmuring, "Anything, anything but the catheter." The difference this time, though, was that they were going to put it in and leave it in. And wouldn't you know it, I was never so happy to have the catheter, because what always hurt was the in and out. I had that catheter in for three days, but it was three days of gloriously being able to urinate. I grew so emboldened, I even went to the mall to see a movie, thinking, *This is great!* And then I was in the food court, and I thought to myself, *What am I doing? I have to get the fuck home.*

Good luck suing a doctor, by the way. When I wanted to sue, I quickly realized in the end, I would simply be outspent. So I wrote an article for *Glamour* magazine instead, called "Lipo Sucks." But not only could I not name the doctor, I couldn't even say in what town it happened. The magazine was too worried. You don't see his name here, either, you'll notice. To this day, it feels like a conspiracy among doctors. But I'm here to tell you, I and many of the doctors I spoke to about it after this experience think this procedure is dangerous, and that lipo is the worst thing to happen to medicine in decades. I try to talk everyone I know out of doing it. I'd like to think I scared enough people about it in my act for months afterward when I'd tell the story of what happened and then pull my pants down onstage to show the black-and-blue marks from my stomach all the way down to my ankles.

The irony is that my figure didn't even noticeably change from the surgery. In fact, not one person—from friends to showbiz colleagues—told me I had the lower body of Jennifer Aniston or any of the *Friends,* Matt LeBlanc included. Six months later I looked the same, and it wasn't until I started running regularly that I discovered how to get weight off and keep it off. But nevertheless, ever since then, people will occasionally say to me, "Well, I had lipo and I loved it."

To which I say, "Good for you. It almost fucking killed me."

It was a while before I had the nerve to try plastic surgery again, but in 2003 I approached a doctor who'd been recommended to me with one of my genius publicity trade-offs. Yet again, painful vanity won out over common sense. I said if I could get *Entertainment Tonight* and *People* magazine to cover my plastic surgery, would he do it for free? This guy said, "Not only will I do it for free, I'll add on a bunch of stuff."

I took full advantage of his offer and got an upper eye job (slicing your eyelid and taking the fat away, yum!), a lower face lift (half the work, half the pain, only pulling up the bottom part of your head), a neck pull (incision, incision, *yank*, then feel for a month like someone's always tugging on your neck), lipo on my arms (I know, I know, but it was part of the package and didn't require knocking me out, which was where the problems began the first time), veneers on my teeth, Botox, and . . . who remembers what the fuck I had done, really.

The thing is, I look back now and have a major regret that I came clean with this whole thing. It's just been an annoyance. Definitely a publicity gambit that backfired. Every interview I've done from then on trying to promote whatever I had coming up on TV ended up being a detailed and embarrassing rehashing of my plastic surgery. If I could redo anything in my career, I would not have gone public with that round of plastic surgery. I should have just paid for it and kept quiet. One time a woman came up to me at an airport and started touching my face, saying, "You don't look that bad." I should have just become one of those dames who absolutely swear they've never had any work done. I'm looking at you, Hatcher. Instead it felt like my first reality show, in a way. It's become something I've been asked about— and will continue to be asked about—for the rest of my life. Of all the things I thought I'd get out of that experience, getting asked repeatedly about my stand on plastic surgery, or how I felt morally about it, was not one of them.

My decision to have more surgery was about as deep as, "Maybe I'll look younger and be in a magazine!"

And then the big irony: After years of trying to get on *Oprah*, this was my ticket in. By the way, Oprah, is this the first thing you're reading in my book, you little scoundrel? I can't believe you! You just looked in the index, saw your name, and flipped to this page, didn't you? Gayle, do something! Oh well.

Anyway, here I was with my moratorium on doing interviews about my plastic surgery, and then my publicist calls and says: "Oprah wants you for a show about plastic surgery."

"Can't I just go on and be a regular interview?"

"You're not big enough."

"What if I really opened up about my personal life?"

"No."

"My show business trials and tribulations?"

"It's a pass. It's plastic surgery or nothing."

"What time does my plane leave?"

When Oprah calls, you eat shit and you do it. That's a lesson, people.

Am I right, O?

You can skip ahead now, Oprah. Nothing else to see here. I'll probably move on to writing about Barbara Walters and that black guy she slept with. Gotcha!

Is she gone? Okay, get this: Do you want to know why Oprah has all that money? She's super cheap. This was the big time, I thought, but all they gave me was one coach ticket, they refused to spring for my hair and makeup person, and they wanted to put me in a low-end motel. I thought, *You're kidding! Isn't this a big-budget show where they roll out the red carpet? Isn't this the woman who lives for lighting and hair and makeup?*

Their warm-up person for the audience? It was the segment producer who did my preinterview. I was perplexed. I said, "Are you a comedian?" She said, "No, I'm just trying this out!" I asked to get a picture with Ms. Winfrey before the show, and they said "No." I said, "Okay, but I need a picture. I need proof for my gays!" They said, "Well, we'll take the picture, and then we'll give it to you." They took it. They own it. They could probably ask for it back at any time. (It's why you're not seeing it in the book. Can't piss off the big O.)

In any case, I wanted to look good for my big moment, so I got myself a really expensive black suit. The idea was to keep it simple and look like a million bucks, but not be super-fashiony. When it came time to tape the show, it was ridiculously exciting to hear Oprah introduce me—"COME ON O-O-O-O-O-OUT!"—and then I was on for my little interview. I tried to make her laugh, but she was very dominant and condescending, somewhat friendly. It took her a few minutes to get who I was, and even though we were there to talk about plastic surgery, I got her to chuckle a little. But she's very alpha dog. You go out there and she lets you know in two seconds, "This is my turf." I think she peed on me a little. And she got one of her classic nurturing digs in when I mentioned getting liposuction twice, even though the first time had complications. Like the wise scold she is, she asked me if I was ever going to learn. I wasn't offended, though. It's Oprah, so it was funny. It's what we want from her, right?

The best moment for me came during the commercial break. Our show was taping not long after they'd aired Oprah's insane interview with Barbra Streisand, where the two of them had appeared to go at it like they were in a Mexican cockfight. So during the break I thought, *I have three minutes with Oprah, I'm going to take my shot and ask about it.* But Oprah, being a very smart woman, took questions from the audience between segments. It's obviously her way of denying every guest who wants their private time with her.

I wasn't having it, though. She took a question and then I just blurted out, "By the way, that Streisand interview you did was off the hook."

And instantaneously, I was rewarded. Sassy ghetto Oprah materialized as she turned to me with WTF eyes and said, "You know, she painted my mic *white?*"

It seems Streisand had wanted her outfit to match her microphone, so she apparently had one of her minions take one of Oprah's mikes and spray-paint it white. And it had been eating at Oprah for *weeks.* Yes! That was my Oprah moment.

Do you think Oprah is bragging about her Kathy Griffin moment? Me, too.

13

REINVENTING MYSELF: I'M JUST LIKE MADONNA!

As the millennium turned, my character Vicki Groener mouthed off for the last time when *Suddenly Susan* ended its run on NBC after four seasons. I was sad for my showbiz family to come to an end and I would miss so many things—eating crappy "pasta surprise" meals at the Warner Bros. commissary with cast members, seeing Nestor Carbonell at the studio gym with his shirt off, and having a little thing called job security—but I was also admittedly excited about my career prospects moving forward. Everybody around me—agents, actor friends, writers—thought I was in a great position. I'd done well on the series, my stand-up profile had increased, and the buzz was that I would now be able to star in my own show.

"We're going for the full *Seinfeld*," claimed my shooting-for-the-moon agents and seasoned sitcom writers who I met with. "We're going for a four-camera, million-dollar-an-episode prime-time sitcom called *Kathy*! It's going to center on you and your crazy life, we're going to find two veteran actors to play your parents, it's going to explore what it's like for you to be a female stand-up comedian on the road, it's going to get into your wacky Irish-Catholic family, your home life,

---

Left: When I perform I solemnly swear to swear, so fucking help me God. (Photo: Martin LePire/Bravo/NBCU Photo Bank)

your dogs, and it's going to be as classic as *Roseanne* was in being based on the person's actual life."

I really *was* like Rhoda, because Rhoda got her own show! Sidekick makes good!

Yeah, well those meetings started and ended very quickly. As in, within three weeks. Everywhere I went I heard, "You can't carry a show." "People don't know you well." "You're not young and attractive enough." Even, "Maybe, but we'd need somebody else to play you, someone younger, and you wouldn't participate in it."

A manager named Brian Medavoy, who's the son of famed studio executive Mike Medavoy, said to me around this time, "You know, you're really off-putting. I think that's a problem for you."

When I hear things like that, I always think, *How can I spin this to my credit?* So after hearing I was "off-putting," I felt like saying to everyone, "Well . . . yeah! It's cause I'm *trying* to be the Off-Putting Girl! Your network is going to be on the ground floor of the off-putting trend, and *no one's* as off-putting as I am right now! Everybody's dying to be off-putting out there, haven't you heard? I've got the market cornered on off-putting!"

Let's see, what else? My voice was annoying. My TV Q score—some bullshit number that's supposed to indicate your popularity with viewers—was bad. But always—*always*—I was too old, old, old, old, old. You'd have thought I was on fucking life support. I was forty at the time. You know what they say: forty and fabulous! Or in my case, forty and fucked.

Those meetings really took the wind out of my sails. I don't know if I was ever hot, but that round of talks with pretty high-level network people certainly showed me I was not-hot. People don't want to touch you when you're not-hot, they don't want to breathe in your not-hot stench. They don't want to have to go to the drugstore to get some salve for your not-hot crabs that jumped off your not-hot vagina. They don't want you, and they're not taking a meeting with you. Once this virus spreads through Hollywood that you didn't get a deal at Warner Bros. or Fox or ABC or CBS—because they all talk to each other and play golf together and go to the same lap dance parties—then it's as if

REINVENTING MYSELF: I'M JUST LIKE MADONNA! 189

you're poison. I had gone from *Suddenly Susan* to *Suddenly Cold*. And this happens *fast*. Because when you have those meetings, they're usually all happening within a day or two. You'll pitch your concept to every network in one day, maybe. So if you're at all the studios on Monday, by Tuesday night you know you're either celebrating or drowning your sorrows.

At which point I was left with, "Well, can I be a second banana again?"

The answer was "No."

Thus began my post-*Susan* year of sleeping till 1 p.m., eating buckets of ice cream, and watching *Oprah* every day. It was the worst feeling in the world. Sorry, O. Nothing personal, I just need to work. As tired as I was simultaneously doing the sitcom and traveling for stand-up gigs, it gave me purpose. If I don't have a place to go every morning, I can get depressed after about three days. That's right, my happiness has a shelf life of two days. Even vacations start not to feel like vacations after about five days: They become the thing that keeps me from working. And now I was on a forced vacation, and it fucking sucked. It's not that I wasn't doing okay financially, because I'd been good with money and socked a bunch away, but I hated that I didn't have somewhere to be every day at 8 a.m. I loved driving to the Warner Bros. lot every day, seeing everyone at the table reads, knowing we taped the show on Friday and that on Saturday I'd be at some college gig, having a schedule that told me when I had to be on and when I got to be off.

Remember, I'm the daughter of a dad who didn't think twice about working sixty hours a week in retail, and a mom who held down a job while co-raising five kids. And those are still two of the happiest people I've ever met. For me, my ideal situation is when work and play co-exist. I'm happiest when I'm working hard with coworkers/friends around me, and we're all in it together. Many of my non-showbiz friends criticize me for having so many close friendships and relationships with people who are "on the payroll": my assistant, my tour manager, my mother because she gets paid for being on *The D-List*. Well yeah, I want to hire people I like, who I want to be with after I do a show or finish taping. I had a great conversation with Joan Rivers about this once. She said, "Everyone has to understand. You're the brand, and you're a business, but it's a *community* that we're all in together." Think about it in your own life. If you work at a job where you love the people you work with, you love going to work. That's all I want.

There was a small problem, though, with my thirst to get back on a sitcom. The traditional soundstage-filmed, studio-audience, half-hour network comedy was on its way out, and soon it was "Hello, *Survivor.*"

In the summer of 2000, *Survivor* became the number one show in the country, and rightly so. It was amazing, edge-of-your-seat TV, a competition but also a peek into some quirky personalities. To this day it's some of the best television I've ever seen. A cheap show to make compared to a sitcom, it was pulling viewers and ratings in a way nobody could have imagined. I mean, there was *Survivor* contestant Jenna Lewis in her bikini on the cover of *Time* magazine. That first summer of *Survivor,* your priorities were clear: Thursday night, 8 p.m., CBS, you had to be there.

When reality television became, well, the new reality in television—and all the networks started developing shows to capitalize on it—many of my comedy writer friends got bitter, and understandably so, because fewer scripted shows meant creative people were starting to lose their jobs. There was this sentiment that reality was the enemy. But I was all over it, not only as a fan, but as someone who's been doing her version of reality for years whenever I got up onstage. Think about it: My act isn't scripted, and here was this new genre that was all about being unscripted. That was me. If sitcoms didn't want what I had, then I'd come up with my own way to celebrate reality TV, and give myself a job.

I went to MTV, where I'd had a relationship from years of cohosting their New Year's Eve specials or appearing on *TRL,* and told them I wanted to do a show where I could talk about reality shows, sum them up, interview kicked-off contestants, make fun of them, and just generally tap into this new watercooler TV topic. I said I could do it for almost nothing, I wanted to co-executive produce, and—of course—I wanted my mom and dad on the show, because I thought they were funny.

MTV gave me six episodes that started airing at the beginning of

2001. The show was called *Kathy's So-Called Reality.* (My name was in the *title!* Like a big star!) It only lasted for those six episodes—they didn't pick it up for more—but I have to say I loved that job. I would start with a monologue, usually about whatever happened in reality TV that week, which was always hard because we taped on a Thursday and therefore couldn't talk about that week's *Survivor,* so by the time my show aired on Sunday, we were a week behind with events. Also, it was impossible to get clips from CBS—even though MTV shared a parent company, Viacom—so I usually corralled my mom and dad into performing *Survivor* reenactments from transcripts. Then we'd have guests. Eden's Crush, the manufactured girl group from the WB's *Pop Stars,* performed on our show. (I don't exactly remember you, Nicole Scherzinger, but I'm sure you were very nice.) Elsewhere we had hilarious difficulties booking reality show contestants, an early indication in my mind that these plucked-from-nowhere people were beginning to imagine themselves as A-listers.

Bad ratings got *Kathy's So-Called Reality* canceled, but I'd like to think it was ahead of its time in tapping into everyone's burning desire for this new type of show. Now you have entire networks like Fox Reality devoted to reality TV, and the dude from *Jon & Kate Plus 8* on the cover of *US Weekly.* Well, I was there first, motherfuckers. Not only that, there are elements to *Kathy's So-Called Reality* that acted as precursors for *The D-List,* from featuring my parents to mining humor out of the fact that I'm not a beloved personality. One of my favorite things to do on the MTV show was read aloud my hate mail as a way of doing the opposite of what Oprah would do, offering testimonials as to how some episode she did changed lives. "Dear Big Nose Bitch," one of my letters read, "get off my TV, I hate you." Another one I read to my parents aloud on the air: "Dear Mr. and Mrs. Griffin, why aren't you in a home?" They thought the letters were hysterical. And so did I.

After *So-Called Reality,* it was back to being in career limbo, not sure of where to go or what to do next. I was in a weird place where I was a little too well known to go sit on folding chairs with totally unknown

Me on stage at the Laugh Factory, ready to debrief an
enthusiastic crowd about whatever crazy celebrity run-in
I'd had that week. (Photo: Bravo/NBCU Photo Bank)

girls at auditions—and certainly not for two-line parts anymore—but
I wasn't famous or successful enough to be packaged as part of a series.

But there was always stand-up. And just like when I devised Hot
Cup O' Talk, if I could find a club and grab their worst time slot—not
try to squeeze myself into a high-expectation, traditional Friday or Saturday lineup—then maybe I could come up with another show to
make my own. My stand-up agent said, "Try Jamie Masada at the
Laugh Factory."

I called up Jamie, the club's owner, pitched him, and said, "What's
a time when nobody comes in?"

"Wednesday nights are usually pretty slow," he said.

Without even waiting for him to accept me, I said, "I'll take it."

The Laugh Factory is a castle-shaped comedy club at Sunset Boulevard and Laurel that, like the Improv and the Comedy Store, is one of the premier showcases in Los Angeles for comedians. It was a place that catered to couples and straight guys—not exactly my best crowds—and its roster was heavy on male comics and theme nights like Chocolate Sundays (as in, not for Whitey) or Latino Night. It also has a fantastic L-shaped marquee, one side facing Sunset Boulevard and the other facing the cross street, which means you'd have a hard time not noticing who's playing there as you drove past or sat at the stoplight nearby. The club itself is pretty standard, but a two-sided marquee on Sunset can fill a room.

If I was going to play there on Wednesday nights, just me, no opener, not part of some lineup so that people coming to see Dane Cook, for example, had to like me, too, then I was going to have to sell the shit out of that show. In addition to the marquee with my name on it, I thought it might be helpful for my assistant and me to stand at the corner of Hollywood Boulevard and Highland Avenue—tourist central with Grauman's Chinese Theatre nearby—and hand out flyers personally to people walking by. I was enough of a name to get booked on morning radio shows, but I wasn't able to land TV appearances. I didn't have a publicist at the time because they were expensive and I didn't have a steady job. Instead, Jamie would act as a de facto publicist for those live shows, making calls to the *LA Times* or anyone who'd take his call to try to get a writeup in print. I'd also call the *LA Weekly*—so helpful in publicizing the Groundlings shows—and beg to get into their listings calendar. Lastly, there would hopefully be that crucial intangible: good word of mouth.

I also wanted to do something special as an opener for my performance, to make people feel like they were coming to a show. One thing I'd tried at my gigs at the LA Gay and Lesbian Center that seemed to work was showing a five-minute videotaped clip I crudely edited myself of something I thought was particularly funny—Mariah Carey's insane appearance on *Cribs,* or an outrageously homoerotic

Backstreet Boys video—and playing it to the darkened crowd while I stood at the back with one hand holding the VCR remote and the other holding the microphone. I'd start the tape, pause it, make a funny comment, resume the tape, and if the audience laughed then it soon felt as if we were all in somebody's living room watching TV and laughing at crazy shit. It was a great way to prime the audience for that feeling I love, which is that we're all on the same page about what's funny. And if Mariah Carey talking about her negligee room as if everybody has one, or slinking into a bathtub full of soapy water *with her towel still on* doesn't make you giggle like a schoolchild, then Dane Cook comes on in an hour.

I had been used to gay charity events, gay bingo nights, gay bookstore appearances, where this kind of celebrity razzing went over really well. When I started at the Laugh Factory, I'd cross my fingers that there'd be lots of gay guys in the audience, but you'd never know. It's another reason the video opening worked. If the crowd wasn't laughing at my rolled-eyes voice-over as they watched footage of a makeupless Julia Roberts braving Outer Mongolia to show how she likes to keep it real, I knew what kind of crowd I had, and could figure out what stories to tell from there.

But let's face it, my experiences performing for the unshockable gays helped make those Laugh Factory shows a no-holds-barred outlet for me. Usually there are all kinds of agendas at a standard comedy club: the audience is talking, they're drunk, they're bored, they're trying to out-funny the comedian, the guys are hitting on the girls, the first dates are going badly. But when I'd play at the LA Gay and Lesbian Center's theater, the crowd has already had their wine in the lobby, and they're just captive audiences, ready to laugh. There's nothing like the energy of a gay audience, and what began to happen at the Laugh Factory was that the gays were coming to see me, and then the breeders folded in, and eventually as the show started getting more and more buzz around town, the place filled up regularly. I really believe a lot of couples and straight guys, who normally wouldn't have given me a chance previously, now came to see what I did as funny. Leave it to the gays to scour a major city like Los Angeles and find the one place they could converge on a Wednesday night and turn it into the place to be. They've always had my back. What I love about the gays is that when I've been lost, they've found me.

I had a receptive crowd, and my scheduled hour went out the window really fucking fast. I would often do two-and-a-half-hour shows, and that in itself was great for the show's popularity. People would leave saying, "Wow, I really got my money's worth!" Then I'd do it again the following week, dressing as appropriately as possible for a sweaty club—tank tops, comfortable shoes—all the while thinking, *If this crowd's with me, they're going to have to literally give me the hook to get me off this stage.* I actually lost weight during that period. If that's not an exercise regimen, I don't know what is: standing on stage furiously gesticulating, which is an excellent upper-body workout, and perspiring for two hours or more. Take that, 24-Hour Fitness.

The cocktail waitresses really loved my Wednesday shows. More of me meant more drinks, until the waitresses eventually told me, "I can make my rent because of you." Plus, they loved serving the gays, because they were well-dressed, respectful, and tipped well. Hell, yeah! The gays are there to laugh, not get in fights and fuck around. (Okay, there was that one time when some drag queens scuffled with a Marine who came with his girlfriend. Obviously, the Marine lost.)

As for my material, that Laugh Factory stint, which ran for over a year past its original limited run, was when I *really* started to talk lots of shit about celebrities. That was the most liberating thing about that engagement, because I was absolutely under the radar. On one level I was just another comic at a club, but because I had all this pop culture experience under my belt—the sitcom, awards shows, being on *Hollywood Squares,* my rigorous TV watching from Oprah to every new reality show—it all came out onstage, with new stories all the time. It was ridiculous. Lines were forming around the block to see me, but it never seemed to get out in the press that I was telling tales out of school on a weekly basis—Whitney Houston waving a cracked-out finger at me; Gwyneth looking pissy on the red carpet; getting a sweaty, and I mean buckets of sweat sweaty, hug from Richard Simmons—for anyone who paid $10 and bought two drinks on a Wednesday night. Even if I was asked to do a piece on *Extra* or *Entertainment Tonight*, it was usually "Kathy Griffin's thoughts on plastic surgery!" with no mention about the show.

I was in a strangely great position. I had nothing to lose, and sold-out audiences that couldn't be shocked were eager to hear me report every week on Hollywood crazy people.

It was during this time that I got my first death threat, though. I guess you know you've made it when people literally want to kill you.

Apparently I'd offended someone at one of my performances to the point where a person claiming to be from some Muslim group called the club owner Jamie, who's Israeli, and started spewing anti-Semitic statements and said they were going to kill me the following Wednesday. The FBI and LAPD were called in to investigate.

Jamie was pretty cool about it. "Buddy," he said to me, which is what he calls everybody, "I've gotten so many death threats. But you don't have to do the show if you don't want to. It's totally up to you."

I thought about it, and came up with an even crazier idea: go public with it from the stage! But then again, I didn't really want a Salman Rushdie–style fatwa on my head, so I decided to do the show, but not talk about it.

That lasted about five minutes.

"Hey, everybody, guess what! There's a death threat tonight, so watch your backs! The bomb-sniffing dogs were here and everything!" I talked about it for three weeks after that, too.

I think the audiences were a little freaked out, but I also sensed that they were enjoying the in-the-moment-ness of it all. You have to say those crowds couldn't have thought I was some hack. I wasn't stealing other comedians' jokes and talking about bad airplane food and asking where everyone's from. If you're at my show I don't want to know where you're from. Keep that shit to yourself. I have things to talk about, like my very special death threat. And that was a unique topic those particular audiences weren't going to hear anywhere except from my pretty little mouth.

So while some people care enough about me to want to kill me, it still felt as if nobody in power in Hollywood gave two shits. One night, though, my UTA agent Martin Lesak, who really believed in me—he was one of the higher-ups at UTA, but he usually passed me off to a more junior agent who was more concerned with rescuing animals— managed to get Kelsey Grammer and NBC head Jeff Zucker to come to the show. It was a night that changed my life.

These two TV bigwigs stayed only for the first hour, but I had a meeting with Zucker the next day where he said the magic words.

"I think you should have your own sitcom. I think you can drive a show. And I want you to be yourself. I don't think I should make you a mom. I don't think I should make you an astronaut. I think the show should be exactly what I saw at that club. You, one hundred percent being you."

"Wow," I said. "That's really cool. Is Kelsey Grammer going to produce it?"

"Why should I pay him to do it?"

Yes! I'm disputed territory in an NBC war!

Well, we started talking about writers, and then it was all about the script phase. They paired me with a seasoned sitcom writer and we collaborated on a script, but then she got another job. A week went by. Then months. The scripts weren't getting done, and then when they did, nobody at NBC would look at them. Then I was back in that situation where calls weren't being returned, and here I was with an NBC deal and they're not doing anything with me. It's called development hell, or as I like to call it, the unemployment line.

Things changed when NBC's cable division head Jeff Gaspin called me in for a meeting. (The reason I mention him by name, as if you guys give a shit, is because I ran into him recently at a party. First of all, his lovely wife Karen is really why I have a television career. She thinks I'm hysterically funny, and tells Jeff that, as he is not able to figure it out on his own yet. Shout out, Karen!) I, of course, thought the meeting was going to be, "We're ordering six episodes of your new sitcom!" Instead it was Gaspin being the bearer of bad news from Zucker. The purpose of the meeting was to convince me to let go of my dream of having a million-dollar-an-episode, live-audience, scripted sitcom and consider instead a $200,000-per-episode, unscripted reality show. And could my house be the set for free? "*The Osbournes* are really big," he explained.

Now, I may have been a fan of reality TV and had my brief stint on MTV, but in my head I thought *No, I'm a sitcom person.* That's my training. That's my history. That's who I am. I should have a scripted show. You don't need me for a reality show. You can pick any stripper or little person or freaky Christian who wants to have twelve kids and build a reality show. My training is in stand-up comedy specials and situation comedy. You need me because I know how to find good writers and build a cast and think up story arcs. I really thought situation comedy was my wheelhouse. By the way, what the fuck is a wheelhouse? I can't believe I just used that expression. I am a Hollywood douche bag. I meant to say "Situation comedy is in my wheelguesthouse."

"We're not going to do an expensive sitcom," NBC said. "We think we can do a show with you where we don't have to pay writers or have a set."

"It sounds like you're just trying to get a really big show for next to nothing," I said.

They never really answered that, but that's what it was.

I wanted a show and I wanted to work, so I said, "Okay, let's do it." NBC didn't do it.

But now I was determined. I had begun thinking about how to do a reality show that wasn't the lowest common denominator. At one point Carolyn Strauss, who was then head of programming at HBO, said to me, "I really think you could have a show where people follow you around. You say funny stuff all the time, and that could be the basis for a show."

HBO was never going to give me a reality show, but if someone there was saying it, it must mean NBC's instincts were good, even if their follow-through wasn't so commendable. But boy, was I getting frustrated. My stand-up show was doing well, but it wasn't leading to anything. It was driving me crazy. Then my agents at UTA got bored and wouldn't take my calls.

I started to think about this bizarre position I was in: a hard worker, a showbiz professional, confident of my ability to entertain, but somebody for whom the spotlight always seemed just out of reach. All around me were people like Paris Hilton who were apparently cover-worthy celebrities, so famous and untalented, and the bane of my existence. Yeah, that's right, I was bitter. Paris Hilton? Not that funny. And reality TV was turning out people like this all the time. I remember getting invited to a charity event around the time the original *Bachelor* was airing, and I found myself waiting in line with Lisa Kudrow and Ray Romano to get a chance to talk to the show's star, Alex Michel. I turned to Ray and said, "What's happened to us?"

"I promised my wife I'd talk to him," he said sheepishly.

It felt like a sea change was taking place, where lines were being drawn on who was big and who wasn't big enough. I remember I got to go to the *American Idol* finale for the first season, when it was the hottest new show since . . . well, the first season of *Survivor.* Anyway, I was famous enough to score tickets to *American Idol,* but when I got there, I saw Camryn Mannheim and Jenny McCarthy in the first few rows. I was in row twenty-six. "Okay, no biggie," I told myself. "I have a ticket to the party afterward. I'm in."

I go to the party, and I run into Jenny and Roseanne Barr, and they're wearing wristbands. My little freckled wrist is bare.

"What are those?" I ask.

"They're for the VIP party," they say.

I don't get access to the party within the party? Ugh. I literally had a conversation with Camryn where we were on two sides of the rope. Trying to save the day, she said to me, "Hey, I'll distract the security guy and you can sneak in."

"Uh, no," I said. "I don't want to sneak in like some no-name gate crasher to the wristband party. I'm okay out here."

It was experiences like this (and too many others to tell here) that helped me realize what exactly I was, the insider as outsider. I could get invited to celebrity parties, but not to the VIP circle within those parties. I got invited to red carpet events, but I'd get there early, when the photographers first arrive, in order to get my photo taken. I had an agent who didn't return my calls, but who was happy to send me e-mails hoping I'd rescue a one-legged blind dog. "I have two dogs already," I'd write her back. "But I do need a job."

It was an A-list world, and my life was the D-list.

And then it dawned on me: That's the show!

14
REALITY
CHECK

So get this, back in 2004 I was so D-list that I couldn't even get my then agents to go to pitch meetings with me to sell a show about how I was *on* the D-list.

Isn't that a catch-22? Isn't it ironic? Like that traffic jam when I'm already late? Or ten thousand spoons when all I need is a knife? Whatever, Alanis.

Apparently, I wasn't what they call "an earner." You know how on *The Sopranos* the wiseguys talk about who's an "earner," how they can't kill somebody if he's an "earner," how they're debating whether or not to put up with an "earner"? Let's face it, the big agencies have giant movie stars like Julia Roberts, Denzel Washington, and Will Smith, clients pulling in $40 million a year, and their agents get 10 percent of that. I wasn't pulling in even $1 million a year. No agent wanted to waste their time with me when they could be going to a Scientology retreat with Tom Cruise and John Travolta. (Or Will Smith, if he's been recruited by now!)

Anyway, armed with what I thought was a great idea for a reality show, I was only able to get three pitch meetings: with TBS, VH1, and Bravo. TBS and VH1 weren't too impressed with me being by myself

Left: My husband Matt and assistant Jessica were two people who understood "Lights, camera, be yourself!" (Photo: Michael Grecco/Bravo/NBCU Photo Bank)

and not dragging either an agent or a big-time producer to the meeting, so they passed. I finally got my agent to come with me to the Bravo meeting, but only because he knew the cable channel's president, Lauren Zalaznick. And what do you know? The show, which we eventually called *Kathy Griffin: My Life on the D-List,* got signed that day.

It's tough sometimes for me to justify the 10 percent I have to pay an agent. They certainly don't do 10 percent of my job. They don't do a quarter of 1 percent. But they're a necessary evil, and if that agent had not been with me at that meeting, I don't know that I would have sold the show. He didn't even say anything, either. He just sat there. Nice work if you can get it. In fact, that guy's not even an agent anymore. Fuck him, I'm with William Morris now. I hear this William Morris character is in it for the long haul. I haven't gotten him on the phone yet, though.

Well, I went home and found my assistant Jessica and my husband Matt in the office they shared and broke the news. "Get ready to put on mic packs," I said, "because you're gonna be on a reality show."

Wait, I'm married? I'll get to that story in the next chapter. Stay focused, people.

Basically, I was offering myself up to be followed night and day by cameras. I hooked up with a production company called Picture This, run by a guy named Bryan Scott and a woman named Marcia Mulé. They're both gay. Check, and check. They weren't the most experienced producers in the world, but I figured what they lacked in experience, they could make up in gayness. And their idea was that naturally funny things seemed to happen to me because I gravitated toward bizarre D-list situations. We arranged it so that they'd shadow me for six months, which would be edited down to six episodes. That comes out to a month of taping, and taping, and taping, for every forty-four minutes of content. To put this in perspective, I believe *Sober House,* which is nine episodes long, shoots for a whopping fifteen days. My next show, incidentally, will be called *Kittens Purring,* and I will shoot forty episodes in two days at a local pet store. Stay tuned.

. . .

I did have a template in my mind for how I wanted the show to be: *Newlyweds: Nick and Jessica*. That MTV series was a big deal at the time, and I knew Jessica Simpson a little from the D-list circuit, meaning we'd see each other at charity events where we both performed. What I liked about *Newlyweds* was that it seemed to accurately portray how the couple really was, capturing what was genuinely funny about her—this affable girl who said ridiculous things—and charming about him. It was driven by their personalities, by them doing what came naturally as opposed to putting up a front of how they thought they should act.

I called Joe Simpson, Jessica's dad, thinking, *I'll get the lowdown, cause he produces that show!*

He never got back to me. As if I needed any more proof of my show concept: When Joe Simpson is too big to return your call, you know you're D-List.

No matter, though. I ran into Nick and Jessica at some benefit gig in Jamaica before we'd started shooting *The D-List*, and we had a conversation about what was in store for me.

"Okay, what boundaries did you set for your show?" I asked.

Jessica told me, "Well, we don't let them shoot in our bathroom or our bedroom, because we have to have one place in the house that's completely private, where the cameras will never go. So if we feel we've had it, the crew knows the minute we cross that threshold, they're gonna stop shooting."

Sounds good, I thought. *I'll do that.*

That little rule went out the window immediately. If Matt and I were walking down the hall toward our bedroom and talking, and he's in the middle of a word as we cross into the bedroom, how was that gonna work? Well, it wasn't. So what eventually got instituted was a policy of no restrictions or boundaries of any kind. Is that even a policy? All I know is there were countless times when somebody walked in on me when I was peeing. Or I'd be in a room getting changed, and the crew guy taking lunch orders would walk in.

"Hey, Kathy, do you want the chow mein or . . . Oh! Sorry!"
Yeah, that'd be my tits you're seeing . . . again. Luckily I didn't have
any dignity to begin with.

Truth be told, it was all incredibly experimental, since we didn't
really know what we were doing. The way that first season was story-
boarded was, I handed over my online calendar of dentist appoint-
ments, stand-up gigs, auditions, Botox injections, awards shows, talk
show appearances, and whatever else was going on, to the producers,
and I'd say something like, "On this date, I'm hosting a hospital benefit at a ritzy hotel where Warren Beatty is getting an award. If that's not
funny, I don't know what is." Then the producers would go try to clear
the locations and get permission to shoot. If you've seen season one of
my show, you'll remember that at that benefit event I ran out when
Beatty was accepting his award so I could have a moment with him for
the *D-List* cameras. What you didn't know is how extremely D-list that
gambit truly was: Beatty, who didn't know who the fuck I was, only
agreed to be photographed or filmed for the event while onstage. That
meant the only way to get him in any capacity was to bum-rush him
post-acceptance speech, before he reached the wings. He paused for a
moment, shook my hand, and smiled, while I furiously said, "Blah blah
holy shit, tee hee, dick joke, time's up." Or something to that effect. But
hey, I got my three seconds shaking his hand! Now that's pretty D-list.

It's a delicate balance, filming a reality show. The three of us—Matt,
Jessica, and I—weren't used to having eight extra people around us all
the time, and the crew—made up of people who had worked on bigger
budget shows like *The Apprentice, The Amazing Race,* and *Survivor*—
wasn't used to a house being anything but a set. They were more accustomed to having a catering area, a built set, and a room full of monitors
where producers are watching all the camera shots. A real show, in other
words, not a fucked-up ghetto camcorder operation like this.

Plus, there's something about the experience that I feel like a lot of
reality people aren't entirely honest about. When I hear people from
other shows say, "After the first day, I forgot the camera was there!" I
don't know what they're talking about. I never forget. I mean, I got
used to it, meaning the people and the equipment. But no matter how

hard I tried not to say stuff that was too heinous, it didn't work. I'm not able to censor myself, anyway, but there were definitely many times when I'd say something on camera, and then five seconds later think, *Aw shit, I'm gonna regret that, the network's gonna love it, I'm not going to be able to get it cut, and then I'll be in a fucking fight with* [insert trashed celebrity name here].

The experience of having cameras on you all the time increased my admiration for Howard Stern, since he's on the air at least four hours a day without a filter. He tells a great story where Gayle King confronted him about something he'd said about her on the show, and his response was, "Do you think I can even remember what I said *today*, much less four months ago?"

I completely identify with that. So if anyone is upset with me about what I say on the show, in my head I'm thinking, *Okay, I understand, but there were cameras there from 10 in the morning until 10 at night taping every word out of my mouth for five months. You're damn right I said some awful shit, and I've said a lot worse than that, so relax, Sharon Stone.*

It was such a long haul, that first season, but one thing I believed early on that holds true to this day is that I should not be involved in the editing process. I knew I wouldn't be helpful in that capacity, and it wouldn't serve the show. What if I saw a shot of my cellulite that I didn't want? That kind of regular interference on my part would probably drive everyone nuts, so I knew it was better to let them come up with a rough cut that was maybe five minutes too long, and let them ask me what I really hated. Then I could say, "Well, this is a little boring" or whatever, and that would be the extent of it. I'd rather be involved fine-tuning the edits with regards to comedy rather than worry myself with matters of vanity. The key for me is that it's a comedy-driven show. It's not *The Real World* where I'm getting in and out of a hot tub with somebody. I wanted the show to be as funny as possible.

I felt very fortunate in that I had a really great combination of *D-List* regulars around me, people who provided easygoing leverage against my desperate desire to be famous at any cost coupled with my talking shit about celebrities. My assistant Jessica was this punk rock

Bottoms up, John and Maggie!

girl with blue hair and a really great, dry sense of humor. Matt was, as
my mom would say, very "go-along" in that he had a good attitude
about the showbiz craziness. He got a kick out of celebrity, but wasn't
overly dazzled by it.

Then there were my parents, who I knew would be naturally
funny. By this point my dad had done several national commercials. It
started as a lark, really. When my mom and dad first retired to California, Dad was one of those workaholic guys who ended up being
really bored with retirement. One day in the early '90s I brought him
with me to my former commercial agency, Abrams Artists, and with
my dad seated by my side, told one of the agents there that I thought
John Patrick Griffin could do commercials. Well, sure enough, he
booked the first two auditions he went on. By contrast, I had to go on
seventy fucking auditions before I booked my first commercial. That's
right. Seventy. It was like he was Lindsay Lohan, and I was wannabe
sister Ali. *I'm* supposed to be Lindsay! It was so unfair. Anyway, he
ended up doing several national and regional commercials, effortlessly

displaying his charms, so I knew he'd be able to be himself on camera. To this day, my parents are the most low-maintenance people I've ever had on the show. You'd sit them down on the couch, hand them glasses of wine, and it's like flicking a switch. They're on.

As for me, I'm that comedian that other comedians—those who feel the need to be troubled offstage—roll their eyes at for being "on" all the time. But really, the reason I'm on all the time is that I really enjoy making people laugh offstage as much as on. It doesn't come from a place of need, or about a thirst to be loved every minute. It's about wanting to have fun, and who doesn't enjoy getting people to laugh? My metabolism is such that for me, there's not a huge difference between being onstage and offstage, or on camera and off camera. That made this my perfect job! I get to be funny going to the kitchen to make a sandwich? Sign me up!

The thing I never saw coming, however, was the strain shooting a reality show would put on my friendships, relationships, and family. It's been the most painful thing about doing the show, and really the only negative aspect. You'd think having cameras on me all day would be the biggest minus, but the cameras just make me hyperaware of everything I say. That's just part of the job.

I guess what I was unprepared for was how people who weren't actors would react to being on camera. From the beginning I was always very honest about people in my orbit appearing in the show. Let's say I wanted to shoot a game night or a TV-watching night with friends, since I had regular get-togethers for favorite shows like *The Amazing Race* and *Project Runway*. Some friends were like, "We're not into it. We don't want to be on camera, so we'll see you on the nights you're not shooting." And I absolutely respected that. And for those who were up for it, I was honest about how this was a little ghetto show of six episodes, that I didn't know how it was going to pan out, if it was going to be a good thing or a bad thing, and I certainly didn't know if audiences were going to care or not.

But the camera does things to certain people. Friends and loved ones alike just turned out to act completely differently in its presence. One guy kept pulling the cameraman aside to a little room in my house to do bits like it was a confessional on *America's Next Top Model.* Somebody else who was usually very witty would just clam up. Another person who was normally pretty mellow would start talking in a funny voice. It was something I didn't see coming, and the editors in New York would start calling me about it. They remarked about one person, "He's showboating so much it takes you out of the feeling like you're a fly on the wall." One of the producers flew out from New York once to tell a couple of friends, "Look, you have to tone it down." Those were uncomfortable situations. It was really tough and awkward. I was spoiled by Mom, Dad, Matt, and Jessica, who were themselves all the time, with or without the cameras.

Even more upsetting were the expectations people around me—who had been a part of filming—started having for the show. Friends or colleagues who had joined me for two scenes would say things like, "Well I've emailed all my friends telling them I'm going to be on your show." I also heard others say, "I better get something out of this show." You have to realize, I didn't even know if the show was going to do anything for *me,* and my name was in the title! I remember saying to everybody, "Look, I don't know who's going to make the cut and who's not. I don't know if I'm going to look like an asshole on the show or not. There is no guarantee. I have almost nothing to do with the editing process when they're assembling episodes. I'm not looking to make anybody a star here. So don't be mad at me if the show's not good or your scene ends up being cut." One person told me, "This is going to help me get dates." To which I thought, *We shot for six months and you came over one afternoon. I don't know if that means you're going to get discovered as a great lover.*

And those who hadn't been part of filming were suddenly looking at me like a potential employer. People who I casually knew were now contacting me and openly saying, "I don't have a demo reel, can I get on your show?" Gay guys I would see once every three years were e-mailing me, hearing that I had gays on my show, and demanding to be on, acting like I'd screwed them over for excluding them.

After the show eventually debuted on Bravo in 2005, the touchiness with my family started. When filming began on season one, my brother John was the only one who agreed to be on the show besides my parents. Joyce and Gary openly said, "We don't want to be on the show. If you've got cameras, don't be coming around to my place." But once *The D-List* started airing, my mother was telling me that she was furious that the whole family wasn't featured, that they all should have had their own story lines. I had to remind her, "Mom, Joyce doesn't even like to be in still photos with the family." Besides, the show wasn't about our family. It's the story of a D-list celebrity and the workings of show business from that perspective.

But that didn't seem to matter. Even intimate family members jokingly referred to themselves as The Forgotten Griffins.

Family pressures are what they are, of course. My kindhearted trainer Bobby succumbed to them after the first season aired. We were shooting something and he suddenly wasn't himself on camera, talking nonstop and being really insulting. We stopped filming and I said, "Bobby, I have to be honest with you, you're not being yourself. The reason I have you on the show is because I'm this bumbling person trying to get in shape and you're the sweet, encouraging guy who is supposed to be trying to help me."

"Well, my parents saw me on the show," he said. "And they kept saying, 'Why aren't you being funny? Why aren't you being funny?' "

And this guy's a trainer who'd never thought about being on TV! I remember saying to him, "You'll get clients from people watching this show. But I want them to hire you because you're the nice guy I know. People won't want a trainer who's making insulting quips to them on the treadmill."

Bobby was very cool about it. But I actually had falling-outs with friends over this kind of thing. It caught me completely off guard. I learned on the first season of *The D-List*, more than all my years of sitcom work, the power of fame.

What I hear time and time again from people when this topic comes up is, "Who are you kidding, Kathy? Everybody wants to be famous."

I used to say, "No, that's not true. I have a lot of friends who don't care about that."

Well, I learned that I have a lot of friends who *do* care about that.

In a big way. But what they wanted was to be famous without doing any of the work that I had done: training, going to acting school, years of rejection, countless open mic nights, all that other stuff.

Now, in a few instances, the strange allure of the camera made for some funny moments at the expense of the people who were acting odd. You might remember from the show the scene with the freelance reporter for *Star* magazine who came to interview me at my house. She'd done no research, and she was trying to be funny the whole time, talking compulsively and saying really bizarre things. How D-list is it to not be able to get a word in edgewise for my own interview? Well, at the end she said, "Oh my God, I didn't turn on the tape recorder. Can we do it again?"

"Nope. I'm in the middle of a workday, sweetheart. Moving on."

By the way, she'd never have forgotten to turn that tape recorder on if she were interviewing Nicole Kidman. Or talked over Nicole's—or as I call her, the human clothes hanger's—pearls of wisdom. On a side note, Nicole really does wear clothes as beautifully as a hanger does. Every designer's dream.

Anyway, that's the kind of situation that should be a reminder to everyone who thinks it's cool to be on the show. It doesn't always go your way. There are many, many times looking at myself on *The D-List* where I just cringe: horrible facial expressions, fake smiles, countless remarks that are way over the line as far as viciousness is concerned, among other things. But everyone wants their moment, I learned. I thought only obnoxious show people like myself wanted their moment. I didn't know the freakin' mailman was going to want it, too.

It shouldn't have to be: "Just leave the mail! I don't *want* to hear the song you wrote! I want to read my letter! PUT THE MAIL DOWN! NICE AND EASY!"

Launching a new show is very different from doing season two of an existing show. I've gotten used to it now, but you should know that when you see me on talk shows trying to get you to watch the season premiere of any year of *The D-List,* I'm still filming the season. What made doing press for that first season of *Kathy Griffin: My Life on the D-List* hard was that Bravo kept changing the premiere date. They didn't know what night to put it on because their *Queer Eye for the Straight Guy* show was a big hit, *Project Runway* was also a big hit, and they weren't sure if ours was a comedy show, a reality show, or a hybrid, or something new. That would mean, first I'd tell the press it was "coming in June," then Bravo would change their mind and I'd have to say, "I mean Wednesdays in July!" And when it would change again, then it was "Guess who's on the fall lineup?"

It was frustrating because I wanted the show to have a shot. I was really proud of it. The biggest battle I consistently had with the network was over the advertising budget. Here was my wish list: billboard in Times Square, and on Sunset Boulevard; ads on bus benches across the country; full-page ads in all the national weekly magazines; and commercials on NBC and all their affiliate channels. Plus, of course, my own line of dolls I could sell on shopping networks like Marie Osmond does. Okay, I didn't get the dolls. What did I get? Sharing a billboard with *Queer Eye* for thirty days on Sunset Boulevard, and a full-page ad in *People* and *US Weekly,* which, by the way, they've never done since. But even then I was like, "Is that all?" When I had my HBO special, I had my own massive billboard for nine months. By the way, being on a billboard is so cool that when it was up, I would drive seven miles out of my way just to look at it heading home.

The D-List finally aired in August 2005, and the ratings were terrible. I mean, I wasn't expecting *Project Runway* numbers, but they weren't even a fraction of that. Why hadn't I had the foresight to just cast Heidi Klum as Kathy Griffin and be done with it? What's "Suck it" in German? It was at this point I resigned myself to thinking this little experiment might be a one-season wonder after all.

Then the oddest thing happened. I started hearing from a lot of showbiz people about *The D-List.* I ran into *Everybody Loves Raymond* star Brad Garrett at a taping of *Hollywood Squares,* and he said to me,

"Oh, I love your show." Now, I think Brad is hilarious, and it was a nice thing for him to say, but I never took it seriously when celebrities complimented me on the show. I just thought they were being polite. My response when a famous person says "I love your show" is usually "Prove it." Sometimes, if I'm feeling particularly gracious, it's "Bull-shit! PROVE IT, fucker! You lying asshole!"

I'm not saying I said those exact words to Brad, but he's a come-dian and nine feet tall. He'd have been able to take it. But what do you know, he actually rattled off some specific examples from the show, and I thought, *Oh wow, he really does watch it.* And then he said, "Everybody in Hollywood watches that show."

"No," I said in disbelief.

He slowed down his words. "*Everybody* in the industry is watching your show, Kathy, I'm telling you."

Now, I don't know if the showbiz world was watching it just to see if they were going to be referenced (meaning "trashed") on it—I did do an entire episode around Renee Zellweger's chilling revenge gift of a bouquet of roses—but as I ran into more people, I started to get the impression that the show's viewership numbers were small but mighty. People were really invested in it. Lisa Kudrow pulled me aside at an event during the airing of the first season of *The D-List* and said, "Hey, your show is fantastic! It really captures the Kathy Griffin that I know." It felt like such a compliment when an old pal I hadn't seen in a while said that watching the show was like hanging out with me.

What also meant a lot to me was hearing from my colleagues and peers how I was striking a blow for the portrayal of women on TV, that I was putting out a comedy series where a woman wasn't a housewife or a mom. I wasn't a typical forty-year-old female on television. And at the same time, *The D-List* was clueing everybody in to how hard I worked as a professional in the entertainment industry. Even better, my world as a D-lister was now on view for everyone to understand, and laugh about. People would come up to me and say, "So is that real, that you can't get your agent on the phone?" As sad as that fact was, it gratified me no end to be able to reply, "Let's call my agent right now."

Ring. Ring. Ring. Pick up. "Hello, Kathy Griffin calling!"

Pause. "Well, she's in a meeting and can't take your call."

I'd hang up and say to the skeptical fan, "Is that real enough for you?"

Things were about to get uncomfortably real, though, in my marriage. *Kathy Griffin: My Life on the D-List* was off and running, but a big part of my life was about to come to a major crossroads.

15
MY
MARRIAGE
BEGINS

I never really had a burning desire to get married.

Actually, as a little kid, I used to think, *I'll get married and divorced a million times! How boring to be with the same person forever!* I was never that girl who dreamed of her perfect wedding day, or tried on bridal dresses, or had princess fantasies. The prize I had my eye on was being the girl who got the applause, not the glass slipper. And that feeling was very liberating, too, because I never entered my adulthood thinking I would need a man to provide for me. I was never one of those girls who had to have The Ring to be happy.

Plus, as my friends started getting married and having kids, they also started getting divorced. So I never had an overly romanticized vision of marriage.

And yet, to this day, my parents had the best marriage I have ever seen. It's a running joke among my siblings that my parents fucked us all, because they set a relationship standard so unattainably high that none of us could ever achieve it. I'm not saying they were perfect. But you have never seen two people more in love. Dad never had a sexist bone in his body. He never bitched about changing diapers, never assumed there'd be a hot meal (preferably Hamburger Helper Beef

Left: Matt and I getting married by his father.

Stroganoff) on the table when he came home, never subscribed to the belief that there was woman's work and man's work.

Mom always laughed about those wives from her era who had to put on a show for their husbands, putting makeup on and a cute outfit for their spouses upon their arrival home. She'd just be in her muumuu, making jokes like, "He'll have to take me as I am!"

It sounds crazy, but I've never heard John and Maggie Griffin say anything disrespectful to each other. They had this great ability to start laughing during a fight. If they started to bicker about something, at some point one of them would break down and start giggling, and then the little problem became a running joke to them. They never let something become a bigger problem. They knew when to be concerned about real things—like my brother Kenny—and didn't sweat the small stuff.

My mom has a great story about later in life telling my dad she just didn't feel beautiful anymore, and him gently touching her hand and saying, "Oh Mag, you gave it a good run." Dad could tease Mom about looking like crap one day, then she could throw it right back at him when he was yelling at the TV during a football game. Their message as a unit was of working equally, teasing equally, and mutual respect, and it was pretty unique for its time.

Now, that's not to say they wouldn't have loved it if I'd married a dentist, since I lived with them till I was twenty-eight. But when they realized I was serious about my career, something shifted in them, and they wanted for me whatever made me happy. Mom understood and would say things to me like, "You want a guy who's going to be able to handle your career, who knows that work comes first." My parents supported me by telling me I was all I needed, and never made me feel that I was less because I didn't have A Man. However, to this day, I have to pay for all of my mom's dental work. So I do have A Mom.

But as you know by now, I'd had plenty of men. Often men bearing donuts. But as I got older my promiscuity lessened because I really did want to make it work with somebody. Call it maturity, or career comfort, or just plain being sore. I didn't have marriage in the back of my head, but I also didn't want to be a whore forever. As I became more successful, though, my circumstance as a self-made dame started to weed certain guys out. One time a cute guy who was flirting with me visited me at my first house, and he was really dazzled by it. "Wow, this is really impressive," he said.

"Thanks!"

Then he said, "Now you're never going to get a guy."

What he said hurt, but at least he was honest. He was saying he wasn't comfortable there. He was intimidated, and let me know that most guys' egos couldn't handle a woman who made more money or was more successful than them. When I was younger, my friends would tell me, "You need a guy who's funny!" But what this guy verbalized seemed to speak to what more and more people were telling me after I'd started a regular television gig and bought my own house, and a nice car: "You need a really strong guy."

"Because I'm a ballbuster?" I'd say.

"Yes," I'd hear, "but in addition, you have better toys than a dude has. And a bigger dick." Which is true. I have to use Magnums.

That's when I started to date younger guys. Younger guys are less likely to have those old-fashioned ideas about gender politics. Plus, the younger ones were asking me out, and men my age weren't. By that point I had gotten over bad-boy types, too, guys who might be charismatic or funny or exciting, but just not nice. As in, assholes on the first date. Pile up enough of those and you'll change your tune about charismatic jerks fast enough.

Examples, you ask? I remember being in a coffeehouse with a guy named Dewey, and somehow the conversation ventured into the topic of abusing women, and he said, "I'd only do it if I really had to." This was our first date. I don't think Chris Brown had even been born yet. I had to call a friend of mine to come pick me up. "I don't want this fucker dropping me off and seeing where I live!" I told her.

I seemed to be a magnet for guys who would do things like take a phone call from another girl during a first date, or comment on the hotness of other girls. One jerk did that when he was driving around looking for a parking space, and when we parked I just started walking home, which was about four miles. A lack of courtesy was a big problem in guys I'd date, too. I'd be at the dude's place that sported some gross futon, an Atari with the joysticks, and a couple of roommates, and he'd make me run out at 8 in the morning to put a quarter in the meter so I wouldn't get ticketed. "Aww, don't make me get up!" he'd say in a baby voice. I could go on and on.

But one day I thought, *What if I tried an exercise where the number one requirement for the next guy I go out with is that he be nice, not anything else?* Well, that decision changed my life. I dated a guy named Andrew for two years, and though the relationship didn't work out— I fucked it up by being the one who was the asshole—what I took away from it was the nice guy part. I'd made the switch to nice guys, and my relationships from then on improved dramatically. Even when they ended, there was nothing overly dramatic about the breakups.

By my late thirties I was single and looking for a fun way to spend the break between the third and fourth seasons of *Suddenly Susan,* so I decided to rent a house in the Provence region of France. It seemed like a thing famous people did, and I had a whole *Big Chill* fantasy that I'd invite friends, and we'd cook fabulous meals and throw plates at each other and play Motown music, and there'd be a lot of hanky-panky and falling in love and teary late-night confessionals. Naturally I saw myself as the Glenn Close character, and was preparing for when I'd have to cry in the shower for hours. So I booked a seven-bedroom house, and invited ten people. Then, as it got closer to the date, the invitees started flaking. It got to the point where it was going to be me and one other person in a huge house, out in a field, alone for three weeks.

At this point, I got less discriminatory and started going through my address book. I eventually assembled a fun group, which included a girl I really only knew tangentially from running into her at the Warner Bros. lot. Her name was Rebecca, and she was an assistant editor on *The West Wing.* During one of our chats she mentioned that she was going to be at the Cannes Film Festival with the filmmakers of an animated short film she'd edited, and it fell right in the window of time when I'd rented the house. I invited her and her friends on the spot, and it helped make that Provence trip what I'd hoped it would be: a good time with all of us shooting the shit and having fun.

At one point I was bitching about how I couldn't meet guys, and Rebecca said, "You should meet my brother. I think you'd really like him. He's really, really smart, and he's really, really funny, and he's just gone through this transformation where he lost a bunch of weight, he's running marathons and wants to change his life and maybe meet somebody."

"Where does he live?" I asked.

"Washington, DC."

"I don't really want a long-distance relationship," I said. "Those are really tough."

"Well, he's moving to LA."

Now it sounded better. Rebecca said his name was Matt, and that he was going to be visiting LA for a couple of weeks and thought we should meet up. I agreed, suggesting she bring him over one night to watch some silly television show and eat takeout. Shortly thereafter, Matt and Rebecca came to my house. What I liked about him was that he was really laid back, and seemed like a nice, mellow guy. He was quietly witty, and overall a pretty cool customer, without a trace of arrogance.

The meet-and-greet went well, and sure enough, Rebecca joked that I should babysit Matt when she had to go to work. "Be his tour guide," she said.

I could do that. So I took him around showing him what I thought was fun about LA. We went to a taping of a show, I drove him around beautiful residential neighborhoods, and we ate at this landmark LA Mexican restaurant I loved called El Cholo. All the while I'm going through a checklist in my head. He's charming, funny, and smart. Check. He's a computer IT guy for a small graphic design company in DC, so he has a full-time job. Check. He wants to be more responsible in life. Check. He seems to get me and my showbiz situation and not be freaked out by it. Check.

"What'd you think of my brother?" Rebecca asked me the next day.

"I really, really like him, but living in DC is a problem. So I guess I'm going to have to look for the LA version of your brother, instead."

"I really think he's going to move out here," she said. I wasn't convinced as I hadn't heard him tell me this himself.

Nevertheless, I saw Matt a lot during those two weeks he was visiting in LA, and had a good time with him, but no moves were made, and I wasn't sure if we were friends or what. Then, after he returned to DC, we started corresponding by email and phone, and after a while he confessed that he felt his DC life had run its course and that he was open to moving to LA, possibly in a month or so. Suddenly this seemed like it wouldn't have to be a long-distance relationship. Maybe I'd found my Caucasian Marion Barry, minus the coke and hookers.

Then I landed a role on an independent movie starring Dominique Swain called *The Intern,* which would be shooting in New York and required me to be there for a month. I called Matt in DC, told him about my gig, and said, "Do you want to jump on the shuttle and spend the weekend with me?"

He said yes, and when I finished work on the movie on a Friday night, I took a taxi to LaGuardia and met him there. We spent a great romantic weekend together, walking around Central Park holding hands, going out to eat, nothing super fancy, just really enjoying each other's company. So the next weekend I went to DC, and I booked a nice hotel and we stayed there. Then the following weekend he came back to New York. It was on that trip that we went to eat at a restaurant on Seventh Avenue, and during the meal I could tell he was clearly uncomfortable. As in visibly sweating.

"I have to tell you something," he said.

"Okay, what?"

"I can't afford this place. I can't really afford any of this."

"Well, what do you mean?" I said.

"I had to borrow money to buy my plane ticket here."

Matt's ten years younger than me. He was twenty-eight then, so when he said that, I began to think about my life at twenty-eight. I probably didn't have a lot of money, either, at that age. And we weren't exactly in a diner, or an inexpensive restaurant. This was a mildly upscale place where even if you ordered a burger—which I did—it was $17. I started justifying Matt's situation, and came to the conclusion that I'd rather he lay his cards on the table than put himself into debt.

"Okay, tell me what you can afford and just be honest about it," I

The great Joan Rivers is a close enough friend that I can always ask her for advice about my relationships. (Photo: Joe Kohen/WireImage/Getty Images)

said. "I don't want you borrowing money from friends in order to date me. Let's say you pay for what you can afford. I'm more than happy to go to a seven-dollar burger joint. So when we go to those places, why don't you pick up that tab, and when I choose to go to a nice hotel or more expensive restaurant, or if I feel like going to a concert or a play and the tickets are two hundred dollars, I'll pay for that because I'm choosing what we're doing."

That was the arrangement we made that day. I could see that it bothered him that he couldn't pick up the check and take care of me that way, and I thought it showed sensitivity, that he wasn't being cavalier about it. Early in our dating, I had a conversation with Joan Rivers about Matt, and I said to her, "I've started seeing this guy, and

I really, really like him. He's a good guy, but he has no money. As in *no* money. Meaning, I think I might be about to embark on a relationship where I'm going to be footing the bill 99 percent of the time. What do you think about that? Should I just look for guys with money, regardless of whether or not I like them, or follow my heart?"

She said something I always remembered. "You know, we all make our own deals."

"What do you mean?" I said.

"Look, nobody knows what happens in a relationship except the two people who are in it."

What Joan was saying was, tailor the relationship to the needs of the people in it. Who said it had to conform to a conventional template where the man paid for everything, or the woman had to act like a doormat, or each person had to be taken care of in certain, established ways? We all bring different things to the table.

In my case, I didn't need to be taken care of financially. I didn't need a boyfriend to buy me a necklace. Matt was offering me something I desperately wanted, which I thought was love. He had many obvious qualities: He was smart, funny, and easy to get along with. But what separated him was that he genuinely seemed to be deeply in love with me. More than any man had ever been. I thought, *I'm someone who very much needs to be taken care of emotionally, I need someone who'll put up with my moods and my crap and be a good guy who's there for me because of the pressures of what I do.* Now, I don't like guys who are cheap, but I feel like if a guy is hardworking and poor, that's not a crime. I'm okay with that. If paying for things was a way for me to fulfill a certain role, then I believed it was a deal worth making to be with a guy I considered an emotional partner. Plus, there were probably areas where I didn't meet every one of his criteria. Maybe he'd wanted a tall blonde, or someone younger, someone more book-smart—Matt was certainly brighter than I was—or someone who worked in a field less demanding or chaotic.

Most important, though, we had a good, open conversation about things. He told me what he couldn't do. I told him what I *could* do, and what I was hoping for in a relationship.

Ironically enough, after our talk, the waiter came over and told us there was an Oklahoma family at a nearby table who were big fans of mine, wanted to pick up our check, and just had. I turned to Matt and said with enthusiasm, "And sometimes that happens!"

Matt moved out to LA, and though he spent nearly every night at my house, I felt comforted by the fact that he had his own place, a shared rental with his sister and her boyfriend. As we got closer, it was evident he could handle himself well in all sorts of situations, from being on the *Suddenly Susan* set with me, to going to tedious work-oriented press or network events, to hanging out with my friends. Best of all, at the end of the day, when it was just us, we could share a pizza, laugh at the ridiculousness of showbiz life or something on television, and just be a real couple. I thought he did a great job of being in my world, but allowing me into his world, too, meaning when he'd talk about the things he was interested in, I felt I could just listen to him forever. It was never just all about me. If we had to travel somewhere because of a work engagement, we'd turn it into a vacation where we would go on runs together, eat at someplace wonderful, stay up late to watch movies in the hotel.

Best of all, Matt had a great attitude about Hollywood. He got a kick out of it, but wasn't overly impressed by it, either. It's a unique quality that I'd been hoping to find in a partner.

When Matt moved to LA, he didn't have a job at first, but then he found employment as an IT guy. The fact that he kept going from job to job, though—comments like "They're all idiots" and "I can't work in that environment anymore" kept coming up—was something I probably should not have turned a blind eye to at the time. But I was busy myself, and more and more I realized I needed somebody to be with me at events like the awards that I hosted or various stand-up gigs around the country. I'd ask Matt to come with me to these jobs, and he did because I think he sensed my need to have a supportive presence with me. But it admittedly caused problems with him keeping jobs back home.

I really felt our relationship was working, though. One day, on a wonderful vacation in Mexico, we were in a beachfront hut—romantic, calm, beautiful—when Matt turned to me and said, "You know, Kathy, I love you and you mean the world to me. I'm so happy to be with you, and I feel that you've made my life better."

Matt often said loving things like that. "I love you, too," I said.

"I'd like to know if you would be my wife."

I was completely unprepared for this. "Are you doing a bit?" I joked.

He laughed and said, "No!"

"Seriously? You're asking me, or is this a bit?"

"No, I am not doing a bit!"

We were both laughing hard now, and then I said, "Did you ask my dad yet?"

"No."

"You're supposed to ask my dad first."

"I don't want to call your dad."

"Well you have to. That's the rule."

The whole thing was light and fun, and we just kept laughing about the formality of marriage proposals, and then I said, "Yes, I would like to marry you!" Pause. "But you have to call my dad."

We went back to LA. Matt called my dad, and Dad made some joke about somebody finally taking me off his back, and that was the start of our engagement. Since I wasn't inclined to have a typical wedding, I came up with an idea from an *Oprah* segment where a couple got a free wedding by promoting all the vendors on all the place cards at the tables. Well, I could afford a wedding, so getting a free one was pointless. But I always felt that shelling out tens of thousands, if not hundreds of thousands of dollars, on a one-day party was a waste. What if I took the money I would have spent on a nuptials bash, donated it to charity instead, and then got people to sponsor the wedding?

I got the venue, the booze, the cake, everything donated, and in return these people got publicity because the wedding was covered by *People* magazine and *Entertainment Tonight,* and I talked about it everywhere I could. I then turned around and wrote a check to

Again with Brooke and looking kind of gay. God help me, I married the wrong person.

amFAR, the Foundation for AIDS Research, for $50,000, and requested all guests donate to them directly rather than give me gifts. In addition to being romantic and fun, the day also benefited an important organization.

I made Brooke Shields my maid of honor, because her celebrity would help the charity tie-in cause. "Are you sure you want my face to be the last face you see as a single woman?" she responded, when I asked her to play this role.

The wedding party. On the right is Matt's best man. On the
left is my best man.

"If I can get you a great loaner Richard Tyler dress, then yes, I'm
sure." What I meant was, if I could tell *People* magazine that model
Brooke Shields would be wearing a Richard Tyler cocktail dress (*People*
eats that shit up), then I was one step closer to getting a publication to
cover it. By the way, both my beautiful wedding dress and Brooke's
black cocktail bridesmaid dress were designed by Richard Tyler. She
got to keep hers. I had to give mine back.

Of course, Brooke being Brooke, she wanted to throw a bridal
shower for me, even though I told her she didn't have to do anything
but show up on my wedding day looking beautiful. With only a week's

Dad walking me down the aisle. Who knows what inappropriate joke he just cracked.

notice, she decided to host a shower for me at Chado Tea Room, with tea and scones and all things girly. Well, it was so D-list, it cracked me up. Get this: *two people* showed up: my hair and makeup person Lisa, and my mom. I thought it was awesome, really more a "luncheon" than anything as high and mighty as a "shower." But Brooke felt terrible. "Everybody I invited was unavailable!" she said.

I sort of couldn't believe it. "*You* called people up personally and they said no?"

"I know," she said dejectedly.

"Well, that's a testament to how people feel about me," I said, and we all laughed.

February 18, 2001, was the big day. We held the wedding at a restaurant on the top floor of a building in Hollywood, and it was really casual and fun, just like I'd hoped. I loved the tongue-in-cheek elements, like walking down the aisle to Night Ranger's "Sister Christian," and Bill Maher toasting about how he hates marriage and thought I was marrying Matthew Modine. But Brooke rocked her toast as only Brooke could, saying how she felt Matt was this great calming figure in my life, and brought out my best side. *People* magazine and *ET* were thrilled with the celebrities in attendance: Jenny McCarthy, Camryn Mannheim, Eric Idle, Jane Krakowski, the cast of *Suddenly Susan*. The food was wonderful—although the cliché is true, neither Matt nor I had a bite of any of it—my dad gave a funny speech, and I was surrounded by my friends and loved ones. Plus, when Matt and I got home, after hitting a drive-thru to eat something, we discovered Brooke and her husband Chris had surprised us by putting rose petals all over the bed. It was undeniably romantic and gorgeous.

The first years of married life with Matt were, I have to say, blissfully happy. We got along great, and even when we didn't, we were able to talk about our problems and come to agreements. He wasn't a screamer. He'd be bright and rational about it. Our disagreements were hardly fights.

There were red flags, though, that I wish I'd paid more attention to, like Matt's work situation and his inability with money. After he quit his last job, he started expressing an interest in opening his own computer/IT consulting business. We had a pretty serious discussion about it one night. I told him it was obvious this was really his dream, and that it seemed he was better suited being in business for himself rather than working someplace for someone else.

"How about this," I said. "I will foot the bill for your new business entirely for a year. We'll build you an office downstairs in the house, and I'll do everything I can to support you."

For a year or so it didn't bother me that he wasn't going to a regular job job, because he was ostensibly starting his business, most of his clients being friends of mine I had hooked him up with. Plus, with *Suddenly Susan* in the past, I was taking more road gigs, and he could accompany me because he was making his own hours.

Matt's mother, however, wasn't so sure about him starting his own business. "I don't think it's a good idea," she said to me once.

"Why?" I said.

"Matt needs structure. If he's just running his own business and accountable to no one but clients, that's not enough structure."

"Well, I believe in him and think he can do it."

I thought, if it doesn't work after a year, he could go back to an in-house job. But what was beginning to worry me was that he could never seem to amass any kind of savings. Sometimes he'd get mad that being on the road with me didn't allow him to service his clients properly. I'd agree and then he wouldn't go on the next trip. But after a month I'd ask him if he'd saved anything. I was covering at least 95 percent of our expenses. He'd say, "I have eighty dollars in the bank."

He was charging his clients $100 an hour. He'd tell me he was working five hours a day. He'd have made $2,500 that week. Where was the money, I'd ask?

He never had an answer. "I don't know, I don't know," he'd say. "I'm not good with money." This was such a foreign concept to me, being an adult and not knowing the basics about how to manage money.

I suppose I knew he wasn't good with money because I had gotten a different call from his mother before we got married, about his car. She told me then that Matt didn't have good enough credit to get a loan for his car, so she'd cosigned, but then Matt began defaulting on his car payments and it was beginning to affect her credit. This surprised me, because while I knew Matt wasn't making much money, I certainly thought it was enough to make car payments.

"I thought you should know this," Matt's mother said to me, "because I don't think Matt realizes that it made my interest payments on my house much higher. After you marry him, this is going to become *your* problem," she joked.

I said, "Well, I'm sorry he did that to you, but I'm not going to co-sign a car for him. I can't have him or anyone destroying my hard-earned credit rating." It's at those moments that I can't help but hear my finance-savvy mom's voice in my head saying, "Keep your money separate. If he's bad with money, don't commingle it. Use your head." I didn't tell Maggie about this, but I'm sure her radar would have gone off louder than mine did at the time.

When I confronted Matt about the car payments, he was remorseful, saying, "I didn't realize," but he also said his mother was exaggerating and being overly dramatic. But I had to stress to him, "Matt, this is a serious thing. You're a thirty-year-old man, you shouldn't need your mother to cosign for a car, and you never told me you'd defaulted on payments."

He said he'd pay her back, and I believed him. His finances were never my business, anyway. We didn't have any joint accounts. Frankly, I've never understood joint accounts between spouses. I can't imagine wanting to add my name to anyone's bank account, checking account, or credit card for any reason. Remember, folks, I was no spring chicken when I got married. I was forty. I thought the best way to make it a nonissue was to make it a nonissue and keep things separate. So I never asked to see paychecks, and I wasn't over his shoulder micromanaging him beyond occasionally showing concern for whether he'd saved money or not. But I really thought between not paying for the house and sharing my insurance, and only having a few bills—a car, a cell phone, not much else—that there was no way he couldn't make that work.

Those "I have only eighty dollars in the bank" conversations were worrisome, but I never saw them as the end of the world. Remember, when you're in love with someone, you tend to overlook things. Mind you, when it came to his business, he was always getting up to go somewhere for it. He seemed to be on the phone constantly talking to clients. When I'd speak to friends I'd hooked him up with as clients, they always expressed that they liked Matt and thought he was really nice. I never got into business specifics with them.

Things started getting tense when Matt started having trouble getting clients on his own. Pretty soon he was blaming me for the failure of his business, because as he put it, if he was at Newark airport with me, how could he get to a client's place in forty-five minutes if their computer crashed? I'd feel bad, and started thinking maybe his mother was right: Maybe he did need structure. But from what I could tell, he was always down in his office working, or going off somewhere to work. I trusted him.

The other big red flag, though, was that Matt gained about a hundred pounds in the first two years of our marriage. *A hundred pounds.* When I met Matt he'd been training for a marathon, so the change was striking. I don't care about a guy having ripped abs or anything, but he was putting on the weight so rapidly that I went from thinking, *Oh, he's just getting comfortable,* to me saying, "Matt, is this a sign that you're unhappy? Is something going on?"

He always maintained, "I haven't worked out in a while."

"Well, I'm not always working out, either, but you seem to have quadrupled your intake of food. Is it the classic case of you stuffing down feelings? Do you need to express yourself more? What's up? I love you, anyway. You know that. I'm attracted to you, any shape. But are you bothered by something? I would be asking you these questions if you'd had a dramatic weight loss as well. What's upsetting you?"

His steadfast response was always, "I've just got to get back to running."

I'd try to get him to go jogging with me, but he'd keep making excuses for why he couldn't go. What could I do? I couldn't force him to stop eating. Instead I just put faith in him coming to terms with whatever it was that was making him overeat.

When *The D-List* started filming in late 2004, we actually made his weight a story line, that Matt was going to have gastric bypass surgery. He never did, but I knew that filming in general would be another strain on a normal life for him—especially growing his business—so I made sure he was financially compensated by Bravo (Jessica, too), and I thought that would help him feel better about earning a living.

He seemed comfortable with the mic pack on, and I thought he was very natural on camera. *Maybe this will be our life,* I thought. *He makes a living, whether nominal or good, and I subsidize the rest.* That was fine with me. I never held it against him that he wasn't going to become a millionaire. I never thought, *I'm going to put my foot down until he makes this level of money.*

Instead, I thought, *You know what? We're lucky. We're in a position where I can carry the financial burden, and he can be the guy who's there for me. This can work.*

When *D-List* filmed, all those potential worries about Matt's ways with money, his weight gain, and his struggles with business seemed to evaporate. Here we were, having fun together, but also working together, as a real team.

One afternoon, a phone call from my accountant changed everything.

16
MY
MARRIAGE
ENDS

It was the end of a shooting day on season one of *The D-List,* and the crew had just left the house. We'd been in Las Vegas that morning filming as well, so it really had been a long day.

The phone rang, and it was my accountant. He said, "Hey, I just got a call from your bank, and somebody tried to use your ATM in two different states today."

I appreciated the concern, but I felt I was able to nip that call in the bud. "Oh well, we were shooting in Vegas this morning, so that was me," I said.

"Well, somebody tried to use that same card this afternoon at a Universal City ATM."

That sounded odd. "I've never gone to a Universal City ATM."

"Well, I'm looking back now on your withdrawals," he said, "and I see several from a Universal City ATM. I just assumed it was the one you went to."

"I rarely take cash out," I explained to him. "I'm more likely to put stuff on cards and get the miles. But actual cash, I might withdraw $500 a month at the most."

"Well, I'm seeing two different ATM cards, used back-to-back at

---

Left: Matt and I holding on, perhaps a little too long. (Photo: Bravo/NBCU Photo Bank)

this machine. One has a withdrawal of a thousand dollars and one is for five hundred. Someone is using those cards approximately once every three weeks, and they're taking out fifteen hundred dollars. With the receipts I'm looking at, it looks like whoever this was withdrew about twenty thousand. And I've only gone back a few months."

I immediately got a sick feeling in the pit of my stomach. This wasn't a case of my cards being missing and I call it in to the bank. This was twenty grand stolen out of my account. Shit.

"Who has your PIN number?" my accountant asked.

"The only people who have my PIN number are me, Matt, and Jessica."

Sometimes I sent Jessica out to get cash. Other times Matt and I would be running around doing errands and if I was driving, I would pull over and ask him to go to the ATM and get cash out for me. That's why he had my PIN number. Oh, and he was also *my husband*.

My mind was racing at this point. I'd have to ask Jessica point-blank if she took the money, which didn't sit well with me. Could there have been a worker in the house who might have gotten hold of the cards? While I was talking to the accountant, I went to my wallet.

"I'm holding those ATM cards," I told my accountant. "They haven't been stolen."

"Well, if Matt and Jessica are the only ones who have access to your ATM cards, and they both have your PIN numbers, you'd better ask them. You've got twenty minutes, because I've called the bank, and they're going to screen the tape of whoever the person was who went this afternoon and withdrew the fifteen hundred dollars."

I hung up the phone, and steeled myself for an incredibly uncomfortable moment. I found Jessica walking up the stairs with a file in her hand, and I leaned over from the railing and said really off-handedly, "Jessica, I have to ask you a really weird question. I just found out somebody got my ATM cards and they've withdrawn twenty thousand dollars from my bank account. So I've just got to ask you, did you ever take my ATM cards?"

She said, "No! *God* no," and I'll never forget this, Jessica's whole neck got this red rash instantly. She had a look on her face of utterly genuine confusion. To me it was completely the physical reaction of someone innocent. I knew it wasn't from guilt. First of all, Jessica's a terrible liar, thank God, and second of all, if someone wrongly accused me of something, I'd get sweaty and nervous and shake, too, probably, thinking, *Oh my God, what do I have to say to defend myself?* I know I would. This was a girl I'd been working with for three years, who was legitimately flipped out that this had happened. In any case, she took a beat and said, "Is there anything I can do to help you find out?" Also not something a guilty person says. I told her I'd get back to her when I found out more.

Well, being pragmatic, I couldn't completely rule out my husband, so I decided to ask him directly, too. He could certainly ask the same of me if something like this came up. I called him into our bedroom, closed the doors, and he sat down. He was pretty large by this point, and he cut an immense figure in the chair. "Okay," I said, "I have to ask you something, and it's a really hard question, but just be completely honest with me, no matter what the answer is."

I still really didn't think it could be Matt. I was already thinking of who had been in the house over the last few months, and my mind was racing. "I just got a call from the accountant, and what they're telling me is somebody has taken my ATM card, gone to a Universal City ATM and systematically taken out twenty thousand dollars from my accounts over the last few months. So I have to ask, have you been taking my ATM card and stealing money?"

"No."

"Okay, because you and Jessica are the only ones with my PIN number, and I've already asked Jessica."

"It wasn't me," he said.

For some reason, the phrase "due diligence" came into my head. I was trying to think rationally. Suspicion started creeping into my mind, so I just wanted to stay with the facts. I wanted Matt to know everything that I'd been told by the accountant. "All right. Well, you should know the accountant is on the phone with the bank, and they're going to look at the tape, and he's going to call me back in about five minutes. So, I know it sounds crazy, Matt, but if you're on that tape, they're going to know, and it's going to be all over their office."

That's when he said, "It was me."

I have to say, that moment was absolutely like being socked in my heart. Not like being punched in the gut or the face, but cold-cocked in my heart. My heart started beating really fast, the way it does when you're faced with having to realize something you don't want to accept as true, that a horrible inevitability is at hand. I couldn't pretend I didn't hear it. He came right out and said it. But only after . . .

That's when I thought, *My God, he only admitted it when he knew there was a tape and he would get caught.* Ouch.

The accountant called back, and all I said was, "Matt admitted it. I'll call you later."

I was physically shaking. But I wasn't crying. I wasn't hysterical. Several things were flying around in my head. Number one, obviously, was *why*? Number two, *what have I done to set the stage for this? In what way have I created an environment where this could happen?* Number three, we're in the middle of shooting a reality show. The crew is coming back tomorrow morning at 9 a.m. *How does that work?*

When shitty things happen to me, I go into processing mode. I wouldn't say my approach dealing with the situation was matter-of-fact, but I started thinking about the actions I needed to take right then and there. I set aside feelings and emotion and instead began taking care of business. I wanted to tell Jessica immediately that she was off the hook, because I felt it was my responsibility to put her mind at ease after my uncomfortable inquiry. But that meant, by process of elimination, that Jessica was going to know it was Matt. I wanted him to know that I had to go do this.

"I understand. You need to do whatever you need to do right now. I've done a horrible thing to you, so whoever you need to tell, whoever you need to process this with, I understand. You've earned the right to get through this however you see fit."

"Okay, then," I said. "Let's take this one step at a time. Why did you do it?"

"I don't know, I don't know, I don't know."

He was very still. He didn't cry, he wasn't cavalier, and he seemed to be grasping the gravity of the situation. I told him to walk me through it, and while his reaction wasn't exactly shifty—meaning he wasn't making up crazy lies about it—what he was saying just wasn't adding up. "My business isn't going well. I'm not really making money. I just didn't have any money."

"Okay, but what made you think that you were entitled to just take money from me?"

All he could say was, "I just felt I needed more money."

My head was spinning with big questions. *What did that mean, he needed "more money"? Did I now have to start questioning everything with this guy? Did I marry the wrong man? Did he really love me? Ever? Did I think I was overlooking a small thing when in fact I was overlooking a giant thing?* Because I don't know why just because there's a piece of paper saying we're married that I have to lose half of my income to someone, half of what I earned from my own hard work. In fact, if Matt had asked for a joint account—which he didn't—I would have been instantly suspicious. If I'd married Steve Wozniak, I certainly wouldn't have expected half his money, or half his earnings during the time we were together. I know California is a community property state, but these were ATM cards that had my name on them, that were accounts to which only I had contributed. Matt had his own ATM card, and his own income from his job, as far as I knew.

At this point, I asked Matt to walk me through the process of obtaining this money. I was obsessed with wanting to know the details of it all.

He said he would get up early in the morning and while I was asleep—because if I can sleep in, I will—he'd sneak into my wallet, take out both ATM cards, and race to that Universal City ATM, which was three minutes from the house. He'd then take out the maximum amounts you could—$1,000 from one card, $500 from the other—and return home with the cash, put it in his pocket, then put the ATM cards back in my wallet. Then this man—who knew more than anyone in my life how hard I'd worked to earn that money, who'd witnessed all the crappy gigs, the exhaustion, the long days that started early in the morning with filming and ended with getting on a plane at night to fly to the next show—would crawl back into bed with me.

Does that not sound like a betrayal of trust? You can argue the whole "his money is your money, your money is his money" thing all day long, but I'm not sneaking into anybody's wallet and taking their personal ATM cards.

This was not a situation where he'd come to me and said "Can you loan me twenty thousand dollars?" It's the secretiveness that got to me. Regardless of California state law, I'm sorry, in my book it's stealing. I was beginning to feel like a wife from one of those *Dateline* episodes where the husband has another family in Wyoming.

After I confronted Matt, I did say, "Why didn't you just ask me for money?"

"Because I knew I couldn't justify why I didn't have my own money."

This seemed a bigger issue than I realized. "So not only do you need money, but you're now telling me that you haven't been working as much as you led me to believe? I thought you had several clients, and you were making three hundred dollars to five hundred dollars a day."

Shaking his head, "No."

Okay. I began steeling myself for the next revelation. "How many clients do you really have?"

"Sometimes I have weeks where I make two hundred dollars," he said.

Okay. "Well, you're getting up every single day at six or seven in the morning, and you come home at five or six at night. What are you doing? Where do you go?"

"I drive around."

Okay. "Drive around where?"

He told me he'd go to the movies, go to the park, and go to the drive-thru. This is where he confessed to compulsively overeating. I remember him saying one thing that did make sense. He told me the real reason he had put on so much weight was because he felt so guilty about taking the money. Now I knew where the 100-extra-pounds issue came from. But then I remembered how he'd tell me in great detail about his clients and workday, the computers he was fixing, the people causing him trouble, how he was trying to get $110 an hour instead of $100, all of it.

I didn't know what was true anymore. This bright, capable guy was apparently living and building a life that was this very intricate lie. It seemed so odd to me. Why couldn't he put all that energy and time and thought into his work instead?

"Matt, I have to ask you, what did you do with the money? It was cash. That's a lot of tax-free money. Did you buy stuff? Do you have anything to show for it? Is there anything else you need to tell me?" I was desperate for answers.

"I just kind of pissed it away."

"On what?" Because it's not like Matt ever showed up with a Rolex, or a sports car, or a $1,000 suit. I never saw any evidence of what he did with it, aside from the occasional trip to the electronics store to buy some new gadget for his computers, but it never seemed exorbitant. He just kept maintaining he didn't know how he spent the cash. To this day, in fact, I have no idea what he did with it. Later that day the accountant told me that at that one Universal City ATM alone, the withdrawn amount was $72,000. So that's $72,000 completely unaccounted for. He says he has no idea where it went. He never really gave me an answer.

At this point I went into fix-it mode. That's what I know. It's my comfort zone. Yes, it was devastating emotionally. Yes, I was in shock. But like so many people who the night before found out their partner was cheating or lying or stealing, or who received some sort of earth-shattering news and still have to get up the next morning and make breakfast and drive the kids to school, I was no different. I didn't have the luxury of falling apart and bringing everything around me to a halt, anymore than anyone else does in these situations. I believed we should continue with the show, because I wanted Matt to continue making money from the show, and I needed the stability of work. I didn't think the answer was for both of us to quit working and cry in separate homes for two years. Besides, I just couldn't make a colossal decision only an hour after getting the initial call from my accountant.

I started spewing whatever suggestion came into my head. I was trying to make sense of everything at this point. I needed an action plan.

"Here's what you're going to do," I said. "You're going to go to a program called Debtors Anonymous. It's exactly like AA. It's twelve steps, and it's free. Or maybe one dollar a meeting. You never have to give more than that. It's a program that helps all kinds of people that are having all kinds of money problems." I was hoping he'd get the tools he needed to help him through whatever problem this was. I was grasping at straws, but I knew that I had friends who had had great success in various twelve-step programs. I told him he had to go tonight, and could go to a meeting every day if he needed to. I also suggested he go to Overeaters Anonymous meetings, because it was a program that I had attended several years earlier and found incredibly helpful in dealing with my own food issues.

He agreed, and then I went to talk to Jessica.

"Look, I can't go into the details, but I know it's not you," I said. "You probably figured out that it's Matt. There's no sense in trying to hide it."

"I'm so sorry," she said.

"Well, let's see if this is an insurmountable problem or not."

Matt and I started couples therapy shortly thereafter, and I began to feel good about the future of our marriage. During those sessions he'd express remorse, saying what he did was a bad thing, although when the therapist would ask if he had a reason for what he did, he'd usually give the same response over and over, "I don't know, I don't know."

Through the course of therapy, he did admit to entitlement issues. "I understand it's not a healthy thing for me to feel entitled to all of your money and everything you have," he said. "I understand you worked really hard for it, and I basically goofed off."

Times like these made me think we could work things out. I took our marriage seriously, and while I'd been hit with a real whopper, I knew couples could have big problems and still be together for decades. One of my attorneys, however, did try to have the "come to Jesus" talk with me. He's an attorney. I'm his client. It's his job to be direct. And I'll never forget the way he worded it. "I know you love Matt," he said. "He hit you for seventy-two thousand dollars this time. Next time it could be five hundred thousand dollars. And at that point, you have no one to blame but yourself, because you won't be able to act like you didn't know what you now know." It was the whole fool-me-twice-shame-on-me scenario. But I didn't want to believe it. I couldn't argue with his logic, but I still wanted to make it work. At the insistence of my attorneys, who were thinking more rationally than I was when it came to protecting everything I'd worked so hard for, I filed for divorce. But the idea was still to try to work it out. Even if it led to some uncomfortable moments, like on *Jimmy Kimmel Live.*

"I heard you're getting divorced but you're staying with your husband," Jimmy said.

"Well, you know, Jimmy, love is odd! Sometimes it's not till you get divorced that you realize you really love the person!"

But it was kind of true. It's what I was feeling. So Matt and I kind of carried on as we had, with not a lot changing on the surface. Matt seemed to understand why filing for divorce was in my best interest, but he also appeared to go along with the notion that we were trying to mend the relationship. Sometimes we'd fight about what happened, and there'd be tears. But he never denied his actions, never said I was crazy or I made things up. He didn't argue about the fact that he did it. If it came up, he'd say, "Yeah, I've got to work on that."

He started leaving the house on a regular basis, and while I never attended OA meetings with him, let me tell you something: I have never seen anyone in my life so dedicated to healthy eating and rapid weight loss. He dove into that program headfirst. He shed pounds so quickly, that it led me to believe that he really wanted to change his entire life. That gave me a lot of encouragement. I was actually concerned that he was getting a little too obsessive about losing the weight—he took his own low-calorie food with him everywhere—but I thought, he's bettering himself. Good. What I didn't know until later was that while he *was* committed to a weight-loss program, he had been lying about regularly meeting with folks to deal with his money issues. It became the same old thing. He'd say he was going to Pasadena for a DA meeting, tell me the details about it: about his new sponsor he'd had coffee with, the work groups he'd joined, the columns of numbers they'd have him write out on notepads. Then a month later he'd admit, "I didn't go."

"What about two nights ago when you came back at nine thirty and told me about the meeting?" I said.

"I didn't go."

"You made that up?"

"Well, I just drove around."

"Look, Matt, it's great that you're steaming broccoli three times a day, but I think the debt and the compulsive lying is your core issue to deal with. The overeating is a symptom of that. I think DA is the program you need to focus on. Matt, if you can lose one hundred pounds, then you can do anything. You've clearly got the discipline and the strength."

He would agree halfheartedly, but it was clear that he had completely thrown himself into losing all this weight. If actions speak louder than words, then by his rapidly shrinking body it was obvious he had focused on his weight-loss program over anything else.

But he'd also tell bizarre *little* lies, too. Small things that made no sense. Matt would say he talked to a mutual friend of ours, then I would talk to the friend and they'd say, "No, I haven't talked to Matt in weeks."

When I'd ask Matt why he said that, it was again with "I don't know, I don't know."

What did he gain by telling little lies? Would it ever end? When I tried to discuss it, and God knows I tried many times, he seemed very shut down, and really, you can't force someone to give you answers. So anytime this came up, I would liken his reaction to that of a little kid who's gotten caught doing something, has just checked out in his mind, and tries to end the conversation as quickly as possible. While I was frustrated by these moments, I kept thinking there must be an answer; I just hadn't figured it out yet.

A big change happened when Matt and I were watching a program on compulsive liars on *Oprah,* of all things. Of course, it made me uncomfortable. The similarities to Matt were weird. Well, one of the liars on the show wound up in prison. When the show was over, I turned to Matt and said, "You know, Matt, if I wasn't your wife, you'd be in jail right now. I hope you're smart enough not to embezzle from one of your clients, cause they'd put your ass in jail in two seconds."

And incidentally, when we were initially dating, Matt told me that when he was in the army and stationed in Germany, he'd gone to military jail, for stealing a buddy's ATM card and trying to use it. At the time he told me this, I just chalked it up to being nineteen years old and stupid. Now, in retrospect, I realize I didn't have the appropriate reaction. I focused on the honesty of him telling me it, rather than the fact that he was caught stealing.

Anyway, when I mentioned prison to him, he had the oddest reaction.

"I think I'd be fine in jail," he said.

"Oh come on, pasty white guy," I said. "What are you talking about?"

"I really think I could survive in prison," he said. "I would know how to assimilate, I would know how to blend in to the point where I just don't think anyone would bother me."

That was a chilling moment for me. The fact that he'd given consideration to how he would assimilate in prison scared the shit out of me. What it told me was, *this guy's not afraid of anything, and more important, not afraid of getting caught.* I don't know about you, ladies, but I'd want a husband who's actively taking steps to stay out of prison. It freaked me out enough that I made a drastic move that night.

"This is really hard, Matt," I said. "But you have to move out."

Matt found a roommate to share an apartment, but I still held out hope for a miracle reconciliation, because despite the gravity of the situation, I couldn't stomach the notion that things wouldn't work out. Filming for the second season of *The D-List* was coming up, and I wanted my husband to be at home, and to be honest, I was determined not to act out my divorce for a comedy-driven reality show. Like anyone else, my responsibilities were such that I couldn't afford to take an infinite amount of time off to fix my personal life. I actually thought we could film the show during the day and when the cameras left, we could run to couples therapy or somehow work on the damaged part of our relationship off camera. Besides, that's not what the show was. Then we had a therapy session in which the therapist actually told Matt, "You have to start doing things to help Kathy. I'm suggesting you go back to work, Kathy, and Matt, probably the best thing you can do for her is go back to work as usual."

So when the crew began filming again, they never knew that Matt would arrive at the house half an hour before the call time, and he'd leave twenty minutes after they left. It was excruciating, really tough. At one point I took him back for a few months, then we'd be back in therapy, and I'd believe him for a while and be optimistic, and then I'd catch him in another lie. It wasn't some coldhearted decision where I hated him and he just showed up to support me. I was hoping for the best the whole time. And that went through the entire season.

I can hear the naysayers now: I was filming a reality show, but deceiving people. Well, I honestly never felt that, because number one, the show is not A&E's *Intervention*. It's not a show that claims to help people. Just like my act is given to exaggeration, the show films heightened comedic experiences in my life. My first responsibility is to make people laugh, and a show where I'm crying or hashing out serious problems in my marriage with my husband is not what an audience signs on for. It's not *Breaking Bonaduce*.

Well, as filming on season two came to a close, things hadn't been very good between us. We hadn't been getting along, and we were both starting to realize it wasn't going to work out. Pessimism was finally settling in with me. Matt seemed emotionally out the door. But a part of me still saw him the same way I did the first day we met, or the day he proposed, or the day we had some other great time together.

We had our wrap party for season two in Vegas, because we'd been shooting my appearance at a very D-listy casino outside of the city.

Matt was there and when it came time to make the party happen, he was at the height of his greatness. He got all the food and the booze, and when people started showing up in my suite, he was a wonderful host, making people laugh, telling stories, and I was proud to be with him. It was the guy I'd said yes to on that beach in Mexico.

The next morning, though, we had a really bad fight. I honestly don't even remember what it was about, but it was a doozy. Matt said, "I can't take this anymore. It's over. I'm going back to LA and moving my stuff out for good."

I was sobbing hysterically, and I had a show to do that night, so I couldn't follow him. One of the crew saw Matt get on the shuttle for the airport, and I made some excuse for him. The crew still knew nothing. Thankfully I had a couple of nice gays with me and they both said, "Kathy, you've got a show tonight. Focus on that. Matt's not coming back today. We'll stay with you one more night and fly home with you tomorrow."

They kept me company, and it was really wonderful and comforting. When I got back to LA, Matt already had been there with his sister and her boyfriend and they had taken all of his stuff. Matt and I made an appointment to get together and talk that night. We sat down and I was hysterically crying and despondent, and he said something at that moment that was in retrospect probably the kindest thing he could have done.

"Kathy, it's not going to work," he said. "Stop trying to make it work. I don't love you anymore."

"I want to try again!" I said, rattling off all manner of ideas I had for trying to prop this thing up one more time.

"We've tried everything," he said. "It's really, really over."

When he walked out the door, I just fell apart. But it's what I had to hear. I needed him to sit me down and say in no uncertain terms that it was done, and that he didn't want me to try anymore. He hadn't wanted to try for a while. "Now it's just ridiculous," he'd said. "You're trying to force something."

He was right. One of my worst character flaws is that it takes me too long to "get" things. I have to be hit over the head with a sledgehammer. It is this very quality of never accepting defeat, going against the odds and not always listening to reason that while serving me so well in my career, has screwed me over in my love life.

I was still a wreck when later that night I asked a friend to come over for support. He helped me out in a great way by saying, "Okay, you've got to cut Matt off entirely now. You have to act like Matt is not reachable." That's because even through our separations, I'd call him if I missed him, or he'd call me if he missed me, or if I'd forgotten where I put something in the house I'd contact him. All those little bits of knowledge that I'd counted on him for—facts about meetings I'd had, who worked where, who said what when, computer know-how, the way something operated—I was suddenly worried about. My friend said, "There's nothing we can't figure out ourselves."

That talk with my friend was very liberating. Because I would never see Matt again. Our divorce was finalized in May 2006. I had begun the process of moving on.

Looking back at it all, I really had been a complete pussy about realizing it was over, even though in the back of my mind the trust that should exist between a married couple was 100 percent shot. I wish I had one of those *Stella Got Her Groove Back* moments where I turned to him and said, "Get out!" But in the end it was Matt who had to hit me over the head with the fact that we were through.

It was an equally hard decision to appear on *Larry King Live* and go public with the details of our breakup. I don't know if that was the right thing to do then, but my ego just couldn't take the speculative chatter—in the public and even from friends—that somehow the old battle-ax nightmare Kathy Griffin ran her poor, sweet husband into the ground until he had to leave. Certainly there are women classier than I who would have taken what happened between us to the grave, but my whole life has been putting my reality out there and owning up to it. For better or for worse.

17

A WIN,
A LOSS

My Life on the D-List, or as I like to call it, "My Little Ghetto Fake Network Show," has actually been the best thing that's ever happened to my career. Through the show, I've gotten to meet some of the greatest people, and have experienced some truly hilarious moments. It's led to some high points in my life, and been there to capture some low ones, too. Let's start with the highs.

Hi, Oprah. I didn't notice you walk into the room. You and Gayle came in at a great time. I was just about to start my EMMY STORIES!

It was the summer of 2006, and season two of *The D-List* had been airing on Bravo, when I hopped on Rosie O'Donnell's gays-and-lesbians-and-children-of-gays-and-lesbians-and-the-straight-people-who-love-them cruise to Alaska to perform. Now, even when I was on a sitcom for four years, I was never one of those girls who got up at 4 a.m. on Emmy nomination day and got my hair and makeup done so a crew could film me jumping up and down when they announce the nominees at 5 a.m. It never occurred to me in a gazillion years I'd ever be nominated for *anything,* much less an Emmy award. Nothing against the kind citizens who once gave me the key to Louisville, Kentucky, or the kind citizens of the gay porn community, who gave me an Honorary Gay for a Day trophy. Represent!

Left: My daughters Emmy and Emily.

Well, I'm sleeping in my cabin on Rosie's ship when I wake up and see the light on my phone blinking. Jessica had called from her cabin and left me a message. I played it back and listened to her very casually, very dryly go through the litany of things I had to do that day.

"Okay, Rosie wants you to go to her room in a couple of hours because you two are going to go over the show later. We're supposed to go watch some iceberg, and I'm not sure I want to stay up for it. The dry cleaning's going to be ready on Thursday. And congratulations, you got nominated for an Emmy. Bye!"

I was like, *"What??"*

I called her back. "What was that last part again?"

In her uniquely deadpan Jessica delivery, she said, "Yeah, right, that's so great."

I had to say, "Jessica, I think that should have been the *first* thing on your message! And I think you should have knocked on my door and woken me up! Hello?"

Of course, I was convinced it wasn't real. Somehow there'd been a typo. Kathie Lee Gifford was the real nominee. There's a sound engineer somewhere named Katey Griffith who got a technical nomination. It didn't help that I was on a freakin' boat in Alaska where my cell phone wouldn't work, all the while trying to find a landline that didn't have static.

Once I got the nomination confirmed from about seven different people, I believed it. And man, was I over the moon. Really bursting with excitement. I called Mom and Dad first, of course, and they were thrilled. I was flooded with emails from the network, and of course the mucky-mucks like Jeff Zucker and Jeff Gaspin who couldn't wait to tell me how they knew all along.

The reaction across the entertainment world was both clichéd and surprising. I knew I'd get plenty of "She's horrible! Why her?" reactions. But I can't tell you how many coldhearted old-timers—agents, publicists, veteran actors, people from my Groundlings days—who said to me some variation of: "Out of all the people I know who have been kickin' around, you really deserve this." That was my favorite thing. Nobody was saying I was going to win. I mean, nobody thought

I'd beat *Extreme Makeover: Home Edition* for Best Reality Program, including me. But it was really nice to hear from people whom I had known from around the way—casting directors who told me to get a nose job, agents who'd told me I was too fat, my peers who had surpassed me in television—that whether they'd ever liked me or not, I'd worked hard and deserved to be recognized.

Plus, simply put: The show was good!

Now, the reality show category I was nominated in is part of the Creative Arts Emmys, not the main draw Emmys you see in prime time where mercury poison-sensitive Jeremy Piven wins every fucking year for *Entourage.* The Creative Arts Emmys are for the technical awards and guest performers on series. And, obviously, the ugly stepchild that is reality programming. It does, however, have a red carpet, but more like a red rug. You'll recognize some of your *Grey's Anatomy* faves, as long as your faves are Nurse #4, Dead Patient On Bloody Gurney, or Respected Character Actor Whose Name You Don't Know. That meant the event I was going to was in the afternoon, where there's only one camera covering the ceremony, and E! runs a clip show from it that no one watches. In fact, in a truly inspired comedy moment, one of the Bravo network executives said, "Oy. We call them the Shmemmys."

But it's a nomination. Where do I sign, lady?

The other thing I didn't know was that I'd have to sit there for *hours* while sixty-six awards were handed out before they got to Best Reality Program, the second to last category. That's a lot of time to sit and think about how you're not going to be walking up onstage. It doesn't mean, of course, that when they get to your category, you don't all of a sudden have a strong desire to win. When they read *The D-List* as a nominee, along with *Extreme Makeover: Home Edition, The Dog Whisperer, Antiques Roadshow,* and *Penn & Teller: Bullshit,* I couldn't help but think, *What if I hear my name?*

With no expectation to win, I assumed I'd be pretty calm and collected when they got to our category. But let me tell you, that all goes out the window when the presenter announces your name with the other nominees. Sure enough, it was Ty Pennington and his *Oprah*-beloved show that won, and I couldn't help but be disappointed. Their posse all screamed, and as I turned around and looked back—cause I was in the front row—I couldn't get over how big their group was: there were more than two dozen people running down the aisle. Well, the Bravo people were all behind me, and at that point I just wanted to make them laugh, and maybe even make the audience laugh. There's this period of about ten seconds when the applause has died down, and you're waiting for all these people to make their way from row thirty to the stage. I wasn't mic'd, so I just started screaming, "This is bullshit! I was robbed!" I flipped off the *Extreme Makeover* folks, and said to Jessica, who came with me, "Get my bag! We're outta here!" It was all very dramatic, especially because my dress had a train that dragged behind me as I stomped off, and I could hear the twenty-five people behind me laughing their asses off. I think the rest of the audience probably thought I was a psycho bitch, but I didn't care. I "stormed off," diva-style.

I didn't even go to the Governor's Ball, but instead went straight to In-N-Out Burger, thinking, *Triumph!*

Weeks later, I ran into one of the interior designers from *Extreme Makeover: Home Edition,* who let me know in no uncertain terms that he did not think what I did was gracious. I said, "Dude, I was kidding. How could you not know something so over the top like that was a joke?"

It was then that I learned how little a sense of humor Hollywood truly has. So I told the guy to fuck off.

Well, the little show that could came through again, and we were up for an Emmy once more for season two. Only now I decided I was in it to win it. I campaigned every waking minute, and would openly beg television academy members to vote for the show. Bravo had pretty much stopped promoting *The D-List,* so I bought my own billboard above the Mel's Diner sign in Hollywood for one month. It cost me $50,000, but I wanted this show, which I thought was good, to have a shot. Friends in show business thought I was crazy, but my take was, nobody else was going to do it, and this was a major opportunity.

The network started telling me, "We really think you have a shot." There was all this talk of "good feelings" about it. It seemed that our

Iraq episode, where I went to Baghdad and Tikrit to entertain the troops—a show that could not have happened without the help of my good friend Lt. Col. Todd Breasseale—was impressing everyone. I was certainly proud of it, and you certainly weren't going to see something like that on *Antiques Roadshow.*

Nevertheless, I attended the afternoon Shmemmys absolutely convinced I was not going to win, that it would be "Extreme Fuckover" for the third year in a row. With me were Jessica, plus new Team Griffin members Tiffany, my second assistant (because I'm that high maintenance), and tour manager Tom. Also with me was a game plan for what crazy bullshit I was going to pull if I lost again, since I felt like I got some good comedy mileage out of my fake fit the year before. This year, I thought, if I lose, I'm going to run up onstage and start an acceptance speech before *Extreme Makeover* and their boatload of people knows what hit 'em. I know the audience will get really uncomfortable, my peeps will laugh, and it'll be a great Andy Kaufmanesque moment, if I really sell it.

But what I'd also planned for was what would happen if I won.

Because then I'd have everybody's attention legitimately.

I wanted something watercooler-worthy. So the day of the Emmys, I emailed three really funny writer friends, which included a guy named Eric Friedman, who wrote for the Disney Channel show *Zoe 101* starring Jamie Lynn Spears. The reason I asked them to help was because I'm not really good at sound-bite-style comedy, that kind of extreme short form, one-liner stuff. And for an awards show, you don't want to ramble, like I do in my act. You want something short and sweet. Or in my case, short and incredibly shocking.

Well, Eric came up with something I thought was hilarious and subversive:

A lot of people come up here and they thank Jesus for this award. I want you to know that no one had less to do with this award than Jesus. He didn't help me a bit. If it was up to him, Cesar Milan would be up here with that damn dog. So all I can say is suck it, Jesus, this award is my god now!

I thought it was laugh-out-loud funny. I read it to Mom before-hand. "Well, I think it's funny," she said, "but I think you're gonna have trouble."

"Good. Perfect. That's exactly what I'm looking for."

I can't remember if my mom rolled her eyes or not. Probably.

On the red carpet, as I entered the awards show, I got asked about being upset last year that I had lost.

"I wasn't upset, I just wanted to cause a bit of a scene," I said. "But watch this year, it's going to be good either way. Trust me, you'll want to cover it."

I wanted the press at the Shmemmys that night to think they needed to stick around for my category—even if it was sixty-seventh or whatever—because something might happen. Even in the green room, I had Jessica running interference, making sure celebrities didn't leave after they'd made their appearance or won their award. Appar-ently she said to Seth Green, "If I were you, I wouldn't leave. Kathy's going to say something you're going to want to be here for."

My category finally came up, and I was so convinced I was going to lose that I had my right leg up like a pointer dog, ready to run on stage to horn in on Ty Pennington's moment. Then they announced my name. *My* name! We won! Now I was going up onstage in com-plete shock! And what was so wonderful was that we got a huge round of applause. As much as I love to make fun of Hollywood and every-one in it for being cynical, I really felt like the people in that room—and these were my D-list peers, this being the afternoon Shmemmys, not the A-list nighttime Emmys—were happy for me.

But I could also feel an anticipation like, "Uh-oh, what's she gonna say?" Which I loved. I took a second to recover a little bit because I wanted to do Eric's speech justice. I didn't want to dishonor it by screwing it up. I said it verbatim, and it got a big laugh, and I thought it was awesome. That was on a Saturday afternoon, and I enjoyed my-self the rest of the weekend. Everyone I ran into was congratulatory toward me, and I was prepared to get all settled in and wait for a nice mention in the trades about my hilarious speech.

Monday morning, still in the glow of victory, with my Emmy curled up next to me in bed, one of my attorneys called.

"So what happened this weekend?"

"Well, you're not going to believe it, but I WON!"

"Yeah. What happened?"

"*Well*," I beamed, "I was wearing a silver dress, and at first my feet hurt because I was in those heels for so long, but let me tell you, when you hear your name it's like you have a second wind! And everybody was—"

"WHAT DID YOU SAY?" he interrupted.

I guess he wasn't calling me for a fashion recap.

"I've been getting some calls," he said.

"Ugh, not this again," I said. Here was the shitstorm. At this point, it was like that tornado-measuring rod in *Twister.* I knew there was a storm a-comin' but I just didn't know how high it would measure. Visions of getting fired from the E! channel for the Dakota Fanning business—next chapter, people, hold tight—were swirling in my head.

"E! isn't going to air your 'Jesus, suck it' comment," he said.

"All right. That's their choice."

Then he rattled off the list of people I'd offended, who'd been calling him. Mostly religious groups. I can't even remember the names now, because I have a no-apology policy with jokes. I said, "Who cares about them? I'd be nervous if I lost my job, but what do I care if some religious group is offended? It takes nothing more than a stiff wind to piss off those fucking phonies!"

That probably didn't help things.

Then the interview requests started pouring in. I was a hot talk show guest! I did Larry King for the whole hour, Jimmy Kimmel was clamoring to get the first crack at me, and CNN wanted to do a whole debate about my speech! (They wanted me to participate, but I said "Nah, you should work that one out on your own, Wolf Blitzer.") It was so much fun watching the fallout. I remember being at home one night in my pajamas eating cookie dough and turning on CNN and hearing about how "controversial comedian Kathy Griffin stirs up

Tiffany, Jessica, me, and Tom backstage at the Emmys, post-win. What is wrong with Tom?

My mom thinks she just won an Emmy for "her" show.

Hollywood as well as the religious community!" Yay! Sounds like good TV! I turned around as if to call to some imaginary watching buddy— "Hey!"—but there was no one there. I was so excited I forgot I was by myself.

I heard everything in those television back-and-forths, from "How could she offend the Lord?" to "She's funny and it's her first amendment right!" Bill O'Reilly made me Pinhead of the Week. My mother's dream: I was practically on the *O'Reilly Factor*! There were demands that advertisers pull out of our show, which I thought was hilarious because it's not like Fortune 500 companies are buying ad time on *My Life on the D-List*. Seriously, it's, like, foot powder companies and late-night dial-a-date lines. Big deal. Then a religious group in Tennessee took out a full-page ad about me in *USA Today*, and *quoted the speech*. It's the full-page ad Bravo would never have paid for to advertise the show! I was like, "Hey, I got my ad!" I loved being able to call Eric and say, "Hey, your speech is in *USA Today*." I was delighted and so was he. It was like getting an award all over again. Shall I mention the name of the religious group? They were kind enough, after all, to pay $90,000 to promote me and my sense of humor. Nah. Fuck 'em.

Plus, I have to say, my little fake network Bravo that I love to make fun of and have had my problems with, absolutely had my back on this thing. I heard Jeff Zucker was flooded with emails demanding an apology, and he never flinched. For all I know Bravo bitched and moaned behind my back, but never once did they say to me, "How dare you." I think they were very smart. They knew it was ultimately going to be good publicity, and besides, it fits the tone of the show. This isn't as if Nickelodeon had flipped out if Miranda Cosgrove from *iCarly* had said, "Suck it, Allah." I don't think I lost one audience member, and I think it gained me several new ones. There's a market out there for people who are willing to stick their middle finger out in the air to the establishment.

All in all, there really was no downside to my little Emmy broadcast outburst, although I was scheduled to film a commercial for DirecTV, and they called me and rescinded the offer. They actually offered to give me a kill fee, but because they wanted me to sign a confi-

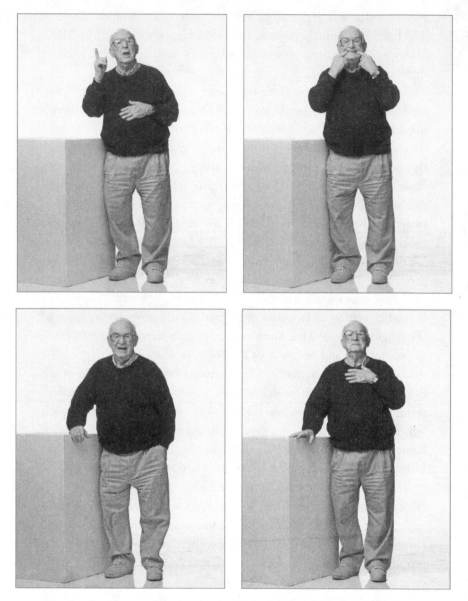

Dear Old Dad (Photo: Michael Grecco/Bravo/NBCU Photo Bank)

dentiality agreement—basically saying I couldn't talk about how they asked me not to do the commercial—I didn't sign it. You know me by now. I don't usually turn down cash. I could have gotten a nice check. But I knew that would haunt me down the line. I'll whore myself out, but I won't censor myself, and especially not in writing.

My feeling is, keep your money, DirecTV. I'd rather be able to put it in the book!

That Emmy win was a glorious time, but there was one person who wasn't around to share it with me: John Patrick Griffin.

We were all nervous as filming started on season three, because Dad's health hadn't been good. The two mantras for that season had been me as a divorcee, openly going on dates with D-list celebrities for the purpose of getting publicity, and the evolution of Jessica into someone closer to me than just an assistant.

But it was Dad's congestive heart failure that was the pervasive issue everybody had to deal with. Questions of scheduling and shooting were always fraught with the tension of: What happens if we all have to go to the hospital suddenly? Can we even include Mom in things? Do I go out of town? We'd shoot Dad where we could, usually at his and Mom's condo so he could sit comfortably in his favorite chair. And the one thing that I was very touched by was that he really seemed to perk up for the show. I know he enjoyed it, and the thing I'm perhaps most grateful for when it comes to *The D-List* is that it's given my family the greatest record of my dad's final years. They always captured the best in him, his humor, his charm, his sweetness.

The last night my dad was completely his old self—lucid, talking, being funny—was when the crew went without me to Mom and Dad's place for an hour-long sit-down interview, the kind that gets used as interstitial bits between the action on the show. He had his arm around my mom, and he was making her laugh—which he did every day of their sixty-five years together—and now that uncut hour is something we'll always have. Later that night he didn't feel well and made one of his then frequent trips to the hospital. He never went home again. He'd really only been ill the last year of his life, and was an unusually healthy guy for freaking ninety. He probably exerted too much energy that night. But I'll bet he forgot about his problems for that hour on film.

It was touch and go for months after that. My family wanted the shooting stopped, so I had to have an important talk with my producers, because John Griffin was such an integral part of *The D-List*. I wasn't going to infringe on my family during this difficult time, but I didn't want it to seem like my dad disappeared into thin air. We had to come up with some way to deal with his imminent passing that was sensitive and realistic. I just couldn't shoot a show where I'm crying when the cameras are off and then acting like everything's fine when the crew follows me to get Botox or do a gig in Des Moines.

My brother John agreed to be taped visiting Dad in the hospital. Mom was off-limits because understandably she just wasn't up to it. Same with Joyce and Gary, who also justifiably didn't feel like it.

Funnily enough, one of my last conversations with Dad was him joking, "Where are the cameras? Where are the cameras?" I know he was kidding, but I felt a lot of guilt during those times because I was working out of town so much. None of us knew which day would be his last.

I was on a plane to Miami to go do Rosie's cruise again and when I landed, I got the message from my sister that Dad had passed away. By the end, Dad had also gotten multiple myeloma—which is a cancer of the plasma cell—and that's what really killed him. I turned around and flew right back, and I told the crew they could tape me getting the house ready for his wake, but that they couldn't film my family, or the memorial service at the church. Nobody would be mic'd, either. But I allowed them to tape the outside of the church. And then the producers did the most wonderful thing: They put together a reel for my dad's memorial, and it was beautiful. By that point Mom had gotten fed up with *The D-List* show in general because in her opinion they were keeping me too busy and away from the family—she obviously had different things on her mind—she didn't want to be on the show anymore, and the show should stop forever because she'd never get over the loss of her husband. But I think she had a change of heart when she saw what the producers had done with all that footage of Dad. It was old commercials, family photos, some great Irish music laid over it. Then I talked to my family about doing a good-bye-Dad episode, which they agreed to, and we arranged for Team Griffin to go to Ireland to bury Dad's ashes at one of his and Mom's favorite places in the old country. I'm very proud of that particular show.

There was no question as to whether I'd go back to work or not. I was shooting the day after the memorial—which was a week after Dad had passed—and then I wanted to honor my contract to perform at Mandalay Bay for two live shows. A lot of people think that's cold and calculated, but know this: My dad was a workhorse. He was a sixty-hour-a-week retail guy who had five kids and shared child-rearing duties. Probably the last conversation I had with Dad, which was via scribbles on paper, because he wasn't able to talk, was me telling him I'd finally booked Carnegie Hall. He struggled to wave his arms, making a circular motion like he had a New Year's Eve clicker in his hand. He couldn't say "Wooo, Dolly!" like he would have whenever he'd share in someone's good news, but I knew he meant it. Then he took a long time writing something on a pad of paper. It was, "Next time, Shea?" As in, the stadium. I still have that piece of paper. My dad's last words to me were about work! Dad got me. And I got him.

I was grateful for the support I got from those shows in Vegas. The news about dad's passing had just gone up online, so I told the crowd, "I'm sure a lot of you know that your beloved John Griffin, my dad, passed away. I just want to thank you guys, because if it wasn't for you here tonight getting my mind off it, I don't know what I'd be doing. Probably just be sobbing. So let's just laugh as hard as we can." I did the show, took a break, then did the second show. One foot in front of the other.

What did my dad mean to me? This may be my favorite story about him, one that exemplifies how important he was to who I became, as in, someone who gets fired, stirs up trouble, and gets debated about on CNN for saying bad things on awards shows. One way to look at it is this: Who I became is really his fault. See, my mom and

Dad and I sticking to our "never pose seriously" policy.

dad have very different senses of humor. My mom is funny because she's a character and doesn't know it. She just naturally says funny things. My dad was more like a comic, and was able to be funny on cue. It was the perfect combination.

When I was a little kid, maybe eight or nine, my dad was constantly working around the house fixing up stuff, being a real handyman. He had a knack for it, but mostly Mom was grateful that it saved us money. One of the other families on our block, the Gillians, had about eight kids. Mr. Gillian had just finished fixing up their rec room. He was proud of his work, and wanted to show it off to my dad, handyman to handyman. So one Sunday after church, my dad brought me over to the Gillians', and they were all there—from the little kids to the parents—sitting in the rec room that was the dad's pride and joy. Mr. Gillian asked my dad, "So, John, what do you think?"

I was standing next to my dad, facing the Gillians, waiting for my dad to say something like "Nice job, Sam!"

Instead, he blurted out, "Wha-a-a-a-t a SHITBOX."

His delivery was dry, his timing was impeccable. It was perfection. The whole room laughed. Mrs. Gillian didn't yell at him or tell him he was inappropriate. He didn't get fired from the block. He didn't get banned Barbara Walters–style from their house. He just taught me that swearing plus shocking plus good timing equals funny.

He killed, and that's when I knew I had the coolest and funniest dad in the neighborhood.

18

FANNING
FLAMES IN
HOLLYWOOD,
AND YES
I MEAN DAKOTA

"Kathy, you're so mean."

"Oh, Kathy, can't you be funny without swearing so much?"

"But Kathy, David Hasselhoff is so sad, why do you have to make fun of him?"

"Come on, Kathy, how can you say that about that sweet Halle Berry?"

And my favorite: "For God's sake, Kathy, Angelina Jolie has *children!*"

Welcome to a typical day in the life. Unfortunately, these are things I've never said to myself. I don't have to. Other people say them to me constantly. I keep it simple. My number one job is to be funny. I try to be funny more than mean. To me, there's a world of difference and it's perfectly obvious what "the line" is. However, sometimes when I'm trying new stuff out, I end up moving the line a few feet and then crossing it. Oh well.

Now, for all you celebrities who *want* to be in the act, it's very simple: Do something crazy, preferably in front of me and a few other people. When Whitney Houston came up to me backstage at the Billboard Music Awards and waved a finger dangerously close to my face,

---

Left: Backstage with my co-presenter Don Rickles, a legend, at the 2008 prime-time Emmys.

saying, "Don't ever make fun of me," how does that *not* go into the act? She obviously wasn't afraid to do it in front of people, because there were three other people who saw it.

I once asked the great Don Rickles how he's dealt with this issue over the course of his fifty-plus career making people laugh and pushing the envelope. What would he do if a celebrity came up to him and said, "Don't talk about me in your act again"? And of course he said, "Put 'em in the act."

I couldn't have said it better, Mr. Warmth!

But I do get asked a lot, how do I determine who's fair game?

Britney Spears is an example of someone who may never be out of bounds, she's such a delicious font of crazy. I've met her a couple of times, and I can safely say, she's dumb as a stick. I wish I could say there was a side of Britney you don't know about, that really she's a Rhodes scholar who hides her love of classical music and French literature because it doesn't go with her image. The truth is, she's a complete moron, and I'm surprised she can even function.

And what stood out when I met her is, she carries no shame about being an idiot. That's what makes her funny. I mean, if I'm caught not knowing something, at least I feel guilty or embarrassed about it. But this girl, with her gum-popping and malapropisms, has no concept of thinking the way most of us would. That interview with Matt Lauer, the one she did without any publicists to guide her, was proof positive of her cluelessness. She's sitting there popping that gum, her fake eyelash is falling off, she's wearing the prerequisite denim mini with her gut hanging out, weird shit is coming out of her mouth, and I'm thinking, *Okay, not so much a victim, Britney.*

And if you're going to go on the Video Music Awards and lip sync your new hit with crazy dirty hair extensions and not know the dance moves, Bingo! You're in the act!

I can hear it now. "You can't make fun of her. She's a mom!"

Really? Well, can I make fun of someone who barely appears to be conscious most of the time?

But I will say, when the reports came out that she was on suicide watch, I backed off. If someone's in real danger, it's just not funny to

Dec 28, 06
SILVER LEGACY   RENO
SECRET SANTA
SHARON STONE CALLING ME
ROSIE VS TRUMP

LARRY KING

MARY KATE!
BRIT's PUSSY
MICHAEL RICARDS
MEL GIBSON
OPRAH + GAYLE

TODAY SHOW

LINDSAY

IRAQ

Westbury LI, 9-23-06
Clay's on Paxil
Bloomberg

Larry King   Suzanne's letter
The View
Paltrow + Joy Z
Christie Brinkley's house
Today show
Big Emmy loser
Oprah!
Paula Abdul
Iraq
Les love letter

A couple of examples of my set lists, which I use as topic points when I perform.

me. But many of the stars who go into rehab and clearly don't take it seriously, and you know who you are, they're fair game. Most of those, by the way, have the last name Lohan, and they reside on Long Island.

Anna Nicole Smith exemplifies how I feel about boundaries, since she was a tabloid figure who was fun to razz until it clearly wasn't fun anymore. When Anna Nicole had her reality show, she was the kind of loopy train wreck you couldn't not talk about. The gays loved her cause she was a big girl and beautiful and sexy and had that mixture of crazy, drug-induced Texas twang and garden-variety stupidity. I'll never forget getting to go to her Christmas party, the one they shot for her E! show. What a juicy hub of insanity that was: That troubled female ex-wrestler Chyna was there, Rip Taylor was helping in the kitchen, and Anna Nicole herself was like a whirling dervish. I was actually pretty impressed at how she was filming and running around and getting drunk and being ridiculous and yet actually spearheading an authentic Southern meal. The food was fucking delicious. She was really cooking it, too, the turkey, ham, stuffing, and what she called "puh-taters."

When things started to get really nuts with her toothless cousin Shelly flying off the handle and getting into an altercation with the makeup girl, my friend and I decided to split. As much as I love a good scene, this one got too crazy even for me. I can observe all day long, don't get me wrong, but I have no desire to be immersed in crazy in a way that's scary or threatening. That's why I'd never do something like *The Surreal Life* in a million years. It's not fun for me to get into a screaming match with Omarosa, and even if I wanted to, I'm not sure I could even track down her crazy ass at this point. Now, in the case of the Anna Nicole holiday wingding, if I could have gone across the street with some FBI surveillance equipment, I would have watched the goings-on all night long. But I don't think my audience wants to hear about how I manufactured a scene. They'd rather I take notes on what I experience, then comment on it.

Anyway, Anna Nicole was someone I'd had a few experiences with over the years, and though she was almost always out of it, she was also always nice. The claws came out with her attorney Howard K. Stern, and my personal belief is that while the general perception is that he was some Svengali who had her under his control, from my observation *she* was calling the shots, putting him in his place, and yelling at him, while he followed her around like a puppy dog.

I heard about Anna Nicole's death when I was on tour, as I was pulling into Cleveland and checking into a hotel. I went to lunch and the news was on television in the restaurant. I couldn't believe it. I don't know why, but it hit me like a ton of bricks. I remember the bartender saying to me, "Now you've really got to go for her in your act!" I thought that was interesting, that this guy assumed I would gun for her harder. Somebody else that day said something similar to me, and I replied, "You know, I knew her. Not well, but I did know her."

There were a million things about her that were funny and outrageous, and when she'd do something bizarre in my presence, I couldn't *not* talk about it. But when somebody dies that day, I'm not rubbing my hands together saying, "Oooh, a new chunk for the act!" It's really the opposite, and in fact, I haven't talked about her onstage since. That's not to say there's a steadfast rule about this kind of thing, but instinct was telling me it wasn't funny. The first show I did after her death, which was only hours after the announcement, I started by saying, "Okay, everyone, let's address the elephant in the room. I know you guys all want me to talk about Anna Nicole." And there was a lot of clapping. I said, "Well, you know, I sort of knew her. We're not going there. Okay, on to the next subject!" It was uncomfortable, and I understand why the audience would expect something hot off the presses being addressed, but I'm telling you, if I had started in on her, I would have lost that crowd two minutes in. I guarantee you people would have thought, *Bummer,* and then it clouds the entire show.

So in my own way, I have boundaries.

But really, there's nothing I won't talk about, and what happens is you have to know your audience, and you have to be able to read their temperature. When I started at the Groundlings, there was a steadfast rule when it came to improvising: no cancer, no AIDS. There was no way to put a funny spin on those two topics, so don't bother even mentioning them by name or talking about them. Then when I went into stand-up, I figured the same rule applied. But it wasn't until I started doing charity work in the gay community, meeting so many people afflicted with AIDS and hearing them tell the most filthy, disgusting, and horrible jokes about AIDS, that I realized that for them, that's what they needed to get through it. That when you have a disease that grave, your threshold for what's funny is probably so much higher than everyone else's that you almost need a pushing-the-envelope type of joke to get you to laugh.

When *SNL* alum Julia Sweeney's brother Mike was dying of cancer, and then through a terrible coincidence she got cancer, too, I would call their house, and they would take turns answering the phone, "House of Cancer." When Mike was ill, it was so important for him to laugh that he had no tolerance for small talk. He wanted to hear the most out-there jokes he could.

I've mentioned my late friend Judy Toll before in the book, but when she was sick with cancer, she once said to me, "Will you come over and make fun of my illness?"

"What do you mean?" I asked.

"All those years you thought I was a hypochondriac, and here I am dying of cancer. But it always made me laugh. So will you come over and make fun of me?"

"Of course, but . . . I don't want to be mean."

"No, it won't be mean. It's going to make me laugh. It's going to get me out of my head."

It's held true so many times that when I meet people suffering from AIDS, they don't want to hear a knock-knock joke. They're in a battle, so they want the jokes to be fearless, too. I have a friend with full-blown HIV, and to this day he calls it the butt flu, and it always makes him laugh. Things like that really changed my attitude about what's on the table and what's off. I don't go out of my way to do jokes about certain subjects, but I also realize that depending on the audience, I may not have to hold back.

Consider the men and women I met when I performed for the troops in Iraq and Afghanistan, or for those recovering from war injuries at Walter Reed Army Medical Center. Soldiers in the field are people whose lives are in danger every day. They wake up thinking there's a 50/50 chance they could die that night. Imagine if you were in that situation. You'd need something pretty hard-core to make you laugh if you were carrying that around all day. "So the dog's thinking . . ." jokes aren't going to cut it. You have to make fun of everything: the insurgents, the officers, the location, the food, and the soldiers themselves!

That's why I'm just blown away when things like FanningGate happen. When you've been in a war zone making men and women in uniform laugh, hurt feelings in Hollywood are not high on your list of things to worry about.

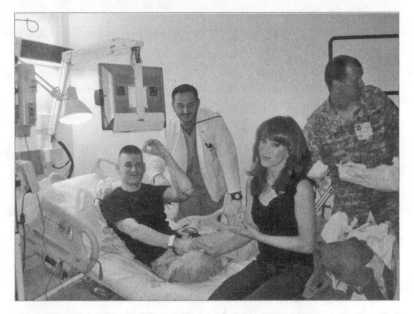

Me at Walter Reed Army Medical Center surrounded by heroes.

Here's that ridiculous saga:

For the 2004–2005 awards season I was hired by E! channel to be their replacement for Joan and Melissa Rivers, who had gone on to sign an $8 million deal at TV Guide channel. In reality, E! considered me number two to Star Jones, whom everyone at the channel was excited about because she'd be able to talk about impending awards show coverage on *The View*. But at least they knew I'd be the funny one. Legitimately funny, that is. I was thrilled.

I have to say, for whatever trouble I ultimately caused at the 2005 Golden Globes over Dakota Fanning, it was Star who was the pain in the ass. On *The View*, we'd gotten along fine, but it wasn't until we did the red carpet coverage together that I found her to be unpleasant, humorless, and kind of a malcontent. I'd hear her being snippy with the crew, complaining that she wouldn't rehearse for more than half an hour. And there was a hilarious diva moment during rehearsal when she and a whole posse of minions were walking by, and when I said "Hi," she barked to her people, "We're WALKING, we're WALKING, we're WALKING."

I, meanwhile, was just happy to be in a pretty dress and meeting celebrities. My idea for questions on the red carpet, though, was to avoid the what-are-you-wearing kind—because I'm not a fashionista—and do something sillier, more offbeat. I didn't even want to try to do Joan's shtick, because she's the master of that. I don't know designers like she does, nor do I have those relationships with stars like Dustin Hoffman and Robin Williams. I wanted to see who would play along with me. Could I ask Kanye West, "What's your favorite meal at the Olive Garden?" E! was fine with that, so I got together a couple of friends to help me come up with those kinds of absurdist questions to ask celebs on the red carpet.

One bit I thought would be funny was to come up with some fake news that celebrities could comment on. I love those moments when some famous person is getting their fucking tonsils taken out or something, and celebrities send them special shout-outs to the camera: "Good luck with your tonsil surgery! God bless you!" Insufferable, right? Well, I wanted to start a rumor that the most unlikely celebrity you could imagine had gone to rehab for drug and alcohol abuse, and then solicit those messages from celebrities right to camera. I couldn't say Lindsay Lohan or Britney because those basket cases you'd believe. Then I thought, *Of course. Dakota Fanning.* Little Dakota Fanning: ten years old, angelic face, impeccably mannered, kind to a retard, er, special needs retard, or whatever, in *I Am Sam.* Perfect.

When the cameras started rolling and we were live, the silly questions turned out to be really fun. People like Clive Owen and my former student/victim Mariska Hargitay (who sustained no injuries that day at the Groundlings) were great, and even the panicked reactions from celebs like Michael Chiklis and his wife, whom I asked if they were getting a hooker later for their hotel room, made for great TV. Then I started my rumor about Ms. Fanning, and every celebrity I said it to laughed. Some even added their own spin. Sean Hayes from *Will & Grace* said, "All I can say is, Dakota, you don't want to go south. Uh-oh, South Dakota!" We were laughing, and I'll admit I was pretty proud of this running bit.

When we went off air, the people from E! said, "How do you think it went?" Which is usually the beginning of a "You're fucking fired" conversation. But I just said, "I thought some of it worked, some of it didn't, but overall kind of fun."

They said, "Okay."

Monday morning my attorney called. "Well, I got a call from Camp Fanning."

"Who's Camp Fanning?" I said.

"Dakota Fanning's camp."

"Wait, you're saying there's a Camp Fanning? What do you mean, like a summer camp? You got a call from a bunch of counselors?"

"No," he said. "She has a movie coming out, a Steven Spielberg picture called *War of the Worlds* with Tom Cruise, and they're extremely upset. Did you say she was a drug addict?"

"Yes."

"*What?*"

"Yes. I said that she went to rehab for drug and alcohol abuse. Why?"

"Well, they're upset that you said that. She's ten years old and she has a giant blockbuster coming out, and they feel like it could affect the box office."

That seemed like bullshit. How was a movie with the biggest star in the world and from the biggest director in the world going to be hurt by my joke? Which was, I remind you, a *joke*. Nevertheless, someone from the channel called and said, "We'd like you to issue an apology."

I said, "Okay, here's my statement: 'You'd have to be a complete fucking moron to think I was serious. The end.' How's that?"

"That's not an apology," he said.

"Well, that's the best I've got. I'm standing by it. What idiot would think I was serious about ten-year-old Dakota Fanning going to rehab? Have you seen her on *Oprah*? She's so innocent-looking it's ridiculous. She practically wears a lacy doll dress and looks like she's going to her first Holy Communion. And by the way, I'd like some credit for not saying it was Lindsay Lohan, for once."

Well, the calls to my agents and attorney wouldn't stop. Team Fanning was upset, as well as Camp Fanning, and Fanning, Ltd., and Fanning & Roebuck, and Fanning Amalgamated, and whoever the fuck were her peeps. My reaction was always, "Whatever publicity anybody wants to throw my way about how awful this is, please go ahead, because I'm super excited that this could blow up into something big."

And it did, because I then heard Spielberg was personally furious with me. I read in the *New York Post* that Spielberg's publicist issued a statement to Page Six: "It was a very upsetting thing for a young child and her family. Obviously, to Kathy Griffin it was a joke, but why make a joke out of [Fanning]? She's a terrific young lady who was there with her family, and it was very upsetting."

That "young lady" part was better than anything I could have come up with. Calling a ten-year-old a "lady"? How much would I have laughed if I was ten and everyone called me a "terrific young lady"!

Also, I was so thrilled that somebody as powerful as Steven Spielberg knew who I was. I thought, *This is great!* Seriously, that was a career high. But I think this means I would not do well in a Mafia situation, because if a hit were put out on me I'd be too excited. I'd just be walking around saying, "The Gottis know my name! The Gottis know my name! Woo-hoo!" As blood came gushing out of the hole in my head.

Well, E! didn't fire me right away, but when it came time for me to cover the Academy Awards for them, they stuck me on what they called the "media bridge"—a bridge that hovered over the red carpet by several dozen feet, and in my case was a euphemism for "you're not getting anywhere near those fucking celebrities"—and eventually after the Oscars I was replaced by Giuliana Rancic née DiPandi.

But I did live off that brouhaha for quite a while. There was a funny moment at a gift suite for the Golden Globes—back when doling out free shit to famous people was respectable, and none of it was taxed—when a woman came up to me as I was getting my free under-eye cream and said, "You know, you upset Dakota Fanning so much that she couldn't leave her bedroom for days, and she wouldn't let anyone open the curtains."

I just looked at her like she was batshit. "What are you talking about?"

She said, "She cried and cried for days in her room."

"Uh, I'm pretty sure you're making that up," I said, and walked away.

Someone who saw all this said to me, "That's someone from the Hollywood Foreign Press Association." The group who chooses who wins Golden Globes.

"Well, I don't care. I think that was someone from the Fucking Crazy Association."

Big deal. Spielberg won't let me star in any of his movies, and I won't win any Golden Globes for the Spielberg movies I'm not in. I'll take my celebrity rehab jokes any day, thank you very much.

And by the way, I have nothing against Dakota Fanning, who's obviously a very gifted and talented young actress. I mean, lady. But I would like a muffin basket from all the Lohans, because it would have been so much easier to make that joke, and nobody would have flinched.

As a side note, I'll tell you just how vicious Hollywood really is. One of my agents actually said to me, "You know, if you had just made that joke about Haley Joel Osment or Jonathan Lipnicki, it would have been fine. Because they're not hot anymore."

Ouch. Can I just say, that is *way* more harsh than any fucking Dakota Fanning joke I could make. That Hollywood would have given me the stamp of approval if I had just picked on a kid whose "career" had cooled instead of a kid who was behind a giant blockbuster where they could all make money, was really an eye-opener. So for the record, my apologies are to Jonathan Lipnicki and Haley Joel Osment. Stay off the smack, boys.

Since people often ask me whether I pay the price for my offending celebrities, I will reveal that I did have an interesting run-in two years later regarding the Dakota Fanning incident. I was working in

Las Vegas on a Friday night at Mandalay Bay and the next night Jerry Seinfeld was performing at Caesar's. I wanted to go see him, so I put in the call to his people and asked if it would be possible to say hi. I was told to come by backstage before the show. Although friends had come with me on this trip, I was nervous about dragging them to see a superstar, so when it came to seeing Jerry one-on-one, I just went by myself.

Big mistake.

I head to Le Celine Dion lounge—I will always call it Le Celine Dion lounge, no matter who's playing there—and see a table full of people. And at that table is, of all people, Steven "I Will Protect Dakota Fanning At All Costs" Spielberg. I walk in and it's literally just me, and a circle of them sitting at a table eating. So I immediately head to the farthest corner of the room, like I'm a second grader in time-out, and quickly vowed to myself never to go to any Hollywood back-stage area, green room, party, or even casual costume fitting alone again for the rest of my life.

Of course, it seemed like Jerry was taking forever to come back and say hi, but he was preparing for his show, which I understood. I just kept talking to the bartender, ordering Diet Cokes and making chit-chat. How was his day? Where did he live? What a nice shirt! I proba-bly looked like a meth addict the way I was furiously babbling at him.

My plan was, let Jerry come in and have his private conversation with Spielberg, and then the Spielberg posse will leave, and I'll be able to say hi, and what the fuck was I thinking and this is what I fucking get and great, I have fucking ass-crack sweat now, and God, why can't I keep my big fucking mouth shut. I'm regretting this whole thing. Re-ally, I'm regretting my whole career at this point. I'm about to pay the piper, and his name is Steven Spielberg.

Sure enough, Jerry comes in and he's got his suit on, and everyone's excited to see him. He deals with the Spielberg party first, as he should, but I knew he'd seen me. Well, it seemed like they were talking for what felt like forever. No one else was there, remember. Then, sud-denly, Jerry starts to wave me over. "Kathy, come on over!" he says.

I'm gesturing like a lunatic, "Oh no, I'm okay over here! Heh heh! This Diet Coke won't drink itself! Heh heh! I'll be right here! Come find me when you're done!"

Then he talked to the Spielberg group some more, and again he called out to me. "Kathy, come on! I know how you like celebrities! Don't you want to meet Steven Spielberg?"

"Oh, you guys probably want to catch up! Don't let me . . . [gulp] . . . get in the . . . heh heh . . . way, I mean . . . [gulp] . . . I would . . . never want to . . . impose!"

I knew Steven Spielberg knew it was me. And I knew he knew I was nervous. There had to be a part of him that was loving this.

It got to the point where it was going to be weird if I said no anymore, so I walked over, and it was that horrible timing where the minute I approached Jerry, Spielberg stood up and Jerry started a brand-new story. So there's Spielberg to his right, Jerry in the middle, and me to his left, and I just kept looking at Jerry, nervously focusing on his tie so as to avoid even being in Spielberg's line of vision. I'm sure that made me look even more normal, right? Everybody was laughing, and I was, too, but probably at all the wrong moments, looking like I was trying to join the in crowd, when I clearly had no membership qualifications, whatsoever.

Finally, Jerry says, "Well, Kathy, this must be an exciting moment for you, because I know how much you love meeting famous people. So, Kathy Griffin, Steven Spielberg! Steven Spielberg, Kathy Griffin!"

I just thought, *Here we go.* I looked at him and chuckled, trying to acknowledge that I'd been busted. "It's so nice to meet you," I said with a little giggle.

He looked at me, and with a very serious tone said, "Nice to meet you, too."

And that was it. He wasn't a jerk. He could have said, "You were out of line," but instead he looked at me in a way that my dad would look at me when I came home late from a beer bash, and I don't even drink. It was the look of someone grounding me. I felt like one of the "Peanuts" characters whenever they're nervous and have a squiggle for a mouth. I was shaking and squiggle-smiling at the same time. And Jerry was so proud of himself, thinking he was doing me this big favor by getting me face time with Spielberg.

Finally it was time for him to do his show, and he said, "Come with me." He said good-bye to the Spielberg party, and then I followed him to his dressing room. We sat down and I just went off on him. "*What the hell are you doing introducing me to Steven Spielberg?* Don't you know he actually issued a *press statement* against me? Didn't you remember that thing where I made that joke about Dakota Fanning? How could you drag me over to make me say hi to him? Were you fucking with me? Is that it? This is so *typical*!"

And then Jerry, in his best Seinfeldian rant mode, was throwing it right back: "How am I supposed to keep track of who Kathy Griffin gets along with in Hollywood? You have so many fights with people, how am I supposed to know? You get along with this person one day! You make fun of somebody else the next! *Am I supposed to have a chart of the people who can't stand you in Hollywood?*"

This got us laughing, especially Jerry thinking that my little fight with Spielberg would possibly be on his radar in a million years. Of course it wasn't. You could even argue that unwittingly Jerry had gotten me back for talking shit about him in my special all those years ago. But if it had to happen, I'm glad it was with Jerry, somebody I could laugh about it with afterward. By the way, Jerry told me that he and his wife watch every episode of *My Life on the D-List*. Take that, Fanning.

Did the humiliation end, though? No way. Sure enough, when it came time to take my seat for Jerry's show, guess who was sitting behind me?

Spielberg.

You know that bottleneck that always happens in the aisle after a packed show ends? Well, now I had to trudge my way out of the theater with Spielberg *right next to me*. So I turned to my friend Todd, who came with me to the show, and said "Go! Go! Hurry up!" But what I forgot was that Todd legitimately knew Steven Spielberg, because he'd been a consultant on *War of the Worlds*. So suddenly Spielberg turns and says, "Todd?"

Poor Todd looked over and said, "Oh, hi, Steven!"

But I nipped that in the bud and just pushed my friend Todd up three stairs, practically knocking him over, and out of the theater. I explained it all to him later, but basically I robbed my good friend of having a normal friendly conversation with Steven Spielberg. Because when it comes to me paying the piper, it will not last any longer than it absolutely has to, come hell or high water. Sorry, Todd.

19
THE
WIZARD
OF WOZ

In the summer of 2007, I was on tour, going through my emails, when a woman named Kris Gunderson contacted me through my publicist. She said she was a friend of Apple co-founder Steve Wozniak, she had seen my act live, and based on that, decided he and I would be a good match. That was all I needed. Soon afterward, when the *New York Post* put to me the question what kind of guy asks Kathy Griffin out, I got a little ahead of myself and blurted out, "Steve Wozniak is in love with me!" Oh boy.

Below is a condensed version of our relationship via cyberspace, and when I say "condensed," I mean that I had to take a meat cleaver to some of Woz's emails. Sorry, Mac heads, but I had to consider readers who may not be able to take seventeen pages in a row about his Segway polo match stats, or dozens of recollections detailing his golden age of laser-pointer pranks. And if the rest of you still can't hack reading what he's got to say, that's because you're no billionaire computer genius, are you? As for the spelling errors, I left in all his and mine, because that's how I roll. Okay, here we go . . .

Left: Woz with his passion, and I mean the Segway polo, not me.

From: Kathy
Date: August 18, 2007 10:30:56 AM
To: Kris Gunderson
Subject: Oh dear god!

Please pass on to Steve:
    How are you enjoying our love affair? Ok, here's what happened. I did an interview last week and one of the questions was "What kind of guys ask you out?" That's it. I don't know where the *Post* got the details. Hope you're not too bothered by all this. XXOO, Kathy G

From: Woz
Date: August 18, 2007 9:06 PM
To: Kathy
Subject: Re: Oh dear god! From Kathy Griffin

You are really ridiculous.
    I assumed it was all very deliberate comedy and I loved it so much. Now you tell me it was accidental. I'm all bummed out.
    It took me a day to respond to this email because I'm currently hosting a Camp Woz at my home. Some young kids, 13 to 17, from a New Jersey social program, are being treated to a special camp. Most of them have been badly abused in various ways.
    They create their own music and do their own choreography and have a big record deal now and do N-Sync like dancing and singing and work with Justin Timberland.
    Hope to hear from you,
    Steve

From: Kathy
Date: August 20, 2007 5:37:44 PM
To: Woz
Subject: Re: Oh dear god! From Kathy Griffin

Steve- you're what they call a "wierdo", correct?
    Wired.com is reporting that were not Dating anymore WTF??? I was planning our Life magazine "At home with Kathy and Steve" pictorial. oh

right, Life magazine doesnt exist anymore the photos would be 1) me holding a ladle of my home made soup up for you to taste 2) me on stage with a stand up mike and you watching me from the audience with your arms akimbo, like I've just said something very outrageous 3) the two of us in your living room counting your money.

P.S. Its Justin TimberLAKE grandMA!

From: Woz
Date: August 23, 2007 6:45:52 PM
To: Kathy
Subject: Re: Oh dear god! From Kathy Griffin

help!!!

You are a hero of mine. I'm afraid to talk to you. It's like my fear of talking with heroes like Bill Hewlett of Hewlett and Packard. My long standing philosophy is that the best measure of life is smiles minus frowns. I once was being inducted as the first member into my High School's Hall of Fame and I gave the students my formula H = F cubed, meaning Happiness is Food, Fun and Friends. The kids started laughing and I had to admit that there might be a 4th F. (Family?). I heard in later years that the school administration did not like my speech because I talked of the smartest students being rebels and why I refused to say the pledge of allegiance, etc.

Anyway, your jokes have made me laugh and laugh so you are truly a hero in my book. The good medicine is better than other effects, like PC stuff. I don't think you are PC. I really see you as a Macintosh person. Oh, wrong PC.

hasta whenever,
Woz

From: Kathy
Date: August 30, 2007 8:59:10 PM
To: Woz
Subject: Better than the lnar eclipse

Steve- I'm so thrilled you're going to the EMMYS with me. The EMMY is an award given out to various television shows. Television is a new and exciting way of transmitting entertaining images in to the homes of humans. You should watch one some day. XXOO, KG

From: Woz
Date: August 31, 2007 1:14 AM
To: Kathy
Subject: Re: Better than the lnar eclipse

Kathy, you are a genius for this one. I probably wouldn't do this if you had not brought me laughter in your comedy. I am truly honored. I have downloaded your D List shows. I will be straightforward at the event. My sense is that this will be successful, since I'm more of an unknown in the entertainment world. We are an interesting couple in that sense.

I like genuineness, or at least a feeling of it, so some (only a few) reality shows are the only ones I've watched in ages. My withdrawal from TV happened in the early days of satellite TV, before you could even buy it. You had to hand-make huge dishes. I discovered that movies delivered that way had much better acting than TV shows for the most part. Heck, the movies weren't even encrypted or charged for when I got into it, in early Apple years.

As for my background, many know that I founded Apple but avoided running a company to stay in the laboratory. I generously gave lots of my stock to other employees who had none. I was the founder of the Children's Discovery Museum and The Tech of Silicon Valley and The Silicon Valley Ballet and more. I wanted to give back to the city I was born in (San Jose). They named a street after me. I went back to college after Apple and finished my degree at Berkeley under the name Rocky Racoon Clark. I got my diploma in that name. I had always wanted to teach 5th grade and felt it was more important to donate yourself and your own time so I taught for 8 years with no press allowed except once for People Magazine. I don't hang around with CEO's or financial types. I prefer interesting creative people, starting small companies or doing other projects, sometime even homeless people. If they have interesting stories, that's more important to me. Oh, I'm also well known in the San Jose for supporting animal causes and the humane society. That's a short summary of my background.

This will be fun. I even bought a suit. What a great thing and it wasn't even my own idea, which is unusual.

xoxo and smiles,
Woz

—tv is wake zone (anagram of my name)

From: Kathy
Date: August 31, 2007 11:45:11 PM
To: Woz
Subject: Re: Better than the lnar eclipse

—Yes, it's Kathy Griffin here. Can you hear me? I downloaded, or I guess just listened to your interview on the Segway fansite ot whatever the fuck that was. Christ, talk about a niche market! I figured I should do some homework if you're going to watch "My Life on the D-List" You are a very smart guy and that's probably why whatever is wrong with you is wrong with you. I hope you can take my gentle ribbing, because hon- estly, I can't get enough of it. I cannot WAIT to give you shit in person about staying at the Universal City Hilton. If you play your cards right, I might let you take me to a theme restaurant there.

I hope you know a few people will assume you're gay just because you're with me. Can't help that. It will broaden your fan base. Speaking of, I find it so funny that at the mention of your name there are only two reactions. "Who" or "He's a GOD!" Nothing in between. Congratulations on buying your first suit . . .

XXOO, KG (my initials)

From: Woz
Date: September 2, 2007 2:34 PM
To: Kathy
Subject: Type A

I mean Taipei . . .

I actually watched 6 D List shows on the flight over instead of sleeping.

I understand the stress of performing. The same goes for my own category. I just toured the world speaking for 20 years but it was phony because I did it all at my own expense, first class travel and all. I wanted to give back to the clubs that Apple came out of. But it got to be so much travel all the time that I started saying they had to pay my way. It's still so full-time that I try to cut back more by asking for fees but I'm still overworked at this and thank god that I'm patient.

I used to carry long knives onto airplanes. In Tokyo I bought ceramic knives that fold up like switchblades. They are so health-driven there that many people don't like metal utensils. I'd take everything metal off my body and walk through the metal detector in airports just fine. I'm sure it would work today as well but I haven't tried this since 9–11. On the plane I'd rub the knife (metal back then) and comment to the stewardess that the knife was pretty dull and how I hoped the steak was tender. Then when the steak was served I'd pull out my ceramic knife, with about a 6-inch blade, and it worked great. The most a stewardess ever said was "wow, a plastic knife" but sometimes passengers had very upset looks across the aisle.

love to your whole crew,

oops, it's been an hour and I'm hungry again here.

From: Kathy
Date: September 2, 2007 10:33:57 PM PDT
To: Woz
Subject: Re: Type A

I've never been to Taipei. Do you explore a city much when you're there? When you're here will you please explain Greenwich time to my in a way

I can understand. In fact I'd like it if you'd pretend I was one of your fifth graders when answering most of my questions. When you ask me a question about Hollywood or celebrities, I will, however, look at you like you're a complete moron. It just makes me feel better.

If I ever see you in an airport or fly with you I'm going to act like I don't know you. Do you really like to travel for work this much? I get road burn out sometimes. On those days I cry for no reason. That's why I'm such a hotel JAP (Jewish American Princess. I'm not Jewish, but I'm jew-friendly.) Unlike you, I must have the largest suite possible in the nicest hotel in town with the best room service. If I don't, I have trouble relaxing. I also like to do lots of online research about the food. I refuse to do chain restaurants on the road. No Cracker Barrel, no Coco's, no fast food. I love Mom and Pop places. I watch the food channel and take notes! I can't cook at all, but it's the best place to find the good places to eat all over the U.S. I really like basic food, but very well prepared. Sometimes my Gays and I have a "tuna meltdown" and search for the best new place to get a really good tune melt. Promoters and hotel manager's usually want to send me to someplace to get duck confit with a raspberry reduction or some shit. God, I would so like to talk to you about money. My mom is staying over at my house tonight. I have depression parents. My Dad actually passed away last Feb. My whole life, their depression ethic has been drilled in to me. Anyway, she has convinced me once again that if I spend one more penny, I'm going to lose everything, live in my car and eat dog food. I don't spend that much money, relatively speaking, but I believe her none the less.

You probably figured this out, but I'm not interested in you for, nor do I need your money.

Why don't you speak at Comdex(sp?) and functions like that where you will be treated like a god and your jokes will kill? I know, you're not in to that, but c'mon, once in a while. Let the geeks love you.

XXOO, Kathy

From: Woz
Date: September 3, 2007 9:10 AM
To: Kathy
Subject: Re: Type A

I hate it when hosts book my travel and it's not non-stop, etc. So every trip that's contracted we have them pay us an estimate for travel, an estimate for food, etc. They often write in the same for Steve's assistant, Julie. For the last trip to Las Vegas they paid us $3700 each for travel I think (maybe $3700 total) and we drove Prius's which get there and back for about $150 each. We have them pay estimates for travel first class and then I can use my credit card for tickets and take advantage of 2-for-1 ticket deals. I don't have to save any receipts this way and submit them. I'm so bad at that. I don't think I've ever done it once because I just don't want to. But Julie is a type A person and she has been pulling some data from my AmEx bills to get me recompensed. ugh.

You are lucky you have the time. I love Dunk'n Donuts because there are about none in California anymore. In foreign countries I like to eat foreign food, which means McDonalds when there. Not exactly but sometimes. It's usually room service. I love mom and pop places but I'm usually alone and not willing to take the risk. God, I took the risk in New Orleans last March and wound up unable to move for 2 days with food poisoning.

Tuna salad sandwiches and Tuna melts are my favorites. When I'm not eating red meat, you can get this at Subway and Togo's and I have my favorite places at home. So I have one thing in common with you or your Gays.

We're different. I never think about money. That goes back to before Apple. We had no money when we started. No savings, no car, no house, no nothing. I had to pay cash at my apartment because of bounced rent checks. We would make computers with 30 days credit on the parts and then sell them to a store for cash after 10 days. We made our first $10K that way. I don't like money.

I had philosophies against having too much money, how it changes you and your ethics. I also had determined at a young age that nothing would change my strong sense of who I was or corrupt me. So when we had so much more money than anyone could need I resented it. I had not sought it. I had started the company reluctantly and only after first giving my computers away without any copyright or patents. I was not even 30. I started giving to every needy cause and started various museums and the like and put on some huge rock concerts and got divorced 3 times so you can trust that I don't have all that much. I talked to friends at Apple about this after it went public and told them that my goal was to give to worthy causes until I had enough to be comfortable but not more than could ever be explained. I'm still in that mode although my accountant doesn't like it. Frankly, I don't think about money. I avoid it. I'm not frugal but I'm not excessive. I don't think I'm excessive. But you can't compare yourself to anyone else or it gets to be like a pissing contest.

I have keynoted at many shows like Comdex. I can't remember if I did Comdex ever but I might have. One big appearance was in the '90's to the the national education computer conference, EduComm. It was to an audience of about 5,000 live. This was in Seattle, near Microsoft. But Seattle was a Macintosh school region. Bill Gates gave one keynote and was boring and got a polite applause when done. I got a standing ovation before and after my speech. They respect me but they won't after my prank book, ha ha.

12 days before something (it's Tuesday here),

—steve

—ok a new size tv

p.s. I got to ride a Segway on stage today!!!! This lady who used to be the CEO of HP in Taiwan had one there. I have to talk them into forming a Segway polo team but she said only about 6 people have Segways in Taiwan.

From: Kathy
Date: September 5, 2007 2:03:17 PM
To: Woz
Subject: Re: hi

Last year I wore this dress to the Creative Arts EMMYS that I'm going to "recycle" and wear to the primetime EMMYS this year in hopes that one of the magazines will do a "what was she thinking" picture. In Hollywood, it's unheard of to be photographed in the same dress twice. What I didn't realize was that I gained 10 pounds from last year. So now Entertainment Tonight doing a "can she get in to the dress by EMMYS" piece, so when we go talk to them on the red carpet, I'll be in that fucking dress. As of 5 days ago, I could zip it up, but not sit in it. The point is, my work is much more important than yours.

The girls (Jessica and Tiffany) and I are very excited about the list of duties we have for you to do when you come to the house, while I'm getting hair and m/u done. Please bring your A game, because you have never quite seen a challenge like this. One of them is to put my favorites on my laptop in alphabetical order. Good luck, and just be yourself. I have been Google news-ing you every day lately. After I do my own name, of course. Some of the articles and interviews are so heady, I just laugh. To me, it's almost like you speak another language, but a dead one like latin or Gaelic. Because it's not just foreign, but difficult to me to even find a translator. I especially like the one about your crazy pine house that you're building. But I like to sleep in 65 degrees, not 71. I mean, honestly, Steve. Sometimes I forget that I'm the brains of the operation, and you're just some bimbo on my arm. XXOO, KG

From: Kathy
Date: September 8, 2007 10:28:07 PM
To: Woz
Subject: Guess what?

I won! I won! I won! Oh wait. Today I won the Creative Arts EMMY. What we're going to next week is the primetime EMMYs. Hope this isn't confusing. Xxoo, K

From: Kathy
Date: September 10, 2007 7:20:11 PM
To: Woz
Subject: Fwd: Kathy Griffin comment request

Steve- Oooh, I'm really in trouble now. Can you handle a real social outcast on your arm? XO, KG

From: Woz
Date: September 10, 2007 10:32:38 PM
To: Kathy
Subject: Re: Fwd: Kathy Griffin comment request

Short answer: yes

You are hardly a social outcast. You did get one-upped by Brittney Spears today.

Whenever I sense everyone going one way, I always try to oppose them with logic and facts, if there are any. I even signed a petition to the governor to pardon Paris Hilton because everyone was so upset that they wanted her punished just to hurt her and not out of logic as to whether it was fair and equal.

You entertain and you are at times irreverent? I totally love it. You had a good joke, even comment, about Jesus. I hate it when you tell a joke and people take it too seriously. That happens all the time.

The more I learn about you yourself the more I like it! I'm into genuine and that means saying things as they are. For the sake of art that offends at times. I'm also of a shy background and that means quiet and polite, which goes the other way.

Anyway, I may not be at your level but you will be surprised at what you find in me! I make sure it's never predictable. If someone could predict what you'd say or do in any circumstance, then I'd change and try to do something else. Except that I'd eat a Big Boy Combo at Bob's Big Boy.

I got the room I wanted here at Disney World. I wanted something near room 4404 and I got 4406. That's HARD to do since it fills up on a first-come first-serve basis. I suspect that my assistant got the word to my hosts and the held the closest room they could. I never could reserve the rooms I wanted here in the past. I'd usually fly out a day or two ahead of my family to play games and switch rooms as other people departed and I'd sometimes get the right rooms. This time I think the Disney people, my hosts, helped. It's late here but I'm still on CA time I told them.

I hope you are floating and very happy as you fall asleep tonight. Just being close to this whole EMMY thing as it happened is one of the greatest things in my own life.

I feel a lot of the significance of the award with you and it's almost overwhelming. I look forward to sharing fun times.

XOXO,
Steve

From: Kathy
Date: September 11, 2007 12:25:04 AM
To: Woz
Subject: Re: Fwd: Kathy Griffin comment request

I just had the crew from D-List over tonight for a poker night. It was really fun. A great group of guys. I regaled them with stories about how I'm making you alphabetize my favorites on Sunday. They want me to break all my gadgets and make you rebuild them. Your hotel number has to be a prime number stories are freaky. When I tell my friends, I tell them I'm trying to get you to like a whole new hotel number. Four, as in Four Seasons. Oh, my Steve Wozniak chunk is coming along nicely. I'm excited that you know who Britney is. I imagined Sunday would be me translating everything that's happening around us, like you're my foreign exchange student or Starman. I do not have any honorary doctorates. I only went to Jr college for 6 months and started working in commercials.

Do you understand, I guess it's physiology? I have some very embarrassing questions for you. Not questions, so much, but a really weird thing to tell you. I started menopause a few months ago and I'm completely fascinated by the whole thing. I know, creepy. I have this cream that I put on my arms once a day. It's called bio-identical hormone therapy. My hot flashes went away and my skin is clearing up and my period came back. I should delete that whole section, but I think you can handle it. I'm on the "Ellen" show tomorrow. I don't know what time it's on in Florida . . . I loved your email, as always. Have a funnel cake for me tomorrow. XXOO, KG

From: Woz
Date: September 11, 2007 1:10:16 AM
To: Kathy
Subject: Re: Fwd: Kathy Griffin comment request

I do plan on bringing you a small gift. It's pre-made origami but with a nice wood stand. I hope you can appreciate origami.

I write all my dates as 2007.10.11 because it's the only way they sort alphabetically into date order. You have to have all 4 year digits and 2 digits for the month and day, even if they are less than 10. It's also logical to put the slowest changing part, the year, to the left. We put the slowest changing parts of numbers to the left.

Computers are so good for things like sorting. They can do millions of things a second. A human can only count about one number a second but a computer can do maybe a billion. (I can count from one to a million in less than a minute but I have to count by hundreds of thousands). Well, the first program I ever wrote was a chess problem and no answer came out and then I did a calculation which showed that I'd get an answer in ten to the 25th years, longer than the universe has been around.

Now what is the embarrassing question you had? It should be something that I even have a clue about.

As for bio-anything, very few people recognize that DNA is a stereoscopic isomer that can twist light and repolarize it, changing the color. A minor example is that a red laser spreads throughout your finger but a green or yellow laser doesn't. I can do a demo for you of how passing laser light through my body can change its color. I do this sometimes in speeches and it leaves the audience aghast. They sometimes ask if it well work on them as well and I hand them a laser and it does work. Beware of my lasers as they are used for sterilizing cattle and removing tattoos.

What the heck is a funnel cake??? I'm in Florida. is that at all like Key Lime Pie? Is it in the shape of a funnel? I will not be able to sleep now.

XOXO,
Steve

From: Kathy
Date: September 11, 2007 7:43:10 PM
To: Woz
Subject: Re:

You know how to send pictures from your iphone???

Kathy Griffin

From: Woz
Date: September 11, 2007 8:07:43 PM
To: Kathy
Subject: Re:

Experimental Prototype Community Of Tomorrow.
    One of the worst acronyms ever.
    The worst may have been PCMCIA cards for computers. Everyone just called them PC Cards in the end. Nobody knew what PCMCIA stood for. Two possibilities were Personal Computer Manfacturers Create Impossible Acronyms (I remembered that one) and People Can't Memorize Computer Industry Acronyms.

praying for you,
Steve

From: Kathy
Date: September 11, 2007 11:20:19 PM
To: Woz
Subject: Re: Re:

You didn't have a funnel cake? Fried dough with powdered sugar on top? You are soulless.
    Are you and Julie driving to LA Sat night or Sunday morning? You're supposed to be at my house at noon. How fast can you type? If you can't fix anything, maybe you can do some light dictation. XXOO, Kathy (big Jesus hater, but EMMY winner) Griffin

From: Woz
Date: September 12, 2007 1:43:45 AM
To: Kathy
Subject: Re: Re:

Sunday morning, departing at 5 AM.

I'm probably very slow now, like 40–50 wpm. But in high school, when almost no boys typed, I even took typing 2 and beat the girls. I was so motivated that I once typed a page of "the" and one of them was tne (with an 'n') and it was very hard to find. One bright kid used a piece of paper along each row and actually did find the tne rather quickly. But never does a boy beat the girls in typing on a real type-writer in typing 2.

best to the best, xxoo good (ssoo good in computer talk)
Steve

From: Woz
Date: September 16, 2007 9:29:00 AM
To: Kathy
Subject: on the way

I'm trying to guess how long it takes to get there. Traffic should be pretty good on a Sunday but I"m afraid of speeding after my 104 mph ticket.

Just kidding. Besides, I drove the first leg and Julie is driving now. I'm using my laptop in the car. I have used my laptops to get online from the first laptops and cell phones, even before there was an internet to get onto. I'd just phone in and join my home network, which was interesting but there wasn't much to do with only that. I love to do tethering but it's not some weird sex thing. Tethering is getting your computer onto the internet anywhere through your cell phone. When the first cell phones came out with bluetooth (Sony Ericsson T68i changed the world for me!!!) I could take my laptop to a park and connect it to my phone with bluetooth (no tethering wire) and get through that phone to the internet. That was one of the biggest tastes of technical freedom in my life. No wires, online anywhere anytime.

In other countries, I get to the internet through my normal phones,

RAZR or Blackberry or about any modern cell phone except the iPhone which doesn't do tethering.

Except Japan never allowed the cell phone system of the rest of the world so no cell phones from other countries work there. Ugh.

We'll check into our hotel first and brush and dress and all.

I did the morning stuff at home. The morning stuff is mostly "sh" stuff—shower, shave, shampoo, shit, shirt, shorts (and socks, shoes, skirts . . .).

The best foods start with C. These are the foods sold at C food places, Convenience sores. Chocolate. Chips. Cookies. Cakes. Crackers. Cokes. Coffee. Caffeine. Cholesterol, Cheese, Cheetos, Cheese-Its, Caramel, Chardonnay, Chablis, Cerial, Coffee Cakes, etc.) Everything except PePPeroni Pizza.

xxoo steve

p.s. the planets are named after the days of the week. Or is it the reverse?

From: Kathy
Date: September 25, 2007 5:29:59 PM
To: Woz
Subject: Re: question . . .

I'm so thrilled that you are coming to Vegas, we are going to have a blast!

Are you going to bring Julie? You know I don't think you can function on your own right? I'm just picturing you wandering around aimlessly in the San Jose airport in the Southwest Terminal wearing your orange tie, handing out 2 dollar bills.

I'll have my girls coordinating with Julie regarding your insane room number request as I am sure you will have to have Room 2225 across from Room 4445 or some random mathematical bullshit. I have two shows that Friday night, 8:00 PM and 11:00 PM. You can come to either or neither, it's up to you. I'll probably invite 4 or 5 friends for the weekend. We can plan a few meals together, but in Vegas no attendance is ever mandatory so you can ultimately make your own schedule of course. I assume you watched the Ahmadinejad speech from Columbia yesterday. I hope you saw the part where he said there were no homo-sexuals in Iran. Upon hearing that I canceled my tour dates in Tehran, Tehran Heights and Tehran City at the Chuckle Hut.

Oh, by the way, I told People magazine, regarding our "engagement" that you did in fact give me a ring, that it was NOT an engagement ring, but it was a lovely gesture from a lovely man. I think that's why they killed the story. Next week, I'll tell them I've had my vagina pierced with the engagement ring and that it's one billion carats. As if you can afford it.

XOXO
Kathy Griffin

From: Woz
Date: September 27, 2007 2:44 AM
To: Kathy
Subject: Re: hello

I'm not going to vote next year. I came to a conclusion during the Viet Nam war that voting didn't help, that the bad results came from much more powerful forces of, basically money, and not from who was in of-fice. Those forces acted on everyone who did get elected. I don't hear much in the way of moral leadership anyway. If I accidentally register and vote it might be for someone weird. The few times I did vote I only voted for president and marked Libertarian for everyone else.

Well, I just got my wakeup call. I awoke 5 minutes before it and waited and waited and waited and they finally came through. I'm off to a speech an hour's drive away. It's a happy last day here.

xooooo steve woz

From: Woz
Date: October 3, 2007 8:52 PM
To: Kathy
Subject: Re: competition

I did major bedroom pickup the last couple of days. When I'm home for 2 days I rest heavely but if I get a 3rd or 4th day I'm ready to get into work mode. I picked up clothes that had been washed 2 years ago. So many of them were in bags (bachelors here) that they were totally wrinkled and have to be washed again. I got my closets sorted (I've expanded to using both walk-in closets and I have about as many saved pairs of shoes as any woman) but now that I'm filling them, I have to go through and have a serious throw-out/give-away action.

I also have to go through bathroom drawers that filled up with hotel soaps and toothbrushes and shavers and all. I used to criticize my friend Jim and his wife who took salt and pepper shakers from every restaurant and event, even non-replaceable fancy ones. But I can't seem to pass up taking soap home from every hotel. I've probably taken 100 or more home this year and can truthfully say that I actually used one such bar, part way anyhow.

I'm off to pack and then leave at 5:30 AM for New York. I have no idea how long I'll be gone but I think I have to get back for something coming up mid-month, like in Las Vegas. Oh, now I remember. Just kidding. People ask me if I'm serious when I say weird made-up things and I tell them "yes". After a while I say "I'm always serious when I'm tricking someone."

XOXO steve

From: Kathy
Date: October 4, 2007 1:44:08 AM
To: Woz
Subject: Re: competition

NY? I'm taking a red eye to Philly tomorrow night to do two shows in AC (that's tour lingo for Atlantic City) Friday night. Then 2 shows Sat night in Storrs (sp?) Conn. What brings you to NYC? Are you going to throw shares of Apple stock from the roof of the Empire State building? Ah, spring cleaning. I envy you. I love organization of all kinds. Jesica and Tiffany are organizational whizzes, and it comforts me like a hug from Allah. I think you should give away all of your hotel soaps. Maybe Camp Woz? People who don't get to stay in hotels go ape shit for hotel soaps. Wait, I just remembered, I haven't Googlo news-d you today. Be back in a minute . . .

Jesus, you sure are on a lot of boards, and congratulations on making the Buffalo News. Ok, where were we? I wish you watched Oprah. It's a television show, in a talk format where an omnipotent being, named Oprah solves everyone's problems, as long as you play along with the premise that she is better than you. Anyway ahe did several shows about "hoarders" and I think you may be one. I'm thinking you were driven to be like this because some man did you wrong and one of your 87 cats died.

- Oh, I did a photo shoot today for one of my favorite magazines. It's called "Radar" and it's very sarcastic and clever. I'm getting some sort of ironic award, which is a gold plated urinal, so we did a shoot with me acccepting it in a beautiful evening gown. So I was all done up in fancy hair and make up so I went to a fancy schmancy restaurant so as to not waste my beauty. There were lots of paparazzi, and crews. One of them is called TMZ.com and I'm pretty proud of a joke I came up with about us. They were asking m where my boyfriend Woz was, and if we were going to release a sex tape. So I said we were going to, but Steve Jobs offered us a billion dollars not to. Hope you likey. XXOO, KG

From: Kathy
Date: October 28, 2007 1:15 PM
To: Woz
Subject: Re: At SFO

Pasadena this week??? Wanna get together, dinner of somehing? Xxoo KG

From: Woz
Date: October 29, 2007 12:27:05 AM
To: Kathy
Subject: Re: At SFO

Back to Pasadena, let's please get together for dinner or anything. I'll call you when I get down there. I don't know our judging schedule but it's pretty much all-day for a few days. I'm going to read the binder of submissions that I have tomorrow and make notes so I'll be ready. Each year new members are inducted into the National Inventors Hall of Fame (people like Steve Jobs can't qualify but ones like me can—you have to have done the real work and have patents) and we also select a Collegiate Inventor who wins some money. My judging is for the collegiate inventor. These collegiate researchers do some cutting edge stuff in genomics and other fields. I can't even understand some of the quantum physics stuff they do.

xoxo steve

From: Kathy
Date: November 8, 2007 12:06:53 AM
To: Woz
Subject: Re: Seoul?

60 minutes did a very interesting piece on Negroponte last year. I would think you would like him. Did you?
   I had this big and mortifying meeting with the mucky mucks at NBC last Friday and I'm still traumatized. The sexism is so profound, most of the time, I thought they were kidding with some of their comments. You came up. I met with about 10 of the executives. When I was joking about how little BRAVO pays me one of them said "Can't your new boyfriend finance your show?" Another was "We don't really do female driven comedies here. The numbers tell us, women don't really watch tv." And the kicker "We need to find a role for you that fits you as tight as those jeans" Welcome to 1958. Oh well, I guess it's back to BRAVO for me. So much for me becoming the new Lucille Ball on NBC. Congratulations on your victory over those bastards, the OJD's. With your

skill and finesse, think of them as the 1978 Boston Bruins and you as the
Montreal Canadiens.

XXOO, KG

From: Woz
Date: November 8, 2007 1:38:55 AM
To: Kathy
Subject: Re: Seoul?

I had met Negroponte only one time before.

On his panel they saved me for last. I spoke of his integrity and of
some issues with his laptop program, based on my own experiences. In
his answers to all of us on the panel he actually only acknowledged my
own remarks. Afterward he expressed a desire to get together and talk
so we'll do that in California or Boston sometime. I really think that he
deserves and could win the Nobel Peace Prize in a year or two. Unlike
Gore, he's actually making a measurable positive change in some lives.
My opinion. And he cares about the poorest kids of all. Apple offered
him their OS but he declined because it's proprietary. I do wish him
great success and luck with the program. He had handshake deals with
6 country leaders but they backed out when it came to writing the
checks. So now he's going first with Uruguay. Some of the technology in
his laptop is beyond clever in fact.

I'm rather shocked to hear those NBC comments. I thought they had
to be smart to be successful. At least it should help. If it's about D List,
boy did they blow it.

Oh, one more thing. Those Oakland Junkyard Dogs play dirty. And
they play on slightly larger Segways, the offroad XT models. I hate playing against them because they are so intimidating and the Dogs just
take them in any direction they feel like without looking, like someone
driving a Hummer does. This one guy is the worst. He modified his Segway to go faster and he cuts ahead of me as I head down the field and
he cuts in front of me. it's fair and good strategy to block, but with a
larger faster Segway it's very unfair. Well, I still get right into the frays
and skirmishes, Segway to Segway. At one junction I'd crowded him and

as he tried to turn we were colliding. Well, he actually fell off (hopped off) and I cheered loudly how I'd taken out an XT!!

XOXO STEVE

From: Kathy
Date: November 25, 2007 11:13:06 PM
To: Woz
Subject: Re: Thanks baby!

I think you're coming to my Cupertino show on Friday night, right? I'm getting in to San Francisco Thursday afternoon or early evening. Want to do something Thursday night? XXOO, KG

From: Woz
Date: November 26, 2007 12:53:02 AM
To: Kathy
Subject: Re: Thanks baby!

I have tickets to the show in Cupertino Friday night. I also have tickets to your SF show Saturday night but a huge long-time music hero of mine, on whom I have never seen, is playing in Berkeley that night so it's a dilemma.

I must warn you that I will be at the show with a woman friend who works at Apple in the Education Department.

I still can't get my Google calendar up. It indicates that my friend, who will be coming to your Cupertino show, might be flying in to San Jose Thursday evening. I thought she was flying in Wednesday, but if she's coming Thursday I may have to pick her up. I'll let you know when I find out more.

It's off to sleep for a couple of hours now.

XOXO
Steve

From: Kathy
Date: November 26, 2007 2:09:15 AM
To: Woz
Subject: Re: Thanks baby!

I am more than ok with you missing either show as I get a little self conscious. My "Woz chunk" is growing though. The straight guys who were dragged to the show seem to really like it.

Can you take me for a bite after the show at one of your local haunts? I'm always struggling to find places that serve food after 10PM on a week night. Can your woman friend from Apple's education dept please help mw with my iphone and my mac.com mail problems. Frankly, you're useless in that department. Can she relocate to LA and move in with me? I have a very impressive home.

XXOO, Kathy G

From: Woz
Date: November 26, 2007 6:04:01 AM
To: Kathy
Subject: Re: Thanks baby!

Ha ha. Janet is actually an instructor on iLife and I need her assistance to keep my own computer going.

I don't think that Janet would move to L.A. ever. She doesn't mind it but she's moving now to Cupertino from Iowa/Kansas only because she loves Apple so much and got a job at corporate.

See you soon,
XOXO STEVE

From: Kathy
Date: December 11, 2007 10:01:30 PM PST
To: Woz
Subject: Last night

Did you go to your Monday night supper club last night? They seem like good company.

XXOO,
KG

From: Woz
Date: December 11, 2007 10:27:20 PM
To: Kathy
Subject: Re: Last night

I missed the Monday night dinner due to an important panel at the Computer History Museum. That museum not only tries to preserve artifacts of the history of computers but also captures stories before the parties involved die. They have a regular speaking program. Last night was about a computer of major influence, the Commodore 64. I was on the panel (we offered Commodore our Apple but they turned us down) and a guy from the first IBM PC, another computer from that time frame (1982–1984) and the guy who joined Commodore later and invented their Amiga computer, another great one technically that didn't go so far.

Tomorrow is Janet's birthday and I don't have a card or present but I joked that a concert ticket was her present and she said OK. Whew until I get time. We have been going to shows together and playing cards and all so it's been fine.

I'll probably do all my X'mas shopping at Cosco the day before Christmas. Then I'm flying to Kansas to meet Janet's family. Someday I'll get 4 hours of sleep. I think.

I got a robot guitar the other day but haven't had time to use it yet. I love calling it a robot guitar but more accurately it tunes itself.

XOXO,
Steve

From: Kathy
Date: December 11, 2007 10:57:24 PM
To: Woz
Subject: Re: Last night

That's so weird,. I also was on a panel for the Computer History Museum. We must've just missed each other. My speech was called "the Sharp Wizard, bring back the greatest tech gadget ever invented"

What is your card game of choice with Janet? Texas hold 'em? Ooh, birthday presents are fun. May I suggest a rubber ring from, say Tiffany? You do know that telling me you're going to do your X-mas shopping at Costco is the same as driving that joke right in to my act in your Prius. Thank you Jesus (and you, Woz) Gotta go. I'll finish later. "Hi" to my girl Janet. XXOO, KG

From: Woz
Date: December 11, 2007 11:45:28 PM
To: Kathy
Subject: Re: Last night

The Computer History Museum has a great array of calculators through time.

I was a big fan and user of the Sharp Wizard myself! The trouble was, I didn't want my life to be carried in an electronic device. I resented having a calendar on my person, so I never used it, only showed it off.

You had better check Costco out. Last X'mas I did my shopping the last day there. I got lots of books and CD's and DVD's and house stuff and kitchen stuff and toys and gifts and could even have gotten jewelry there. It was my best X'mas shopping ever.

missing you,
xoxo
steve

From: Kathy
Date: December 24, 2007 4:59:53 PM
To: Woz
Subject: Thinking of you

at Costco just going NUTS! I can't stop imagining you running from aisle to aisle gleefully filling your shopping cart with books, cds, and 20 lb cans of funyuns, carmel corn and french onion dip. I hope you are having a wonderful X-mas and I look forward to seeing you in the new year. XXOO, KG

From: Woz
Date: December 24, 2007 11:03:54 PM
To: Kathy
Subject: Re: Thinking of you

I did much better this year.

A few days before Christmas Julie and I went shopping at a Cosco of her choice and it was a smaller Cosco. I wasn't interested in any of the tech stuff there, iPods, cameras, etc. I got some books and DVD collections but not very much overall. I found lots of stocking stuffer type stuff like magic tricks and candles and back scratchers and forks that can grab your friends' food.

I do love you and all your people and the fun you bring to us all,

xoxox steve

From: Kathy
Date: January 8, 2008 5:51:40 PM
To: Woz
Subject: Hey and Hi

My God, the straight guys love you! I was on kimmel last night and he was beside himself. He went to some convention you were at and said the crowd went apeshit. How is your new year going so far? Back in to traveling?

Have you given any thought to driving down for the Producers Guild Awards on Saturday, Feb 2nd? Please, please, please? Just being next to you at these things is a purifying experience. Besides, you're the only one smart enough to keep up with my high brow, cerebral and environmentally conscience brand of humor. XXOO, KG

From: Woz
Date: February 1, 2008 1:10:01 AM
To: Kathy
Subject: Re: Hey and Hi

kimmel . . . kimmel . . . please tell me who or what he is . . .

I decided today to drive down on Friday but now I'm having such problems with tech at home that I may still wind up coming down on Saturday. Anyway, I can't wait. How fun It will be, and I'm pretty much in the dark. I love all our times together so much!

xoxo
steve

From: Kathy
Date: January 22, 2008 12:20:15 AM
To: Woz
Subject: So many things!

I'm bursting with stuff to talk about with you. First of all, I'm beyond thrilled you're my date for the PGA's. We can really catch up then. Some topics on the table . . .

How was the MacWorld Expo, or as I call it Mac Pride Fest? Granted, it must have been a bitter pill for you when all the tech gays just wanted to hear what it's like for you to be allowed to be in my presence.

I'm dying to know if you ran in to Jobs?

should I get the 3K air thing? What if I drop it??? Do I have to think of everything?

I've been getting a big laugh when I tell the Gays in my audiences that the Mac Enthusiasts are giving them a run for their money.

Did you really invent the universal remote? Finally, something that can actually improve people's lives.

XXOO, KG

From: Woz
Date: February 1, 2008 1:26:53 AM
To: Kathy
Subject: Re: So many things!

MacWorld was good and I got to chat with Steve Jobs for a while.

He was friendly for a photo. I talk to him at all the MacWorlds. I get in early with VIP's and it's easy to talk with Steve. I also talk to him right after as well. Oddly, he suffered some bad publicity when some girl asked him for a photo and he said that it would be rude, which is sort of accurate—it would be rude to the thousands of others that he'd have to turn down.

I made up a joke while there. Q: What do you call Steve Jobs' body-guards? A: Jobs Security.

I am not a big fan of the Apple Air but you are probably the perfect candidate for it. As tech objects get smaller, they get tighter too and don't break as easily when dropped. Look how many times people drop cell phones and they usually survive. Steve Jobs showed the Air by taking it out of an interoffice mail envelope. I joked right away that I wanted a case that had the interoffice design on it and a day later a company announced one. I have it on order but that case may be months off.

actually, yes, [I did invent the universal remote] and there's a story behind it, a normal story

XXOO
SGW

From: Kathy
Date: April 10, 2008 12:53:11 AM
To: Woz
Subject: ep 1

Hey Steve- I just saw the rough cut of episode one of season 4 and you're so cute in it! Thanks for participating. I hear from Julie that it may have caused some discomfort for you with Janet, but you and Janet will see that it has truly been in fun! XXOO, KG

From: Woz
Date: April 10, 2008 7:43:04 AM
To: Kathy
Subject: Re: ep 1

The show was more fun than anything for me! It was so different from the other exciting times and adventures in my life. I hope it does go well.
   xoxo steve

From: Kathy
Date: April 14, 2008 10:00:31 PM
To: Woz
Subject: Holy shitballs!

Are you engaged? Some one from NBC emailed and heard you got engaged. Congratulations, if you are, but let me know as I will have to answer on talk shows etc. XXOO, KG

From: Woz
Date: April 14, 2008 10:06:35 PM
To: Kathy
Subject: Re: Holy shitballs!

actually, yes, but we've been hiding it for some time . . . this NBC source may not be in the know . . . I don't know anyone at NBC . . .
   we are planning kids too!

xoxo Steve

From: Kathy
Date: April 14, 2008 10:34:58 PM
To: Woz
Subject: Re: Holy shitballs!

Steve, I wish all the best for you! Have you guys set a date? XXOO, KG

From: Kathy
Date: April 25, 2008 1:32:53 AM
To: Woz
Subject: Finally!!!

I sent you an email Sunday night, but my iphone ran out and I couldn't
find it in my sent or drafts or anything. Anyway, there's a cute picture if
us in the STAR, so folks online are commenting on your wedding ring
slash not wedding ring. SO, did you two crazy kids actually tie the knot
or not? On the D-List show, we're kind of dating. It's harmless stuff, but I
don't want to be seen as some one who would "date" a married guy.
XXOO, KG

From: Woz
Date: April 25, 2008 8:58:00 AM
To: Kathy
Subject: Re: Finally!!!

not married but it's possible secretly
     I'll have to see the STAR.

From: Kathy
Date: May 9, 2008 2:19:53 PM
To: Woz
Subject: Goodness gracious!

I'm sure youre laughing at the STAR article. Some very funny mistakes,
but did want to let you know I did not speak to them and I would never
say I'm "glad its over" Hope youre well.

XXOO,
KG

King and Queen of Woz's charity event, The FurBall.

From: Woz
Date: May 14, 2008 1:30:22 PM
To: Kathy
Subject: Hi, love!

Kathy,

I have to thank you profusely for the great fun you brought into my life, in many ways.

I can also never thank you enough for helping out at the Fur Ball. The Humane Society raised something like $315,000 after expenses, far above what they had expected. You have done a good things for me by helping them out.

missing you,
xoxo................sw

From: Woz
Date: July 1, 2008 6:04:47 PM
To: Kathy
Subject: Fwd: Re: geeksaresexy.net

Hey, so guess who's going to be on Dancing With The Stars this season?

xoxo steve

20
HOW
PARIS HILTON
CHANGED
MY LIFE

I know Barack Obama had an historic 2009. But really, can it top the fact that the world realized I have what has been referred to as a "bangin' bikini bod"?

I have Paris Hilton to thank for it.

Not many people know this, but Paris Hilton is a genius. She speaks seven languages, including Urdu and I believe Romulan. She's written countless scholarly works under pseudonyms, because she's famous enough as it is without being pestered for her intellectual prowess. I heard she just declined a position on the board of directors of the Rand Corporation because she's too busy advising the Pentagon on delicate international matters. And apparently she's at the forefront of a gene therapy breakthrough.

Okay, that was fun to write. Really, she's an idiot. But she's *my* idiot, dammit. And here's why.

For season five of *My Life on the D-List* we did a whole episode chronicling my harebrained scheme to join Young Hollywood at the tender age of forty-eight. We decided that the quintessential example of living out loud Young Hollywood–style was, of course, Paris Hilton. She really is the generation's best ambassador. (See, she's a diplomat!)

When I brought this idea up to her, Paris and I hammered out a trade whereby I agreed to do a day of filming on season two of her MTV show *Paris Hilton's New BFF,* and she agreed to do a few hours of taping for *My Life on the D-List.* Now, in her defense—and I have to admit, it's killing me to write anything about a celebrity that starts with "in her defense"—Paris was one of the easiest people I've ever worked with on my show. She got the drill. The more Paris-y she could be, the sooner we'd be done, so she flicked the switch when the cameras rolled, laughed at my jokes, and generally took it on the chin. I walked away from my day with Paris liking her, and telling her I would think a little longer before being as hard on her in my act. Then I reminded her that it was still my job to put her into the act, and that if she could go to jail one more time but maybe stay a little longer, I would be personally grateful. A moving violation would be nice, but assault and battery would be ideal.

As we taped our first scene for the Young Hollywood episode on trendy Robertson Boulevard, I got younger with every store. We started out at Kitson, and by the time we ended up at Lisa Kline, I was sixteen and a half years old. Of course, it wasn't just us, but approximately fifty paparazzi photographers. This may have been a little too much for even Team Griffin to handle. I had to roll with an entourage, so of course I brought my twenty-four-year-old assistant and Young Hollywood aficionado Tiffany Rinehart, and beleaguered tour manager and trichotillomania (look it up, freaks) sufferer Tom Vize. They had their marching orders. Tom was in charge of my two eighty-pound, ill-behaved dogs Chance and Pom Pom, and Tiffany was busily Twittering our every move. But I tell ya, it's hard to focus when everywhere around me were video cameras and flashbulbs going off. I get so angry when I think that someone called the paparazzi photographers and tipped them off. If I ever run into that someone, let's say a red-haired lady who lives at my house, I'm going to give her what for.

Spending a day like that with Paris, I have to say, was more of an eye-opener than my 2003 upper-lid face work. Those photographers were pushy, noisy, physically aggressive, fighting among each other, shouting, knocking each other over, and generally unapologetic about causing an insanely chaotic scene. But the way she and her security team handled them, and the onlookers and screaming fans and tourists, was impressive. She'd turn to me every so often and say "Hungry tigers!" in her bizarre, yet oddly fascinating baby-voice affect. Really, that voice is younger than a baby's. It's fetal. A spot on her mother's pituitary gland. Plus, she had her tiny dog with her, who was so calm for such a frenzied situation, the dog must have been on some of my mother's "nervous pills." I don't remember the name of the dog, but I just started thinking of her as Little Paula Abdul.

Paris was sporting a bob, which may or may not have been Paris Magic Hair, and a ringed headband, as if she was a hippie from a commune bankrolled by a trust fund. I asked her if she knew what a hippie was, and she just giggled. She also had on high-heel black Ferragamo boots, and a very trendy peasant top and tights—all very fashionable. As for me, my original idea was to get an outfit of Paris's that she'd recently been photographed in, and wear that. I had a vision of magazines comparing us on a "Who wore it better?" page, and I thought it'd be funny if it was something like, "Paris Hilton 96 percent, Kathy Griffith 4 percent."

But when I called her office to talk to her stylist, to see if I could wear this '20s-era tube dress that she wore for her birthday bash in Vegas, it was, "Oh, you'll never fit into it. She's much smaller than you." Ouch.

Well, they wouldn't send me anything she'd actually worn, but they sent me her own line of clothes, which is ridiculous and must only do well in Asia because it's all so loud and over-the-top and pink pink pink. True, half of it I couldn't squeeze into, but I did pick out the most obnoxiously pink, silly outfit, a dress with a full-on '80s tube top. But because my boobs are real and tend to bounce off my knees, I wore it with an old-lady Maidenform bra—pink, mind you—completely showing. Look, I was going for a joke here, but I'm not that hard up for a laugh that I'm not going to wear a fucking bra.

So we make our way into Kitson past the snapping hordes, and then to Lisa Kline. We hadn't really planned it, but Paris started faux-shopping for me, and began sifting through Pucci bikinis. She picked out a blue-and-green paisley one for me, and said, "You'd look huge in this."

This is an actual Paris Hilton dress that she loaned me.

"Go fuck yourself."

"No, no, I don't mean you're huge like that. You know how I used to say, 'That's hot'?"

I cautiously said, "Yes?"

"Well, 'huge' is the new 'hot.' So if I say you're huge, that's a good thing!"

"Oh, okay. And just so you know, 'go fuck yourself' is still 'go fuck yourself,' but I'm sorry I said that."

Well, she bought the bikini for me, which I thought was nice. Next we were going to go to this trendy hotel called The Avalon and film by the pool, because this is where Young Hollywood grazes. So the show's producer said to me, "When we shoot this scene with you and Paris hanging by the pool, you've got to wear the bikini that she bought you."

Shit. Now all my weight issues were suddenly bubbling to the surface again, even though I have to say, 2009 has probably been my thinnest year since high school. But I started thinking crazy shit again, like how I was five pounds lighter only a week ago! Plus, it was me next to 6'1", super-skinny, super-perfect model-like Paris Hilton, who is a complete stick. How could it not bring up my issues? And in a bikini on top of that?

"I don't think I've even worn a bikini in about fifteen years," I told the producer.

It's true. When I go swimming I'm usually in a turtleneck wetsuit. And if that's not available, I'll wear a mens' suit. As in, a three-piece with tie and vest, and maybe an ascot. And a bowler hat. I'll wear that to take a shower if I'm having a particularly bad body-image day.

And can we discuss my skin for a second? It's not as if I have pale, alabaster-like-a-baby's-ass skin like Anne Hathaway. When I say that my skin is white and pale, that's an understatement. It's translucent. You can see right through to my veins and organs. I'm really no different from an anatomy figure in biology class.

Now, Paris, in all of her skinny Paris-ness, wouldn't even agree to wear a bikini without a sarong for the Avalon pool shoot, so I decided me in the tiniest bikini without any cover-up would be good for a few laughs. I just had to suck it up. Maybe I'd make it onto a worst-dressed bikini list. As you may know, I'm a staple of worst-dressed lists, ever since my days on *Suddenly Susan* when no designer wanted to touch me or loan me anything for awards show appearances or public events. The first time I was ever tagged by one of the magazines for worst dressed—it might have been me in a Betsey Johnson outfit, because those were big in the '90s and I liked her designs—my initial reaction was this bad feeling in the pit of my stomach. Then, about ten minutes later, I thought, *Wait a minute, this is kind of funny.* Such began my many appearances on these lists, usually next to pictures of Margaret Cho in some peacock-feather dress, Paula Abdul in something from her signature QVC line, and Bjork dressed like a swan or goose or

Paris Hilton getting served, Griffin-bikini-style.

some other waterfowl. For the longest time I cut out and laminated these photos and stuck them proudly on my refrigerator.

My only real triumph in the fashion area was the year I was asked to be a red carpet correspondent for the VH1/Vogue Fashion Awards, interviewing celebrities for the moments going into and out of commercials. Because *Vogue* was involved, they wanted to pick my outfit for me. They dressed me in this Ralph Lauren Purple Label girl's tuxedo with Versace heels. Well, *Vogue* editor Anna Wintour fired me the night of the show because I was so offensive on the red carpet—basically none of my segments were going to be used—but months later *Glamour* ran a small item on women who wear suits, and they cited me as someone who did it right! I considered it pretty much a Best Dressed award. So, no thanks, but thanks, *Vogue!* (I stole the outfit, too. Still wear the shoes!)

The hilarious part is, you know what joke provoked Anna to ax me when she heard it in the production booth? I said I was going to try to be a part of the fashion community by going into the bathroom later and doing blow off the Hilton sisters' asses. Luckily, since then I've learned how to talk about celebrities with restraint and grace.

Now here I was with Paris, about to expose to the world my pale 5'3" form in a silly-small bikini, and those damn pesky paparazzi (grrr, who *called* them anyway?) had followed us over here to the hotel from Robertson Boulevard. Then I thought about that old helpful "act as if" rule from the Overeaters Anonymous Big Book, the technique that guided me through more than a few downward spirals after binge-eating. Act as if it's all going to be fine. When it came time to shoot, I just had to say to myself, "Kathy, act as if you have the fucking hottest body there, and every guy in the crew wants to bang you. You are the hottest"—wait, "hugest," sorry, Paris—"piece of ass ever!"

That night, it all began happening online. There I was in photos next to Paris Hilton, and the consensus from *US Weekly's* website to PerezHilton's seemed to be that I have a "bangin' bikini bod." When they drop the "y," on "body," it's like you have something other than a "body." That "y" was holding me back, it seems.

I say this with humility, but I am now in the infancy of my new career as a semiprofessional bikini model.

The press reaction, for one thing, has been the kind you can't buy. The *National Enquirer* featured me on a page of Hottest Beach Bodies. I did a bikini shoot for *TV Guide,* as well as one for *OK* magazine, which wrote, "Kathy Griffin's got a hot body and she isn't afraid to show it!" They brought bikinis *to my house*, because at that point I thought the only bikini that existed in the world was the one Paris Hilton bought me. But when you have a "bangin' bikini bod"—or "bbb," as I'll coin now—they come to *you* with bikinis, and ones that fit, not ones that let your real boobs accidentally slip out so you can trip on them. Did I mention *People* magazine had a "Bikini Body Showdown" and polled readers on whether I, Lisa Rinna, or Tara Reid had the hottest bikini bod, and I won? And I don't take steroids *or* get drunk and fall down in public. Not that they do, of course.

Look, I'm not out to embarrass Gisele Bundchen or Bar Refaeli, or whatever bikini model Leo is or was banging or will bang in the future, and my goal isn't to make any of these women lose any sleep over the contracts they're about to miss out on because of me. But I'm clearly not far away from a Bain de Soleil campaign, some beach towel contracts, and the inevitable pleading from *Sports Illustrated* for a cover shoot and, if the attorneys can work out the details, a tasteful centerfold. Will anyone really be surprised when Tyra Banks simply cuts to the chase next season and stands in front of my bikini-ed self—well, not that close, because she'll be too self-conscious to be that close to my "bbb"—and says, "Kathy Griffin, congratulations, you *are* America's Next Top Model." I'm ready to change lives here, people. Oprah, you're going to be trading in Dr. Oz's scrubs for me in a bikini every Tuesday.

The reality, of course, is that this whole bikini thing has been hilarious and great and bizarre, and it couldn't have come at a better time when my tireless efforts to get the word out about *My Life on the D-List* often meant sitting in a room doing twenty-five interviews in a row with places like *Wake Up, Tulsa! People* magazine would never give me the time of day—wouldn't cover me going to Walter Reed Army Medical Center—but now that I have a bangin' bikini bod, I guess it's all good. If it gets one more viewer to watch *The D-List,* call me the worst or the hottest, I don't care. Although a few extra straight guys turning on my show to jerk off to me would be so great. A pretty lady has dreams.

Here comes the section my editor is making me write. She keeps asking me to explain my "typical routine regarding diet and exercise," and "how you got the bbb." Oh Christ, Pamela. Here it is.

KATHY GRIFFIN'S BANGIN' BIKINI BOD REGIMEN:

Sometimes I work out with a trainer. I get real mad at him occasionally because it's *real* hard. And . . . [sob] . . . I hurt afterward. But I do it, because I'm on TV. If I was still a loan officer in a bank I would be a good fifty pounds heavier and a lot happier. Sometimes I forget to work out for a month. Guess what happens then? I GAIN WEIGHT. Sometimes I'm so stressed out and exhausted I just have a bunch of diarrhea. I'm pretty sure "bunch" is the correct term for multiple diarrheas. Anyway, it's good for at least a jean size. Sometimes I'm out of town and go for very long walks or hikes. Yawn. One thing, though: I find the thinner and hotter I get the bitchier I get. If you see me in an airport and say, "I didn't know you were so tiny!" I might slap you in the face or kick your husband in the balls. It's not personal. I'm just really hungry. In fact, I'm hungry most of the time.

Now for my nutritional regimen: Have you heard of sugar-free Red Bull? Sometimes that's lunch. That's because I have such a crazy upside-down schedule—early morning radio promotion interviews at 6:12 a.m., two shows at night, and in between whatever is demanding my time—that I can't really stick to normal meal times. Some days I have three healthy meals, and make sure a big salad is one of them. Good for me! Wheeeee! Other days I think I will die if I don't have some pizza. I mean I really think I'm going to die. Guess what? At those times I eat pizza. And I haven't died yet! What's really helped me is having "sensible" specialty meals delivered every day. I still adore all my favorite junk foods (shout-out to marble two-layer cake with chocolate chip frosting in between and buttercream on the outside), and I'm never going to love steamed broccoli, but I also know that having a Cobb salad in my hotel room before I do a stand-up show— instead of pigging out on bad things because I'm lonely or bored— means I won't feel like crap onstage later.

All this bikini hoopla doesn't mean I still don't struggle with my weight. Body issues don't just go away. Just the other day a flight attendant had the bikini picture in a tabloid and wanted me to sign it, and there was still that little part of me that wanted to go, "Oh! Well, just so you know . . . heh heh . . . this picture was from five pounds

My first bikini picture, with my cousins Maureen and Nancy. Why do I look like I just got punched in the face?

ago . . . heh heh . . . I didn't get to work out the week prior to this photo being taken . . . heh heh . . . I've worked out so much more since then!" I had to stop myself and say, "Kathy, sign the fucking picture."

God, I could talk about my hot body all day. Couldn't you, Oprah? Don't you find it heartwarming that in this roller-coaster D-list life of mine where talking shit about celebrities and making fun of crazy Hollywood has given me an incredible career, it's a fitting irony that I'm ending this book by offering my gratitude to a celebrity? One who was responsible for getting my picture into so many magazines and TV shows. And by way of a frickin' two-piece, no less.

So to whoever's reading this to Paris Hilton, tell her I say thank you.

EPILOGUE

So what do you think of my life so far? Oh shut up, *you're* too skinny.

Well, I've read my book, too, and here's what I think about my spiritual journey: Cake is awesome. I want some right now.

Actually, it's a little strange to look back so thoroughly on my life and realize I haven't learned one lesson. Instead, I just go by my own creed, which is essentially: Make mistakes (telling Jesus to suck it), repeat them (FanningGate), don't learn from them (got two Emmys), and blame others (the Vatican).

More than anything, the guiding force of my life has been my work ethic. Like a lot of things, as you've probably gathered, it goes back to my childhood. When I was growing up, my family loved watching *60 Minutes* every Sunday, and I remember once there was a story about an old woman who had lost everything. She was so poor, she had to eat dog food. After watching the story Mom turned to me and said, "I hope you're proud of yourself, for Chrisssake."

"Whuh?" I said.

"I know you spent three gahddamn dollars at Woolworth's today on a Barbie outfit. I saw you."

"Whuh?"

"You keep spending money like it's goin' out of style and you're gonna be eatin' dog food outside in our Dodge Dart, cause we're gonna lose this whole gahddamn house. Everybody around here is spending money like it grows on trees!"

Mind you, we didn't have a dog. But the point is, my parents instilled in me their very own prewar, Depression-era work ethic, and along with that goes the daily fear that I could truly lose everything tomorrow. And by "lose everything," I mean succumb to the hot-or-not system that governs every aspect of the entertainment business, that turns A-listers into D-listers faster than you can say, "I'm a Celebrity, Get Me Out of Here."

I'm not eating dog food now, and that is why I want to take this opportunity to sincerely express my gratitude to all of you for coming to my stand-up shows, downloading my CDs, watching my little cable show, ordering T-shirts that say "Suck it," and, of course, buying this book. When I look out into the audience, when I see you at book signings, when I read favorable comments online, get your emails, or notice that more of you are following on Twitter, none of it is lost on me. I see you. I thank you.

Here's why I'm the luckiest motherfucker on earth. I get to do what I love, and I mean I love all of it. Stand-up. *The D-List.* Talk shows. Red carpet. The occasional yeast infection. (That's from performing in polyester blend pants in an outdoor venue in Milwaukee during Summer Gay Pride.) All the people I've gotten to meet. I mean, who else gets to do shit like this:

Yeah, that's me in bed with CNN's John King. And *his* Emmy. It gets better. His wife, White House correspondent Dana Bash, took the picture, then told me I'm her Cher. Sure, it's fun to be in bed with John King, but it's way better to be somebody's Cher.

ACKNOWLEDGMENTS

First and foremost, I would like to thank my friend and collaborator Robert Abele, who did the heavy lifting of shaping this book, while I just mostly bitched and moaned; his lovely wife Margy, who guided us along the way, constantly muttering something about "More detail! More detail!"; my editor Pamela Cannon, who gets how awesome I am; Team Griffin, not to be confused with the Griffin clan, so shout-out to Jessica (miss you!), Tiffany (best laugh ever), and Tom (love); the agent who made this happen, Trena Keating; my WME gang, Nancy Josephson and Ari Emanuel; my beloved attorneys Bill Sobel and Alan Isaacman; my stand-up agent Steve Levine; the entire gay community; Nancy Silverton and the delicious pizza she would serve Robert and me at Mozza after writing sessions; and a pretty, pretty lady publicist named Whitney Tancred.

I also want to thank Jeff Zucker, who has done very little for me but thinks he discovered me. Jeff Gaspin, same thing. The Bravo gang: Lauren Zalaznick, Frances Berwick, Cori Abraham, and of course, Andy Cohen. Now can I get a fucking billboard? I love you freaks. Sorry, gotta go. Les Moonves is on the other line.

My doggies, Chance and Pom Pom.

My Emmys, Emmy and Emily. Yes, I named them. Guys name their dicks, for Chrissakes. Get over it.

A New Jersey Housewife said it best. "Let me tell you something about my fa-muh-lee. We are as thick as thieves, and we protect each other to the end." Or until our annual Christmas fight. Ladies and gentlemen, the Griffins: my brothers John, Gary, and even Kenny; my sister Joyce; a beautiful Irish rose named Maggie, and the man who loved her so.

OFFICIAL BOOK CLUB SELECTION

KATHY GRIFFIN

READING GROUP GUIDE

A CONVERSATION
WITH KATHY GRIFFIN

Random House: State your name and profession.
Kathy Griffin: My name is Kathy Griffin, and I am a teller of dick jokes. And a plumber.

RH: It appears your pen is as profane as your tongue. Where did you learn to swear?
KG: I learned to swear from the masters, the priests and nuns at a little church called St. Bernadine's. I also learned some good swear words from other parishes, but I would say the Chicago parishes and the adjacent suburban parishes really have it down. In addition to that, I would just say I probably learned swearing from the mean streets of Forest Park, Illinois. The other four-year-olds were pretty rough in my neighborhood. I'm not gonna lie. Chicago dockworkers were afraid of them.

RH: This is your first book. Had you ever considered writing anything before? A novel? Or a scholarly work of history? Or a children's story?
KG: I had not considered it, because I'd always been told by the nuns at St. Bernadine's that my cursive was poor. A children's story is an interesting idea. How's this for a title: *Waterboarding Preteens: The Debate Is Back On.* I have a political side as well.

RH: How much did your Irish Catholic heritage play into being a pain in the ass to celebrities?

KG: I feel that while I have never had a drink in my life, I have the audacity of a serious alcoholic. And when I say alcoholic, I am certainly not referring to anyone in my family, who may have ever had a problem with the drink. Because if there's one thing you should know about my family, and all of my relatives, it's that none of them have a drinking problem at all, that I have made it all up, because I am, let's get this right, "dramatic."

RH: When you were a child, you performed for your family. What advice do you have out there for parents enduring their obnoxious brat's self-indulgent showboating?

KG: I am a firm proponent of monitored tasing. I believe it can be done in a controlled, humane way. I am also in favor of having your child on a bridle-style leash in the mall, or just in their room. But if they do insist on doing shows, you should hold them up to a Broadway standard. And if they don't give a good performance, you should be able to pummel them with fruit, and talk to them about how perhaps they could learn a little something from the vaudeville days, when there were no child labor laws. Look, I don't care for children. I don't think they're special, except yours. I don't think they're attractive, except yours. And I don't think any of them are gifted, except yours.

RH: You seem fairly obsessed with Oprah. Is this something you'll ever outgrow?

KG: I will never outgrow my obsession with Oprah. Just as she will never outgrow her cardigan sweaters. Oops, she already has. Now look, that sounds like a dig, but it's not. It's called a struggle, and I'm on it with her. I support her. (Not as much as she needs those underwire bras to support her, because she's got some serious ropes and pulleys going on there.) The point is, I worship her, and fear her at the same time. And believe me, that's how she wants it. Don't be fooled.

RH: Did I miss something? Where's Celine Dion in this book?
KG: I didn't write about Celine Dion, only because of my fear of her husband Rene Angelil. I have an unfounded but constant fear that he could be in the French-Canadian diva-by-association Mafia. Or have French-Canadian diva-by-association Mafia ties, and by ties I don't mean les cravats. And I fear that I may be abducted, whisked away, and held prisoner at a charming little brasserie in Montreal, forced to eat multiple croque monsieur sandwiches until I confess to knowing the lyrics to every single one of her songs.

RH: You mention a lot about wanting to be Rhoda. Did you ever get to meet Valerie Harper?
KG: As a matter of fact, I have met the great Valerie Harper a couple of times. The first time was on a television panel, with myself, Valerie, Cindy Williams, and Diahann Carroll—Dominique Deveraux from *Dynasty*—who loves to tell anyone in that stuffy, almost British-but-mandatory-if-you're-in-an-eighties-prime-time-soap accent, "I. Was. The first. Black. BITCH. In prime time." Anyway, during the panel, one of the questions from the moderator was about reality television. Valerie went on to give a diatribe about how it was really the dawn of a horrible age in television, and that, in the time of Shakespeare, people needed scripted works to entertain them and help raise them to a higher level of intellect. She went on and on, made a very good argument against reality television, and then I rose my hand up and said, "Have you guys seen *Survivor*? It's fucking awesome. They don't even eat for like, thirty days, except sometimes they just eat dirt. And sometimes they have to fuzz out their genitals."

RH: You spent many years in the showbiz wilderness. What's in your "survival backpack" for that kind of journey?
KG: Blame. I feel it's essential to blame others for your failures. It's comforting. Also, as you'll remember from my binge-eating chapter, combining salty foods with sweet foods in an irrational manner, i.e., potato chips and Rolos, which are a chocolate-covered caramel candy, is something that I find helps me get through difficult post-

audition moments. Also, it's important to stay hydrated. But not too hydrated, or else you'll have to wear a catheter. Which I did one time, but for a different reason, as you might also recall from the book. But let me just say this: I am more pro-catheter than the medical industry gives me credit for. So that would be blame, Rolos, potato chips, and a catheter.

RH: Of all the possible stories you could have told about Andy Dick, you chose a balmy spring night at the University of North Florida. Why that one?
KG: I feel that that story has all the great elements of a typical experience with Andy Dick. I cannot tell you how many holiday parties I've had, and especially my yearly Kwanzaa festival, where my comedy world friends sit around and have bizarrely similar stories about Andy Dick. The locations change, but the story's always the same. There's drugs involved, and some vomiting, a lot of confusion and anger, and maybe his fly going down, and Andy taking his penis out. And when the inappropriate behavior reaches its peak, then it's a lot of us looking around the room saying, "That happened to me, too." Mine just happened in Jacksonville.

RH: What do you think gays should take away from reading this book?
KG: I think the gays should be happy with this book. It talks a lot about being who you are, and I certainly mention a lot of gay people. I would say it definitely has strong gay themes, and the gay community should know that frankly it has been a moral struggle for me even to acknowledge the heterosexual community in this book at all. But I am slowly reaching out an olive branch to the heterosexual community, even though I believe everything they do goes against the teachings of Our Lord and Savior Jesus Christ. But I'm trying not to judge them.

RH: Please, one more Brooke Shields story.
KG: No. I think I have more Brooke Shields stories in my book than in hers. What was that one she wrote in the '80s about being

a virgin? *The Brooke Book,* I think? Well, hell, I'm a virgin, too. I'm real scared of vaginal intercourse, because I'm just not ready yet. And someday I'm going to get my menstrual period. Now will you fuckers at Wal-Mart sell this book?

RH: **You've done such an amazing job describing the sights, sounds, and aromas of incredibly bad dates. What are your methods of recall?**

KG: Well, I studied serious acting at the Lee Strasberg Theatre and Film Institute, and they have an exercise there called sense memory. It means I am a much more serious actress than Meryl Streep, or her brother Joe Streep, the little-known Streep no one talks about. And what I cannot recall through my senses, I make up. So I'm a believer in the truth, the senses, and then making some shit up if you think it's funnier than the truth.

RH: **Everyone might be a little concerned that you have nice things to say about Jessica Simpson. Does an act of reflection like book writing soften memories slightly?**

KG: Writing this book has definitely distorted my memories of certain celebrities, so it may surprise you who I have fond stories about. But also, come on, I do a lot of shit-talking about Steve Martin, who I *guarantee* you will never remember meeting me. Nor should he. But I'm kind of proud of that paragraph or two because I think it's really out of left field. I'm hoping someone in Camp Martin will call him at some point and say, "Uh, there's this really weird part in Kathy Griffin's book where she just talks *shit* about you, Steve." And then he'll harrumph and go to a gallery opening with Lorne Michaels, and it'll all be better.

RH: **If we were to call the incomparable Maggie Griffin and ask her for her take on the stories about her in this book, what would she say?**

KG: Maggie Griffin will deny like it's Watergate. Or she will say, "I don't recall." She may actually get Nixon advisor John Dean's wife

Maureen to sit behind her like she did for the Watergate hearings. My mother proudly says that denial is in fact a river in Egypt, and she is on a canoe.

RH: Who did you decide wasn't worth writing about in this book?
KG: I decided it wasn't worth talking shit about talk show hosts, because they're the only people in the book who can actually fuck me by not having me on their shows to promote the goddamn book. So all you talk show hosts, you know who you are, you know what you did, and you're off the hook for now. I'd like a muffin basket from each one of you.

RH: Voltaire once wrote, "Work keeps at bay three great evils: boredom, vice, and need." Do you care what Voltaire had to say?
KG: For a model she sounds like a really smart lady, and I think it's great that she had so many things to say. So she's supercool. I'm gonna sext her later.

RH: Do you consider yourself an inspiration to women everywhere?
KG: If by women you mean drag queens, then the answer is yes. I am an inspiration to women, he/shes, the LGBTQI community, and if you can tell me what the "Q" and the "I" are for, you get a handjob. But I do inspire them. "Q" might be "Queer." It could also be "Query," like you're asking about which sex you're going to be. And I'm not sure, but "I" has to be "Interesting." As in, "Check that one. *Interesting!*" But look, I'm not putting anyone in a box, so gays, stop your letter-writing campaigns right now. I think you're all great. I don't care if you have a penis or a vagina or a pagina, or a venis. You're all great. You're all fabulous.

RH: What do you say to those who think women aren't funny?
KG: I know you're talking about Jerry Lewis, so I say, "Bring it on, old man. And don't forget your meds." Look, all female comics battle the chicks-aren't-funny stigma, all day and all night, and mostly

at night. All I can tell you is that no one makes me laugh in my life more than my girlfriends. When I think about those times as a kid when I was in my pjs at a girl sleepover—I'm talking to you, Patty Sapienza—they would have me on the floor in stitches, everything from making fun of the popular girls—I'm talking to you, Mary O'Hanrahan—to impersonating the meanest of nuns. (I'm talking to you Sister . . . I'm still too afraid to say your name.) So I don't know where that bullshit about women not being funny came from. Whoever says chicks aren't funny has not seen my aunt Irene on Christmas Eve with a few Tom Collins in her singing "Danny Boy," because that's some hilarious shit.

RH: Describe your ideal, make-a-wish day of personal experiences with batshit celebrities.
KG: Well, it would start with some sort of a fit in the hair-and-makeup trailer on a set. I heard a story that when Sharon Stone was working on *Casino,* she got into such a fight with her hairdresser, that after he spent four hours doing this beautiful bouffant hairdo for her, she got up and walked to the sink and put her head under water. I have no idea if that's true, but I hope it is, cause that's some awesome shit I would love to see. Then it would go right to lunch, where I could witness an eating disorder. Maybe a Lohan is purging in a bush somewhere with her finger down her throat. Or perhaps there's an Olsen twin on a scale crying because she finally tipped 100. Any outburst over weight I would cherish. Also, it would be great to see an actress have a workload meltdown. So maybe at 2 p.m. some A-lister saying, "I can't handle this shit anymore." Because I love when actors can't deal with a normal workday, and they think two in the afternoon is like midnight, so I would love to see somebody storming to their car, exhausted because they've put in a grueling four-hour workday of saying three lines and texting their nanny. Then it's maybe off to an illicit affair. At the top of my wish list would be following a rapper or a football player over to his baby mama's house where a screaming match ensues to the point where someone, maybe me, has to anonymously dial 911, and then I take

a couple pictures, and I become an unannounced star witness later at the trial, entering Joan Collins–style in a smashing hat. And then at the end of the day it's a healthy round of clubbing with Janice Dickinson, and then on the way home we go to the Beverly Glen pharmacy and run into Paula Abdul. All three of us secretly take our small white-paper pharmacy bags and put them behind our backs and make uncomfortable small talk. And then we go back to Andy Dick's house and Janice, Paula, and I fuck the shit out of him.

RH: Everyone from Mac-heads to *Dancing with the Stars* fans want to know, what was up with your relationship with billionaire Apple co-founder Steve Wozniak?
KG: Turns out I was banging Steve Jobs the whole time, but I have a really good reason for it, which I'll have to go into in the next book.

READING GROUP
QUESTIONS AND TOPICS
FOR DISCUSSION

1. Kathy's Irish Catholic grandfather left his wife when she wouldn't bear any more children for him. What other ways is organized religion completely fucked?

2. Kathy grew up in a home where drinking was prevalent, encouraged, and embraced. How many of you are drunk right now? Did you know Two Buck Chuck is for sale at Trader Joe's today? Can you pick up Maggie on your way there, please?

3. Catholic school was a source of emotional pain and fear for Kathy, but she rose above it by talking shit to mean girls' faces. Did Jesus start weeping for Kathy then? Or much later, after he was told to suck it on national television? Or is Jesus too busy dealing with Lindsay Lohan—not to mention Ali—to care about what Kathy says?

4. Kathy watched a lot—I mean, A LOT—of television growing up. If the average American child watches eight hours of television a day, how is it that Kathy managed to watch twenty-seven hours a day? Could Kathy have a superpower? Is there anything you used to do for hours on end that's made you who you are? Besides masturbating?

5. When she was in high school, Kathy gravitated toward gays. Did you go to high school? Are you gay? Have you experimented? Are you what Oprah would refer to as "on the down low"? How often and why?

6. Kathy openly discusses a binge-eating disorder that plagued her for years. Have you ever struggled with such a disorder? Do you want to go to Costco later?

7. Kathy has a thing for donuts: hot, sugary donuts. And a thing for donut fryers, as unpleasant as that sounds. Would she have become nearly as famous and successful if she had been really into tofu? Or arugula? Or sushi? Would she have fucked a sushi chef?

8. When Kathy discovered stand-up, she found her calling. Do you think you're funny enough to do stand-up comedy? Well, you're not. Bye now.

9. Kathy blew her audition for *Saturday Night Live* and ruined her shot at being a neglected female cast member on a famous TV sketch show. When have you blown your big chance? Have you ever wondered what it is that makes Lorne Michaels cast people like A. Whitney Brown?

10. In the chapter "Brooke Shields, Don't Read This," Kathy tells stories about television and beauty icon Brooke Shields. Do you have an icon of beauty and perfection in your life who you try to learn from? Are you Brooke Shields? If you are Brooke Shields, did you go ahead and read this, even though you were told not to? How often and why?

11. Kathy was once unwittingly privy to the sight of Rodney Dangerfield's balls. Have you ever been scarred by the accidental sight of someone's genitals who wasn't a member of Young Hollywood? Is Congress doing enough about this issue?

12. Kathy writes that, to this day, Jerry Seinfeld is the A-lister who's taken her jabs with the most grace and humor. Is this because Jerry is secretly in love with Kathy, and obviously miserable in his sham of a marriage, going so far as to have children with that woman simply to make Kathy jealous? Has this ever happened with you and Jerry Seinfeld?

13. In the chapter "Nip/Fucked," Kathy Griffin details her many experiences with plastic surgery, including a near-death occurrence from liposuction. Have you had any work done? Did it help you advance in your chosen field? Would you like me to ask again, Nicolette Sheridan? I mean, Arnold Schwarzenegger? I mean, Barack Obama? Okay, it's just a hunch. I'm pretty sure he only gets a little Botox now and then.

14. Kathy felt really good about herself when Howard Stern told her on his show that he'd bang her. Who makes you feel positive and uplifted by declaring they'd like to nip/fuck you every which way?

15. Kathy has been banned from many talk shows. How do you feel Barbara Walters has managed to hide her pain about dealing with life without Kathy day in and day out? Have you seen Barbara send secret messages to Kathy over the airwaves, begging her to come back on *The View*? And even go so far as to signal Kathy through various hand gesticulations, hoping that Kathy will come to Barbara's apartment one evening and spoon together in her big bed?

16. While many reality stars complain that they were "edited" to come off like horrible people, Kathy maintains that she has been edited on *My Life on the D-List* to look nicer than she is. Can you imagine what a bitch she must be in real life? Have you ever known such a big old bitch as Kathy Griffin?

17. Kathy coined the phrase "the D-list," and happily claims it's where she resides. What lists are you on and why? Are you honest

about it? Come on, girl. Are you happy with your list? Do you really want to be on the A-list? Because if you do, Kathy can send someone over to rifle through your trash, take a picture of you with no makeup on, and videotape you banging the nanny. How do you like your A-list now?

18. Kathy has vigorously campaigned for the right for gay people to be married. However, since her own divorce, she is vehemently against heterosexual marriage, and feels it should be made illegal. Do you think these two beliefs are at odds?

19. When Kathy told everyone that Dakota Fanning was in rehab, she sparked a shitstorm, even though she was making a joke. When will it be okay to say that the Octomom's children are in rehab? Soon? Please? Do you know someone who you'd like to be in rehab whether they need it or not just because they annoy you?

20. When Kathy says she doesn't drink, she's fucking serious. She doesn't drink, so quit offering her one. What do you avoid because it tastes disgusting, ruins lives, and turns loved ones into raving lunatics? But also, what do you abuse? Because nobody's perfect. Have you seen Kathy with a cake?

INDEX

Page numbers in *italics* refer to photographs.

Abdul, Paula, 321, 323, 344
    Colleague, worst-dressed list
African American moviegoer, 69
Agassi, Andre, 123, 124, 125, 157
    Kind of a pill
Aguilera, Christina, 26, 155–56
    Fighter
Aiken, Clay, 100
Alice from *The Brady Bunch,* 29
Alonso, Maria Conchita, 58–59
    My Lee Strasberg rival
Amber-Thiessen, Tiffani, 135
Angelil, Rene, 339
Aniston, Jennifer, 176, 181
    I want her lower body
Apatow, Judd, 97
Attell, Dave, 97
Aunt Florence, 20, 105
    Pop-culture-savvy octogenarian

Baba Booey, 151
Banks, Morwanna, 117
    Almost Brooke's sidekick
Banks, Tyra, x, 65, 326
    FIERCENESS

Barrett, Rona, 20–21, 113
    Keeping Mom in the know
Barrie, Barbara, 121, *120*
Bash, Dana, 331
Bass, Lance, 150
    'NSYNC hottie
Bee Gees, The, 33
Behar, Joy, 146
    On Hasselbeck duty
Berkus, Nate, ix
Berry, Halle, 269
Big Fat Paul, 165–66
    Ass-rape pantomime artist
Bitches of the Century, The,
    161–62, *163,* 165–66
Bjork, 323–24
    Colleague, worst-dressed
    list
Black, Jack, *98,* 99–100
    Fucked him twice
Blitzer, Wolf, 260
Bobby the trainer, 211
Bolton, Michael, 143
    Rockin' the mullet
Bono, Chastity/Chaz, 80
    Theory of her conception
Borowitz, Andy and Susan, 106
    Connoisseurs of rap culture

Bowen, Mr. and Mrs., 4–5, 15
  First audience
Brady, Marcia, 30
  I wish
Breasseale, Todd, 257
Bendewald, Andrea, *120*
Brown, Chris, 219
Brown, Downtown Julie, 117
  Almost Brooke's sidekick
Brown, Julie, 87
Buffett, Warren, 124
  Mr. Kathy Griffin???
Bullock, Sandra, 77, 135
  Ranchy diva
Bundchen, Gisele, 326
  What's up, fat ass?
Burnett, Rob, 144
Buscemi, Steve, 110
  Won't remember me

Cannon, Pamela, 333
Capers, Virginia, 106–7
  Cool old actress
Carbonell, Nestor, 121, *120*, 187
  Cuban hunk
Carey, Drew, 20
  Kissed him once (next book)
  My neighbor
Carey, Mariah, 156, 193–94
  Crazy on Cribs
Carroll, Diahann, 339
Castellanata, Dan, 30
  From Oak Park High to Homer
    Simpson
Cavett, Dick, 20
Chance, 320, 333
  Best guy I ever knew
Cheadle, Don, 109
Cheech & Chong, 66
Cher, 80, 331
  We're both a size 0

Chicago White Sox, 34, 57, 58
Chiklis, Michael, 276
Cho, Margaret, *90*, 92, 96–97, 101,
  155, 156, 323
  Sex shop employee of the month
  Stand-up comrade
  Colleague, worst dressed list
Church, Thomas Haden, 108–9
  Hot, funny, and mean
Chyna, 271
Clay, Andrew Dice, 84
Clift, Montgomery, 21
  Maggie's first gay
Clooney, George, *105*, 109–110,
  113
  I totally fucked him *(J.K., kids)
Collins, Tom, 15, 343
  Uncle Mo's best friend
Conrad, Lauren, 72
  Co-CEO, Fucking Lucky Club
Cook, Dane, 131, 193, 194
  Ugh
Coolidge, Jennifer, 117
  Almost Brooke's sidekick
Corbett, John, 75–76
  Sex in my city
Cosgrove, Miranda, 261
Crawford, Chace, 32
  Love her
Cross, David, 94, 130
  Too alternative to buy house
  Wants my Realtor's name
Cruise, Tom, 203, 277
Cyrus, Miley, 171
  Cutting-edge rocker
Czech, Brian, 26, 27–28
  (Call me!)

Daly, Carson, 146
Dangerfield, Rodney, 131–32, 346
  Guest testicles on *Susan*

David, Larry, 116, 118, 129
  Loves to give me shit
Davidovich, Lolita, 109
Davis, Viola, 110
Deen, Paula, 3
DeGeneres, Ellen, 107–8, 296
  Golfs with Timberlake
DeMornay, Rebecca, 58
De Niro, Robert, 59, 76
  Respected actor, Sally Kirkland
  paramour?
DeVito, Danny, 109
DiCaprio, Leonardo, 326
  I totally fucked him *(J.K., kids)
Dick, Andy, 25, *87,* 94, 97, 100,
  118, 135–36, *154,* 161–68,
  340, 344
  Where do I start?
Dickinson, Janice, 344
Dion, Celine, 280, 339
  Bonjour!
Drescher, Fran, 117
Dr. Oz, ix, x, 326

Edwards, Anthony, 109
Efron, Zac, 32
  Love her
Esposito, Jennifer, 117
  Almost Brooke's sidekick
Everett, Chad, 21

Fanning, Dakota, 259, 275–79,
  282, 329, 348
  Scarred for life by me
Ferrell, Will, 78
  Taught him everything he
  knows
Flav, Flavor, 107
Flockhart, Calista, 17
Frank, Barney, 26
Friedman, Eric, 257, 258

Garland, Judy, 13
Garofalo, Janeane, *74, 87,* 88–89,
  91, 92, 93, 94, 96, 97, 100,
  101, 148
  Alternative comedy's Julie McCoy
  Stand-up comrade
Garrett, Brad, 213–14
Garrett, Leif, 132
  "To the Bone"
Gaspin, Jeff, 197–98, 254, 333
  Discovered me
Gaspin, Karen, 197
  Really discovered me
Gass, Kyle, 99
Gelman, Michael, 145–46
Gertz, Jami, 172
Gifford, Kathie Lee, 145, 146, 254
Gold, Tracey, 17
Goldthwait, Bobcat, 87, 111
Gorney, Karen Lynn, 33
Gosselin, Kate, 5
  Hair-challenged mom of eight
Gould, Dana, 92
Graham, Steadman, x
  Still living?
Grammer, Kelsey, 197
Grandma Griffin 9–10
  Faith . . .
Grandpa Griffin, 9–10
  . . . and Begorrah
Gray, Macy, 161
Green, Seth, 258
Griffin, Gary, 11, 15, 17, 34, 61–
  62, 211, 264
Griffin, John (brother), 11, 17, 34,
  41, 44, 48, 61–62, 211, 264
  Dangler extraordinaire
Griffin, John Patrick (father), v, 5, 8,
  9–10, *11,* 12–17, 25, 30, 34–
  37, *38,* 40–41, 43, 45–50, 54–
  55, 58, 62–63, 66, 85, 94, 99,

Griffin, John Patrick (father) (*cont.*)
111–13, *112*, 117, 173,
189–91, 208–11, *208*, 217–18,
226, *229*, 230, 254, *262*,
263–67, *266*, 281, 291, 330
Handyman
Comedy role model
Griffin, Joyce, 4–5, 11, 15, 17, 34,
36, 41, 66, *175*, 211, 264
Griffin, Kathy, It's my book, do I
really have to list page numbers
here?
Bikini model
Griffin, Kenny, 11, 17, 36, *38*,
39–50, 61, 218
Griffin, Maggie, ix, 4–5, 7–10, *11*,
12–18, 20–22, 25, *25*, 30, 32,
34–37, 40–41, 43, 44–50,
54–56, 58, 62–63, 64, 66,
68, 75, 77–79, 85–86, 94,
99, 111–13, *112*, 117, 121,
126, 130–31, 156, 163,
173, 189–91, *208*, 208–11,
217–18, 229, 232, 254, 258,
260, 263–66, 291, 329–30
Sommelier
Comedy role model
Griffin, Mary, 8
Grisaffi, Christie, 31
Gunderson, Kris, 285

Hagar, Sammy, 142
Alien abductee
Hargitay, Mariska, 78–79, 276
Falling star
Harper, Valerie, 339
Hartman, Phil, 54, 77–78, 118
Groundlings wizard
What a mensch
Harvey, Laurence, 28
Hasselhoff, David, 269

Hatcher, Teri, 182
Hathaway, Anne, 323
Pretty, pale lady
Hawn, Goldie, 166
Hayes, Sean P., 276–77
Henchy, Chris, 127
Hewlett, Bill, 287
Makes Woz's heart stop
Hilton, Paris, 17, 80, 199, 295,
319–25, *324*, 328
I'm her BFF (bikini fake friend)
Hilton, Perez, 100, 325
What doesn't he know?
Himself, 7–8
Hoffman, Dustin, 276
Hogan, Hulk, 132
Holden, William, 55
Who loved him more? Maggie or
Stefanie Powers?
Horne, Lena, 22
Mom's BFF
Houston, Whitney, 195, 269–70
(Hi, Cracky!)
Hubert, Janet, 106
Hughes, John, 31, 66, 77
Hunt, Helen, 108
Hutton, EF, 27

Idle, Eric, 230

Jackson Five, 33
Janssen, David, 22
I totally fucked him *(J.K., kids)
Jeni, Richard, 87
Jesus, 258, 259, 295, 298, 329, 340,
345
Jewel, 75
Jobs, Steve, 303, 304, 311, 312, 344
John and Yoko, 20
Johnson, Betsey, 323
Jolie, Angelina, 269

Jonas Brothers, 20
Jones, Star, 275–76
    I totally fucked him *(J.K., kids)
Jones, Tommy Lee, 77
Judd, Naomi, 174
Judd, Wynonna, 3

Kattan, Chris, 87
Katz, Jonathan, 159–60
    See Prince Charming
Kelley, Kitty, 21
    Mom's oracle
Kennedys, The, 21, 141
Kenny, Tom, 94–95
Kidman, Nicole, 171, 212
    Human clothes hanger
Kightlinger, Laura, 92, 96
    Stand-up comrade
Kilborn, Craig, 149
Kimmel, Jimmy, 245, 259, 310,
    311
Kindler, Andy, 92
King, Gayle, 207
    Larry's sister
King, John, 330, 331
King, Larry, 250, 259
    Gayle's brother
Kirkland, Sally, 59
Kline, Lisa, 320, 321
Klum, Heidi, 213
Krakowski, Jane, 230
Kudrow, Lisa, 55, 82, 83, 85, 101–2,
    199, 214
    I know a Friend

Lachey, Nick, 205
Lane, Diane, 56
Lange, Artie, 151
Lapides, Beth, 91
    Alternative comedy queen
Larter, Ali, 131

Lauer, Matt, 270
    Straight man, gay body
Lauren, Ralph, 325
LeBlanc, Matt, 181
Lesak, Martin, 197
Letterman, David, 138, 143, 145
    Hates the swears
    I'm back in!
Lewis, Jenna, 190
Lewis, Jerry, 342
Lewis, Richard, 84, 87
Lewis, Vicki, 117
    Not me
Lincoln, Abraham, 66
    16th president
Linney, Laura, 94
Lipnicki, Jonathan, 279
    Not hot enough
Lohan, Ali, 208, 279, 345
Lohan, Dina, 113, 279
    Maggie's mom-ager competition
Lohan, Lindsay, 208, 276, 278, 279,
    345
Lonow, Mark, 88
Lovitz, Jon, 68, 76, 82
Loy, Myrna, 113

Mackie, Bob, 80, 80
    I wore one!
Madonna, 60
Madsen, Michael, 110
    Creepy and sexy
Maher, Bill, 141–42, 142, 230
    Creepy
Mannheim, Camryn, 199, 230
Manson, Marilyn, 130
    My goth neighbor
Marguiles, Julianna, 112–13
Martin, Steve, 3, 139–41, 341
    Won't remember me
Mary Ann from Gilligan's Island, 143

Masada, Jamie, 192–93
(Hi, buddy!)
Mastrantonio, Mary Elizabeth, 30
Oak Park High royalty
Maxwell, Tom, 54
McCarthy, Jenny, 152, 199, 230
Playmate/activist
McClurg, Edie, 66
McDonald, Mike, 78
(Hi, Magoo!)
McGee, Hacky, 96
McGrath, George, 68–69
Meaney, Kevin, 87
Medavoy, Brian, 188
Messing, Debra, 108
Michaels, Lorne, 68, 82, 341, 346
Missed the boat
Michel, Alex, 199
Minnelli, Liza, 13
Mohr, Jay, 97
Moline, Matt, *202*, 204, 205, 206,
208, 210, *216*, 217, 221–34,
228, 236, 238–50
Montag-Pratt, Heidi, 76
Co-CEO, Fucking Lucky Club
Moore, Mary Tyler, 29
Morisette, Alanis, 203
Mule, Marcia, 204
Mullally, Megan, 117
Almost Brooke's sidekick
Murphy, Tom, *32*, 33
My first gay lover

'NSYNC, 150
I totally fucked them *(J.K., kids)
Negron, Taylor, 92
Nelson, Judd, 117, *120*, 121, 131
Newman, Laraine, 66
Nick (high school boyfriend), 33
Norris, Fred, 151

O'Brien, Conan, 97, 118, 146–49,
148
I'm back in with him, too!
O'Donnell, Rosie, 148, 253, 254,
264
(Hi, Ro!)
O'Hanrahan, Mary, 26, 343
O'Neal, Shaquille, 82
O'Reilly, Bill, 142, 261
I'm his Pinhead
Obama, Barack, 176, 319, 347
I totally fucked him *(J.K., kids)
Odenkirk, Bob, 94, 97
Olsen, Mary Kate, 64
Omarosa, 272
Osment, Haley Joel, 279
Not hot enough
Osmonds, The, 33
Creepy big-doll lovers
Oswalt, Patton, 97
Oteri, Cheri, 78, 87
Owen, Clive, 276

Pacino, Al, 58, 59, 171
Respected actor, Sally Kirkland
paramour?
Palin, Sarah, 145
Phew, that was close
Paltrow, Gwyneth, 195
Newly British
Parnell, Chris, 78
Peet, Amanda, 94
Pennington, Ty, 255–56, 258
Perry, Matthew, 93, 117
Peterman, Steve, 135
Peterson, Cassandra, 66
Pfeiffer, Michelle, 176
Philbin, Regis, 145–46
(Get me back on, Rege!)
Philips, Emo, 87

Pig Pen
    See Black, Jack
Piven, Jeremy, 255
Pom Pom, 320, 333
    Who's a good boy?
Povich, Maury, 65
Powers, Stefanie, 55–56, 57
    Stalked by Mom
Prince Charming
    See Katz, Jonathan
Pytka, Joe, 81–82

Quinn, Colin, 89
Quivers, Robin, 151

Rajskub, Mary Lynn, 97
Rambo, 69
Rancic, Giuliana, 278
Rath, Dave, 97, 101, 147
Refaeli, Bar, 326
    Hi, saddlebags!
Reid, Tara, 326
    Bikini loser
Regan, Brian, 87
Reiser, Paul, 108
Reubens, Paul, 66
Rhoda, 29, 70, 188, 339
    My idol
Rickles, Don, 146, *268*, 270
    My idol
Rinehart, Tiffany, 320
Rinna, Lisa, 326
    Bikini loser
Rivers, Joan, 131, 189–90, *223*, 275
    Mentor
Rivers, Melissa, 131, 275
Roberts, Julia, 104, 203
Roland the donut fryer, 61
    Don't ask, just read

Romano, Ray, 87, 199
Roseanne, 199
Roth, Tim, 110
Rourke, Mickey, 171
    Dental work?
R-Rated Hypnotist, The, 160
    Comedy Palace favorite
Ruby, 176
Rudner, Rita, 87
Rushdie, Salman, 196
Ryder, Winona, 94, 100
    Won't remember me

Saint, The, 7
Sapienza, Patty, 343
Scherzinger, Nicole, 191
Schumacher, Mrs., 18
    My binge-eating cover
Scott, Bryan, 204
Seacrest, Ryan
    Not mentioned ONCE in book
    (Suck it!)
Seinfeld, Jerry, 113–16, *115*, 118–19, 128, 280–82, 347
    What an asshole
    What a great guy!
Sepulveda, Tony, 117
Serling, Rod, 22, 27, 29, 99
    My future husband
Shakur, Tupac, 132
    I totally fucked him *(J.K., kids)
Shannon, Molly, 87, 101
Sharpton, Al, 141
Shepard, Sam, 84
Shields, Brooke, 116—17, 121–28, 133, 135, 136, 152, 227, *227*, 228, *228*, 230, 340–41, 346
    Some broad I did a show with
    Maid of honor
Shields, Teri, 126

Simpson, Jessica, 205, 341
Simpson, Joe, 205
Shore, Mitzi, 86
Short, Martin, 139–41
   Funny, nice, and friends with
      that prick Steve Martin
Silverman, Sarah, 97, 117, 141
   Guy-comedian magnet
Simmons, Richard, 196
Sister Mary Bitch-and-a-Half, 25
Smith, Anna Nicole, 271–73
Smith, Will, 105–6, 107, 203
   Won't remember me
Smothers, Tommy, 131
Snipes, Wesley, 94
   Decked Dick
Soderbergh, Steven, 109
   Can't be bothered with him
Spears, Britney, 3, 131, 163, 270,
      276, 296
   Fair (but not balanced) game
Spears, Jamie Lynn, 257
Spencer, Diana, 21
Spielberg, Steven, 277–83
   Big fan of KG
Sterling, Mindy, 67, 68, 76
Stern, Howard, 149–52, 207, 347
   (Read this fucking book,
      Howard)
Stern, Howard K., 272
Stiller, Ben, 94, 97
   Comedy hub guy
Stone, Sharon, 72, 207, 343
Strasberg, Lee, 58–59, 65, 66
   See Yoda
Strauss, Carolyn, 198
Streep, Meryl, 13, 341
   Respected actress, pesticide
      teacher
Streisand, Barbra, 172, 184
   Clouds Oprah's mind

Strickland, David, 120, 121,
      133, 133–34
Suleman, Nadya, 7, 171, 348
Sultan of Brunei, 126
   I totally fucked him *(J.K., kids)
Summer, Donna, 33
   Ideal gay-themed date
Swank, Hilary, 75
   Pain in my ass
Swain, Dominique, 222
Sweeney, Julia, 68, 82, 110, 273–74
   Lorne picked her

Tarantino, Quentin, 104, 110–11
   Dated, cuddled with, didn't fuck
Taylor, Elizabeth, 21
Taylor, Rip, 271
   Why the fuck is he in Anna
      Nicole's kitchen?
Tenuta, Judy, 87
Thomas, Richard, 57
   My co-star in Battle Beyond the
      Stars
Thompson, Lea, 116
Tierney, Lawrence, 110
Toll, Judy, 76, 84–85, 85, 174,
      274
   My dear departed friend
True, Rachel, 117
   Almost Brooke's sidekick (Hi,
      Rach!)
Tyres, Mrs., 4, 5
   My first audience

Uncle Maurice, 15, 16, 21
   Enjoys the drink
Unibrow Girl, 163
   Dick wrangler

Van Dyke, Dick, 29
Vize, Tom, 320

Wagner, Robert, 55
Walters, Barbara, ix, 111, 183, 267,
   347
   My memoir is funnier
West, Kanye, 276
Wheeler, Maggie, 117
   Almost Brooke's sidekick
Winfrey, Oprah, ix-x, 20, 26, 65,
   75, 149, 150, 182–84, 189,
   191, 195, 226, 247, 253, 303,
   326, 328, 338, 346
   Where do I start?
Whitaker, Forest, 20
   My neighbor
Williams, Robin, 58, 111–12, 276
Williams, Tennessee, 21
Willis, Bruce, 93

Wintour, Anna, 325
   De-Vogued by
Wozniak, Steve, 241, 284, 285–316,
   344
   Wake up, Mac Heads!

Yoda
   See Lee Strasberg
Young, Andrew, 105, 110
Young, Robert, 21
   Consumed by showbiz paranoia
Young, Sean, 146

Zalaznick, Lauren, 204
Zellweger, Renee, 214
Zucker, Jeff, 116, 197, 198, 254, 261
   I totally fucked him *(J.K., kids)

ABOUT THE AUTHOR

KATHY GRIFFIN, a multi–Emmy Award–winning and Grammy-nominated comedian and actress, is best known for her Bravo television reality show *Kathy Griffin: My Life on the D-List,* her multiple stand-up comedy specials on HBO, Comedy Central, and Bravo, and her four-year stint on the NBC sitcom *Suddenly Susan.* She has hosted several award shows and appeared on numerous talk shows including *Late Night with David Letterman, The Tonight Show with Jay Leno,* and *The View.* She has been nominated for a Grammy for her comedy CD, *For Your Consideration,* and performs to sold-out audiences at venues worldwide.

www.kathygriffin.net